Families Shamed

The consequences of crime for relatives of serious offenders

Rachel Condry

LONDON AND NEW YORK

First published by Willan Publishing
This edition published by Routledge 2011
2 Park Square, Milton Park, Abingdon, Oxon OX14 4RN
270 Madison Avenue, New York, NY 10016

Routledge is an imprint of the Taylor & Francis Group

First published 2007

Hardback
ISBN: 978-1-84392-207-0
Paperback
ISBN: 978-1-84392-501-9

British Library Cataloguing-in-Publication Data

A catalogue record for this book is available from the British Library

Project managed by Deer Park Productions, Tavistock, Devon
Typeset by TW Typesetting, Plymouth, Devon

Families Shamed

CRIME ETHNOGRAPHY SERIES

Series editors: Dick Hobbs and Geoffrey Pearson

Published titles

Holding Your Square: streetlife, masculinities and violence, by Christopher W. Mullins

Narratives of Neglect: community, regeneration and the governance of security, by Jacqui Karn

Families Shamed: the consequences of crime for relatives of serious offenders, by Rachel Condry

Northern Soul: drugs, crime and social identity in the northern soul scene, by Andrew Wilson

Contents

Acknowledgements

First and foremost, my thanks go to all the relatives of serious offenders who participated in the research, both as interviewees and fieldwork participants. I have promised them anonymity and therefore cannot name them individually, but I am grateful for their generous help and hospitality, for sharing details of their personal lives and for having the courage to talk about the difficulties they had encountered. My thanks also go to all of those involved with the running of Aftermath over the years for their openness, support and assistance. A number of people who work with offenders and their relatives gave their time to talk informally and to be interviewed, including the managers of two prison visitors' centres, the directors and staff of various organisations for prisoners and their families, and the staff of the prison visitors' centre in which I worked as a volunteer, and my thanks go to them all. I am grateful to all at Action for Prisoners' Families for their assistance and particularly to Lucy Gampell and Mark Heybourne.

I am indebted to many people for their support and guidance as this project developed. The book is based on doctoral research in the Department of Sociology at the London School of Economics, and particular thanks are due to my supervisors, Paul Rock and Bridget Hutter, for their initial encouragement to embark upon doctoral studies, their constructive feedback on numerous drafts of thesis chapters, and their support and encouragement to develop the thesis into a book. My thanks also go to the academic experts and colleagues with whom I discussed my research as it developed, some of whom read and commented upon earlier drafts of chapters and gave invaluable advice. In particular I would like to thank Stan Cohen, who has been very generous with his time and support and has helped me to see through the fog of motivational accounts theory, and Dick Hobbs, Tim Newburn, and members of the Tuesday crime and deviance research seminar at LSE for helpful discussions and advice. Frances Heidensohn and Ken

Plummer examined my PhD thesis and their perceptive comments proved extremely useful when the time came to write this book.

Nicola Lacey and Paul Rock very kindly read a full draft of the book manuscript and, as always, provided incisive and constructive feedback. I am very grateful to Nicola Lacey for her support and astute advice during my time as a Postdoctoral Fellow in the Law Department at LSE, and to Frances Heidensohn for her guidance and encouragement. I would also like to thank Brian Willan, and the editors of the Crime Ethnography book series, Dick Hobbs and Geoffrey Pearson, for their patience and for supporting the publication of this book.

The research received various forms of funding. The book was written during the first year of a British Academy Postdoctoral Fellowship, and I am very grateful to the British Academy for its support. The PhD on which the book is based was funded by an ESRC Research Studentship (award number R0042983451), and the Department of Sociology at LSE provided financial assistance in the first year of my doctoral studies and towards the transcription of some of the interviews.

There are many friends who have been with me through the years and supported me in various ways and I thank them all. I am particularly grateful to Anna Souhami, Stephanie Hayman, Amanda Goodall and Andrew Oswald, Martina Klett-Davies, and Lucy Mackenzie for their interest in the development of the book and for useful discussions.

Finally, my thanks go to all my family, and particularly to Dave, Isaac and Martha; to my parents, Gregory and Catherine Condry; and to my sister Abi Condry. I am especially grateful to Dave who has seen this project evolve from the beginning and been unstinting in his patience and support, which in recent years has included holding the domestic fort and looking after the children when work ran into extra time.

Rachel Condry
London School of Economics
2007

Introduction

Lionel Shriver's 2005 Orange Prize-winning novel *We Need to Talk About Kevin* is narrated by the mother of a serious offender, Eva Katchadorian. Eva's son Kevin has killed seven of his fellow students, a teacher and a cafeteria worker in a shooting at his high school. The book consists of a series of letters to her estranged husband Franklin in which she looks back to their life before they were parents, the 16 years they had with Kevin before he committed the crime, and how her life had changed afterwards. In her letters, Eva recounts Kevin's upbringing and attempts to unpick what might have led Kevin to kill. The book does not provide an easy answer to this question and Eva's account is brutally honest about the problems she perceived Kevin to have since his birth, her own lack of maternal feeling towards Kevin, her failings as a mother, and her husband's denial of their problems and determination to construct the family as happy and normal. The question of why Kevin did what he did is cleverly left open for the reader to decide (the back cover of the book reads: 'Nature or Nurture: what makes a monster?') and many of the reading group questions that appear at the end of the book are constructed around this central issue.

The book and the character and magnitude of the crime it describes are distinctly American and Eva's predicament, without disclosing how Shriver's book unfolds (several key elements are revealed towards the end), has some significant features that differ from the accounts of relatives of offenders on which my book is based. However, there are parallels between Eva's account and the stories told by the relatives that I met. Eva attracts blame as Kevin's mother, and this blame is expressed in covert and overt ways. Her neighbours regard her with suspicion; her brother won't let his children anywhere near her; and in the eyes of her father-in-law, she says: 'Kevin had proven defective, and I was the manufacturer' (p. 139). During one night a month after Kevin's crime, gallons of crimson paint are quietly splashed across the front of her house. Eva is sued in the civil court for being a negligent parent in a case brought by the mother of one of the victims (this fictional account has a basis in reality; in the US, a number of school shootings have resulted in similar cases against the perpetrator's parents).

Eva is aware that apportioning blame might meet particular needs: 'Blame confers an awesome power. And it's simplifying, not only to onlookers and victims but to culprits most of all. It imposes order on slag. Blame conveys clear lessons in which others may take comfort: *if only she hadn't* –, and by implication makes tragedy avoidable' (pp. 65–6). She herself feels 'exhausted with shame' (p. 4) and describes her guilt, her 'own sense of complicity' (p. 69), and how she feels 'infected, contagious, quarantined' (p. 384). She is constantly aware of the ramifications of Kevin's actions: 'I wake up with what he did every morning and I go to bed with it every night' (p. 12) and feels the burden of having such a story to narrate: 'And one of our consuming diversions as we age is to recite, not only to others but to ourselves, our own story. I should know; I am in flight from my story every day, and it dogs me like a faithful stray' (p. 17).

The book challenges its readers to think about responsibility, blame, empathy, and forgiveness, and to address their assumptions about parenting and family life. It confronts us with perplexing questions: to what degree can we be deemed responsible for the actions of our children and who they become? Would we support – and visit in prison – a child who had committed such a heinous crime? If we were a victim of a crime, or the relatives of a victim, would we hold the perpetrator's relatives responsible? Why? And under what conditions might this vary? *We Need to Talk About Kevin* is of course a work of fiction which weaves one family's story in intricate detail. At the same time, it brings into focus some of the questions that this book will consider: what are the consequences of serious crime for relatives of offenders? How does life change once a serious offence is discovered and how do relatives adjust to and manage those changes? How do stigma and shame flow through kin relationships and why are relatives of serious offenders stigmatised? How do we make sense of our lives through the stories we tell? How do we make sense of 'interruptions' to our self-narrative and our sense of identity? How do we account for our own – and others' – actions? What purposes do our accounts serve?

This is a book about relatives of serious offenders in England. It examines the experiences of a group of relatives of those accused or convicted of serious crimes such as murder, manslaughter, rape and sex offences. A broader literature exists on prisoners' families, but few studies have looked specifically at those related to *serious* offenders, or considered their experience other than as prison visitors. Many of the difficulties faced by the wider population of prisoners' families are magnified for the relatives of serious offenders, by the seriousness and stigmatising impact of the offence itself and by the severity of the consequences, which often include a long prison sentence.

It is a book about relatives like Anne, Jane and Pauline. Anne's son raped and violently assaulted a 16-year-old girl when he was 17. Anne described being in deep shock when she heard the news and barely being able to function. For 18 months before the offence her son had had considerable problems with alcohol, drug and solvent abuse, stealing, suicide attempts and abusive behaviour. She said she had tried to get help for him, and he had been under the care of a psychiatrist and drug support worker. She compared the devastation of finding out about the offence to bereavement, and said it took her two years to start to feel as if she was coping. She had palpitations and panic attacks, and described the impact as 'debilitating'. She struggled to understand why her son had offended, and worried whether she might be in some way to blame, although no-one else in her family, including her other two children, had ever been in trouble with the police. Her son had been released from prison when I met her, and she was providing counselling and support to a number of other relatives of serious offenders.

Jane was very upset when we met and cried frequently throughout our interview. Her daughter was in her early twenties and had just been sentenced to two years imprisonment after being jointly convicted with her partner for inflicting numerous injuries on their 11-month-old son. Jane thought the sentence would have been longer, but because they both pleaded their innocence the court could not be sure who had inflicted the injuries. Investigations showed that Jane's grandson had had previous broken bones and must have suffered prolonged abuse. Jane's grandson was adopted and had no further contact with his birth family, and Jane was heartbroken. She had been close to him and cared for him often, and still kept a room for him, with everything left just as it had been when he was taken away. Jane lived on a council estate and had become a virtual prisoner in her own home as a result of abuse she had received from neighbours following her daughter's conviction. She felt angry towards her daughter, but continued to be her main supporter. Jane was on income support and found the cost of supporting her daughter and visiting the prison difficult to manage. She said she felt very depressed most of the time, but had to keep going because she was a single parent caring for her teenage son.

Pauline's son committed a particularly brutal murder which was notorious in her local area. He killed a young man he met in a bar, and when he returned home he raped his girlfriend. He was arrested quite quickly and is now detained indefinitely in a special hospital. When it happened, Pauline said she did not leave the house for weeks, her 'nerves were shattered', and she was so devastated that if it was not for her other son (ten at the time) she thinks she would have attempted suicide. It was seven years since her son's offence and although she said she could understand her son's anger and frustration, she was at a loss to understand the violence that came with it and was searching for reasons that might explain his actions.

The relationship between crime and the family has received attention in both academic and public discourse, yet very little is known about how offenders' families are affected by crime and its consequences. Academic discourse has been dominated by studies which attempt to identify family factors associated with crime, focusing in particular on the relationship between family breakdown and/or parental failure and youth offending. Within the wider context of public discourse about crime and its control, individualistic explanations for crime have held sway, firmly placing responsibility for crime with offenders and their families, while downplaying structural factors (such as material conditions or unemployment) and the complex processes that might lead to crime (Hil and McMahon 2001). The strongest version of individualistic explanations emerged in the discourse of the New Right in the 1980s which targeted the breakdown of the family as central to moral decay in society and to blame for rising crime rates (Abbott and Wallace 1992). Campbell showed powerfully how these ideas were seized upon in debates about disorder on a number of English housing estates in the early 1990s. Families – and particularly mothers – were blamed and made scapegoats for the young men's actions, diverting the focus from the 'crisis of masculinity' and the political and economic landscape they inhabited (Campbell 1993). Current political debate and policy developments continue to focus on 'problem families', feckless parents and individualistic explanations for crime; I consider these debates in Chapter 3.

We know very little about the home and family lives of offenders' families and how they manage their everyday circumstances. Offenders' relatives often only become visible when they enter a prison or a prison visitors' centre and are rarely studied in their own environments, which echoes the critique of 'courthouse criminology' (Polsky 1998; Hagedorn 1990): the tendency to study research subjects in convenient but non-natural surroundings rather than go into the field. Sitting in the public gallery in court or visiting a prison might be significant and important experiences for relatives of offenders, but only comprise a small part of their lives and one dimension of the difficulties they have to manage. As a population, however, offenders' relatives can be difficult to reach and doing so through a prison visitors' centre or self-help group might be the only realistic option. Even if relatives of offenders are found through visitors' centres or self-help organisations they are usually studied in those locations and not followed into their own environments. It may be possible to locate communities where prisoners' families are highly concentrated, and some work in the US examines the cumulative impact of imprisonment on such communities and the families that live in them (see, for example, Rose and Clear 1998; Clear, Rose and Ryder 2001; Hagan and Dinovitzer 1999) but this kind of work has not yet developed in the UK. Serious offenders' families can be even more difficult to reach. Most of those I met were guarded about their identities, did not want to court publicity and did not know another relative of a serious offender in their everyday lives, other than those they knew through mutual membership of a self-help organisation: this was their 'community'.

In the UK, the organisation Action for Prisoners' Families has worked hard to raise the profile of prisoners' families and the difficulties they face, liaising with government and acting as an 'umbrella' organisation for a number of smaller self-help groups. There is also a growing literature which is sensitive to the difficulties faced by the broader population of prisoners' families (see Chapter 2). Only a small number of studies, however, have specifically considered the experiences of relatives of *serious* offenders. In the UK, May conducted interviews with relatives of eight people convicted of murder and looked at how they accounted for the offence and how they experienced and managed stigma (May 1999, 2000) and Howarth and Rock have written about Aftermath, a self-help organisation for families of serious offenders and the main fieldwork site in this study (Howarth and Rock 2000). In the US, two authors have written about the families of those on death row. King examines the crimes and their consequences, devoting a chapter to each of nine cases (King 2005), while Sharp provides an analysis of the 'complicated grieving process', pain and trauma faced by the families of death row prisoners who endure a cycle of hope and despair with the uncertainty generated by years of legal wrangling (Sharp 2005). Smith and Trepper have written about the parents of five sexual offenders and how they responded to the 'ongoing crisis' in a similar way to those who experience grief through bereavement (Smith and Trepper 1992). In Canada, a professor of psychiatry followed a single family through the suspicion, charge and finally the conviction of their son for murder (MacLeod 1982); in contemporary Germany, Bar-On interviewed 51 children of perpetrators and witnesses of the Nazi Holocaust about the legacy of their parents' involvement (Bar-On 1989). The following book is the first study to combine long interviews with individual relatives of serious offenders in England with fieldwork in a self-help organisation over a number of years.

The emotions that flow through our connections to kin are many and varied. The actions of our close kin can cause us to well with pride or to hang our heads in shame. We might feel pride in their achievements, in a kind act they have performed, or just feel proud of the person they have become. Conversely, we might feel ashamed because they have broken strongly-held norms or taboos, hurt someone, or behaved in a way that appals us. This book tries to understand how, when a serious crime is uncovered, relatives of offenders are drawn into the shaming processes that follow, and exactly what it is that underlies these processes. In Chapter 3 I suggest that their stigma is more than just a shadow of the offender's stigma, and that it has its roots in notions of kin contamination and kin culpability.

Being stigmatised can elicit a range of emotions: anger, sadness, humiliation, embarrassment, for example (Jones *et al.* 1984), but shame is one of the most significant. The title of this book, *Families Shamed*, refers to this as the key factor that defined the experiences of the relatives I met: the stigma and shame they experienced because of the seriousness of the offence. It refers both to the stigmatising and shaming processes to which they were subject in interactions with others, and to the subjective feelings of shame that most relatives expressed. In this book I draw on a number of theories of stigma and shame to understand these processes, including Goffman's theory of stigma as a 'spoiled identity' and as something that can be experienced vicariously as a 'courtesy stigma' (Goffman 1963); Nussbaum's theory of shame and its structure, thought-content and role in human life (Nussbaum 2004); and Braithwaite's theory of reintegrative shaming (Braithwaite 1989; Braithwaite and Braithwaite 2001).

There is no unified single approach to the study of shame: 'theoretical work on shame has occurred across many disciplines and in a haphazard manner, such that well-defined schools of thought have not developed systematically' (Harris 2001: 90). Shame has been conceived in a range of different ways by scholars from a number of disciplines including psychology, psychiatry, anthropology, sociology, law, and criminology. Theorists disagree on shame's key defining characteristics, on how it differs from other emotions such as guilt, and on whether it can be a positive force for good. Harris has provided an organising framework for some of the most influential approaches to shame, based on three key conceptions: shame as an individual's perception of social rejection or disapproval ('social threat conception'); shame as something that occurs when individuals fail to live up to important standards and perceive their whole self as a failure ('personal failure conception'); and shame based upon a recognition that one has committed a moral infraction or breached an ethical value ('ethical conception') (see Harris 2001: 90–93). Harris argues that the complexity in the study of shame can thus be reduced to three key issues: (1) how we feel others think of us; (2) how we feel about ourselves; and (3) views about what is ethically shameful that we share with others, and theorists take different positions on these themes (*ibid.*: 78–9). A similar approach to those classified under the 'personal failure conception' has been taken by Nussbaum (2004), and in Chapter 3 I suggest that although all three of the above themes were important to understanding the shame of relatives in this study, this conception was particularly salient. Because the relatives' shame flowed through the actions of kin and was constructed around their kin relationships, it went to the very heart of their identity and their whole self, and as a result for many it was devastating.

Braithwaite's (1989) theory of shame and its role in human life and in responses to crime has been enormously influential in criminology in recent years. He contends that shaming of a particular kind – reintegrative shaming – can be effective in preventing offending. Reintegrative shaming 'shames while maintaining bonds of respect or love' and 'sharply terminates disapproval with forgiveness' (Braithwaite 1989: 12) Stigmatising shaming, in contrast, amplifies crime by casting offenders out and pushing them towards criminal subcultures. The shame experienced by relatives in this book was largely what Braithwaite would describe as disintegrative, stigmatising and negative in consequence, and as such the picture of the reactions experienced by relatives in this book is perhaps more pessimistic than the one he presents (Braithwaite 1989; see in particular his example of the reactions to the family of an offender in a murder case pp. 75–6, and Chapter 3 of the following book). In Chapter 3 I consider the implications of my findings for Braithwaite's theory, and suggest that they raise particular questions about the involvement of relatives in shaming processes and about what expectations might be right or reasonable.

A further key focus of this book is on what relatives *did* with the shame and stigma they experienced, how they moved forward from the low point of finding out about the offence, and the various ways in which they managed their experiences. Finding out about the offence was an event that disrupted the coherence of their narratives about who they were and how their lives were progressing and was an event that had to be somehow assimilated. Other chapters in the book consider the changes wrought by becoming a relative of a serious offender, how relatives tried to make sense of the offence, how they tried to make sense of their own role and their own shame, and how they came together with other relatives in a self-help organisation to find ways to manage their stigma and to construct a collective story about their circumstances.

The research

The book is based on ethnographic fieldwork with Aftermath, a now-defunct self-help organisation which was specifically for families of *serious* offenders, and long interviews with 32 relatives (I describe Aftermath's work in more detail in Chapter 6, and reflect on my methodology in Appendix 1). Aftermath was based in Sheffield and existed for 17 years (1988–2005), supporting its members through a newsletter, a network of telephone supporters, annual seminar weekends (which took place in a conference centre, lasting three days and having a variety of speakers), various training sessions, and self-help meetings for members known as 'lunches' and held on a Saturday, usually every six weeks, in three areas.

The research fell broadly into four phases. The first was an exploratory phase (October 1997–October 1998) which involved negotiating access to relatives of serious offenders through Aftermath, attending their annual seminar weekend, attending an Aftermath self-help meeting, talking informally with members and spending time in the Aftermath office talking to staff and looking at Aftermath files and records. In the second phase (November 1998–April 2000), I continued to attend Aftermath meetings and interviewed 24 relatives of male offenders, all of whom were Aftermath members. In the third phase (April 2000–December 2000), I sought access to families of female serious offenders. Fieldwork in this phase took place in the visitors' centre at a women's prison and interviews were conducted with eight relatives of female serious offenders. In the fourth phase (January 2001–July 2003), I remained in contact with Aftermath and continued to attend some of their functions.

Aftermath as an organisation was very open to the idea of my research, though understandably keen to protect the confidentiality of members and to stress that participation in the research would be an individual choice. Access to interviewees therefore had to be negotiated individually. In the first instance, I talked informally with members I met at Aftermath meetings and invited them to participate. I was introduced to some of my interviewees by other members, which enabled me to reach several people who had been active members many years previously but had since stood back and taken a less prominent role. One member in particular was very helpful, I stayed at her home for a few days and she made several introductions. Context was clearly important in shaping people's willingness to talk to me and to participate in the research. In particular, a personal introduction from an Aftermath member was important, whether during a meeting or afterwards.

I wanted to include some relatives of female serious offenders to understand whether and how their experiences might differ. Would these relatives be differently stigmatised? Would they experience additional difficulties? Female offenders are often deemed 'doubly deviant' (Lloyd 1995) and violent female prisoners, unlike violent male prisoners, are never glamorised (Carlen 1983; Lloyd 1995). Other studies have found that female prisoners face particular problems which centre on the family. When we look at the wider population of all female prisoners, over 60 per cent are mothers and 45 per cent have children living with them prior to imprisonment (Prison Reform Trust 2000). Studies have found the impact of imprisonment to be worse for their children than for the children of male prisoners and that they are much less likely to be cared for by the prisoners' spouse and more likely to be looked after by other relatives or in local authority care (e.g. Caddle and Crisp 1996; Casale 1989; Gibbs 1971; Player 1994; Wilkinson 1988; Zalba 1964). Women in prison can experience additional pressure because they have failed to live up to traditional expectations of caring and nurturing motherhood (Tchaikovsky 1994), and deviation from an 'ideal' of motherhood might actually contribute to women being imprisoned in the first place (Carlen 1983).

However, access to relatives of female serious offenders was difficult to secure. They are clearly drawn from a much smaller population than relatives of male serious offenders (the majority of the female prison population are held for non-violent offences – in February 2005, for example, only 186 of the 5,792 prisoners serving a life sentence in prisons in England and Wales were women). Aftermath itself only had 49 families of female serious offenders as members (out of 1285 families) between 1988 and 2001, two of whom I interviewed. I approached several prisoners' families organisations and secured one interview through this route, and after a recommendation from the Director of Women in Prison, arranged to work as a volunteer in the visitors' centre of a women's prison for five months which led to five further interviews.

Interviews with the 32 relatives lasted between two and five hours, with three hours being the average. An interview of two to three hours would usually take place in one sitting, while a longer interview might be spread across the day with lunch in between. An interview guide was used to structure the questions, although this was flexible and interviews were allowed to flow conversationally and to diverge from the guide where necessary. The guide covered a number of areas: their experience of being involved with Aftermath or other organisations; whether they thought the experiences of relatives of serious offenders differed from relatives of those who committed less serious offences; their views about why people commit serious offences; what they understood about why their relative had offended; the details of the crime; their relationship with the offender; the effect on the family and on different family members; problems they had to cope with; what life was like before the offence; how people within and outside the family reacted when they found out; whether their relationship had changed with any of these people; how they found out about the offence; their experiences with the police, courts, and visiting a prison or special hospital; their experiences with the media; what they thought about the way Aftermath constructed relatives of offenders and their experiences; how they thought the public perceived families of serious offenders; and how they saw their future.

Most interviews took place in the interviewee's home. Participants would be more relaxed on their 'territory', we could break where necessary for a cup of tea, and they could explain events that had occurred in the house or local area with much more ease. I would often be shown photographs of the offender and other relatives, along with files of newspaper cuttings about the offence and sometimes court or other legal papers; these 'personal props' (Plummer 1995) were important to the telling of their stories. It was also invaluable to be able to talk informally with participants between taping sessions. I was welcomed as a guest in people's homes, and shown hospitality, always offered tea or coffee and sometimes lunch. This welcoming attitude is often neglected in research reports (Finch and Mason 1993; Oakley 1981). Interviewees were spread across England in different locations and several interviews each involved a round trip of around 600 miles and an overnight stay in bed and breakfast accommodation. (Most of the lunches also involved significant travel – one involved a round trip of 150 miles and the other over 300 miles.)

I was interested in how relatives understood their circumstances and how they constructed their experiences. Relatives' responses to particular questions were important, and the transcripts of their interviews would later be taken apart and coded, but I was also interested in how they narrated their lives, how they told stories about their experiences, how they talked about their past, present and future, and the relationship between narratives constructed in the somewhat artificial context of an interview and the everyday narrative construction of life and self-identity.

Recorded interviews were also conducted with people working with families of serious offenders, including the chairperson of Aftermath during the main period of fieldwork; the director of Action for Prisoners' Families, a manager of a visitors' centre at a men's prison, the manager of a visitors' centre at a women's prison, the director of the organisation Women in Prison, and the director of an organisation for prisoners' families. Through these interviews I learnt more about the difficulties facing relatives of serious offenders, how these difficulties were understood by the people who work with the relatives, and what attempts were being made to support families and meet their needs. However, I decided not to quote from their transcripts in this book, but to concentrate instead on using quotations from the relatives whose voices, opinions and predicament are rarely heard (see Appendix 1 for further discussion).

Defining serious offenders' families

All participants in this study had a close kin relationship with someone accused or convicted of a serious offence. The offences in question were violent or sexual or attracted a sentence of four years or more. None was

a property crime and in the main they were non-instrumental. The individual offences included murder, manslaughter, violent offences, rape, and sex offences against children (see the end of this chapter and Appendix 2). Of 32 interviewees, ten were wives or partners of the offender, 17 were mothers, one was a father, one was a grandmother, one was a sister, one was an aunt and one was a daughter. Aftermath defined its membership as the families of those 'accused or convicted' of serious offences, and I decided to follow this definition. There were two interviewees whose relatives were accused but not convicted (Harriet and Angela) and they defined their experiences in very similar ways to the other relatives and had to overcome a number of significant difficulties as a result of the allegations.

It is difficult to quantify the population of families of serious offenders because the category of 'serious crime' is a contested boundary (Francis *et al.* 2001). There are a range of components making a particular offence more or less serious, including the harm caused or risked by the offender's conduct, the offender's individual culpability and remoteness from the harm, and various factors of aggravation or mitigation (Ashworth 2005). There have been attempts to rank offences or allocate a category of high, medium or low seriousness, but this is far from straightforward and gives rise to complex debate about proportionality in sentencing which is beyond the scope of this book (see Ashworth 2005 for a detailed discussion). However, there is some constancy: 'In reality, at any point in time the 'seriousness' rankings of some crimes are being renegotiated while the 'seriousness' of others are being maintained' (Francis *et al.* 2001: 734) and surveys of public opinion tend to find that people give similar rank-orderings to crimes (Von Hirsch and Jareborg 1991). Participants in this study were self-defining as relatives of *serious* offenders and were found either through Aftermath, an organisation specifically for relatives of serious offenders, or, in the case of six interviewees, through a leaflet in a prison visitors' centre asking for relatives of serious offenders who were willing to be interviewed.

A very approximate estimate of the number of relatives of serious offenders can be obtained by looking at the number of prisoners serving longer sentences: in 2004 there were 25,837 prisoners serving a sentence of more than four years but less than life and 5,594 serving a life sentence (Howard League 2006). There were therefore 31,431 prisoners serving sentences of more than four years. Extrapolating from this section of the prison population to the number of families involved can only give a very rough approximation. This might overestimate – we cannot assume that all those prisoners have the support of their family, and we know that with more grave offences and longer prison sentences this becomes less likely (NACRO 1994) – or underestimate because it excludes a number of serious offenders, such as those who are no longer serving a prison sentence but whose families are still affected by what has happened, or those who received a shorter sentence for an offence which would be deemed in the eyes of most as 'serious' and serious in its consequences for the family. One family in this study had their house attacked and their family torn apart by conflict following the conviction of the husband for sexual offences against children – the sentence he received, however, was only two years. But we can at least make a very approximate estimate of tens of thousands of families contending with difficulties of supporting a serious offender.

The relatives

When the research began, it soon became clear that this was a sphere in which women predominated. Almost all the active members of the self-help organisation were women; all but one of the participants who agreed to be interviewed were women, despite attempts to secure interviews with male family members; and as the research progressed it emerged that in most cases one female family member, usually a wife or mother, was taking primary responsibility for the offender and his or her needs and shouldering much of the burden of caring (see Chapter 2). We should not be surprised to find a higher number of wives or female partners taking the role of primary supporter – we know that in crime the sexual division of labour is distinctly marked and there are many more men convicted of crimes than women. In January 2006, for example, there were 4,229 women in prison in England and Wales out of a total prison population of 75,393 (Howard League 2006). We would expect, therefore, to see a higher number of women as primary supporters when the supporter is a spouse or partner.

However, it cannot be assumed that all offenders or prisoners are being supported by wives or partners. Surveys in a men's and a women's prison found that 51 per cent of male prisoners were visited by their parents, 46 per cent by their partners, 42 per cent by siblings and 36 per cent by children (Murray 2003a) while 56 per cent of female prisoners reporting visits received those visits from parents, 43 per cent from children, 39 per cent from siblings and only 28 per cent from partners (Murray 2003b). A discussion of the difficulties faced by offenders' families should therefore not be restricted to wives and partners (Mills 2004; Paylor and Smith 1994). Studies in the US have found prison visitors to be predominantly female: one described a visiting area at a male prison as 'a distinctly *female* space' with approximately 95 per cent of visitors being women (Comfort 2003); one found that twice as many mothers as fathers were prison visitors (Schafer 1994) and another that 'Men in prison are visited by their wives and mothers and women in prison are visited by their mothers and sisters' (Girshick 1996: 24). The predominance of women in the fieldwork locations and in my sample of interviewees is therefore not unique and I consider some of the possible reasons for it in Chapter 6.

The sample of interviewees was slowly built and relatives were selected by availability and opportunity. I was fortunate to gain access to 32 interviewees – one study of murderers' relatives reports taking 21 months to reach and interview members of eight families (May 2000). I was not able to select Aftermath members or prison visitors to provide a random sample, or to select participants on the basis of particular characteristics (other than all sharing a close kin relationship to a serious offender). Certain factors might therefore affect the degree to which the sample is representative. Compared to the general prison population the interviewees showed greater ethnic homogeneity and a higher socio-economic level. Thirty interviewees classified themselves as 'white UK', four of whom classified the offender as 'mixed race', and only two classified themselves as 'black UK'. Ethnic minorities are consistently over-represented in the general prison population; prison statistics 'suggest that around one and one-quarter per cent of the black population in England and Wales is in prison, about eight times that of the white population' (Bowling and Phillips 2002: 241). Work is emerging in the US that highlights the collateral consequences of mass imprisonment for relatives of prisoners, and how significant numbers of African-American women in particular are affected (see, for example, Comfort 2003; Mauer and Chesney-Lind 2002; Sokoloff 2003); the figures from England and Wales suggest there might be a similar disproportionate effect not reflected in my sample.

The relatives I met could be described as working or middle class, but most were not what might be described as 'socially excluded',[1] in contrast to both the general prison population and some of the families I observed at prison visitors' centres. According to the Government's Social Exclusion Unit, many of those in the general prison population have experienced a lifetime of social exclusion with high levels of unemployment and drug use and a significant lack of basic reading, writing and numeracy skills (Social Exclusion Unit 2002: 6). The Government has defined social exclusion as 'a shorthand term for what can happen when people or areas suffer from a combination of linked problems such as unemployment, poor skills, low incomes, unfair discrimination, poor housing, high crime, bad health and family breakdown' (Social Exclusion Unit 2004). Those I interviewed had individual problems to contend with, but these were not of the same magnitude or severity as many of the relatives I observed in prison visitors' centres.

I asked all interviewees for their current or most recent employment with the intention of making some assessment of their class position.

However, this was far from straightforward. Many described themselves as 'housewives'; some had not worked for some time due to illness; some were retired; and others were employed in a voluntary capacity. Only ten out of 32 could straightforwardly name an occupation: a teacher, a care worker, a cook, two charity workers, a social worker, a solicitor, a 'stress management therapist' (working in the sex industry), a counsellor and a childminder. This was not enough on its own to assess the class composition of the sample. It may be possible to make some inference from their housing situation. Twenty out of 32 interviewees owned their own homes, 11 were in local authority accommodation and one in a housing association flat. Those who owned their own homes tended to live in houses with two or three bedrooms.

Appendix 2 records interviewees' characteristics. Only five interviewees were no longer supporting the offender, all of whom were former wives or partners. The ages of interviewees ranged from thirties to seventies (I asked participants to choose age bands rather than specific ages); there were no younger relatives in their twenties or teens. For most participants this was the first member of their family to go to prison, and many spoke of their offending relative having little prior history of serious offending. This may be another factor colouring my sample: it is perhaps more likely that families with less experience of crime would join a self-help group – in particular a self-help group such as Aftermath which claimed that families were traumatised by having a serious offender in the family (see Chapter 6) – or agree to take part in research. Interviewees might also not have known the full extent of their family member's offending history (see Chapter 1).

None of the rape or homicide victims was a member of the interviewee's family, other than Debbie whose husband killed his grandmother. Some of the sex offence victims were within the interviewee's family (nieces, a foster daughter, step-children and grandchildren) as were some of the violent offence victims (grandchildren and a father) but none was the interviewee's own child. I met other relatives through fieldwork where the victim of both homicide and sex offences had been in the immediate family, but perhaps not surprisingly they were underrepresented in a group such as Aftermath where the majority of relatives continued to support the offender.

None of the offenders was part of an organised or professional crime network (as far as their relative was aware). In fact, relatives were keen to distance the offender and their family from these types of criminals (see Chapter 5). This is an important difference. Hobbs describes how the family unit and kinship networks enable and enhance organised crime activity which relies on 'interlocking networks of relationality', trust and loyalty, concluding that 'kinship is as relevant to understanding contemporary British organized crime as it was in the days of the Krays and the

Richardsons' (Hobbs 2002: 27). Examples of families colluding together in crime abound; a book has recently been written by the wife of the notorious drug smuggler Howard Marks, for example, who recounts becoming intimately involved with his crimes (Marks 2006). These were not the families I met, none of whom described being part of criminal networks, or being involved in crime.

Many participants were members of a self-help organisation which in itself raises questions about who joins self-help groups, and how the way they understood their predicament was shaped by the lens it provided (I consider this issue in Chapter 6). However, this also meant I could learn about the experiences of a much larger number of relatives than those directly interviewed, first as fieldwork participants, and secondly as members being supported by those I interviewed. Nine of the interviewees who were Aftermath members worked as telephone supporters of other members, together having supported over 150 families. During the interviews they often spoke about this work and about the difficulties these other members had faced. Conclusions drawn from a sample such as this must be tentative and caution should be exercised in generalising to the wider population, although I did find parallels with a number of other studies of offenders' families and similar experiences were described in interviews with the managers of two prison visitors' centres who had daily contact with relatives of serious offenders.

The long interviews were conducted with 32 relatives who are listed below along with details of the offence. The category of 'homicide' includes murder and manslaughter; 'sex offence' refers to sexual offences against minors (which in some cases included the charge of rape); and 'rape' refers to rapes against adults. For brevity, 'the offence' will be referred to as a single event, although it is recognised that there might have been a series of offences. Where available, documentary evidence (such as court papers and media reports) was checked, but descriptions of the offences and the sentences received rely primarily on interviewees' accounts. Some identifying details have been left out to preserve anonymity.

Ada (rape)

Ada's son was convicted of three rapes of strangers when he was 19. He claimed these attacks were attempted rapes, but was convicted on three counts of rape. He was sentenced to 15 years, and had been released around 18 months before our interview.

Alice (Homicide)

Alice's son was convicted of murder and sentenced to life imprisonment, with a recommendation that he serve at least 25 years. He had a disagreement with someone which resulted in a shooting, although Alice was very clear that he was not a professional criminal and had never been in trouble with the law before. He claimed to be innocent of the crime, Alice was not sure.

Angela (sex offence)

Angela's husband was accused of sexual abuse by his adult nieces, but after a long wait was eventually cleared at a Crown Court trial, several years before our interview. The experience inspired Angela to help others, and she had supported many other relatives of serious offenders through Aftermath and another support group.

Anne (rape)

Anne's son raped and violently assaulted a young girl of 16 that he had met on the bus. He was sentenced to five years, and had been released at the time of our interview after serving three-and-a-half years.

Beatrice and George (homicide)

Beatrice and George's son was in his early twenties when he killed his girlfriend during a violent argument around ten years before our interview. He was convicted of manslaughter on the grounds of diminished responsibility and given psychiatric treatment. I interviewed Beatrice and George on separate occasions.

Beryl (homicide)

Beryl's son was convicted of the murder of a local pub landlord; his co-accused was the landlord's wife with whom he was having an affair. He was 29 at the time of the offence, and served 14 years of a life sentence. He had been released six months before our interview.

Betty (sex offence)

Betty's brother was convicted of indecent assault and sentenced to two-and-a-half years when he was 55. This happened around a year before I interviewed her. She said the victim was a boyfriend who had encouraged the relationship, although he was under the age of 16 when it began.

Beverly (violent offence)

Beverly's grandson was convicted of attempted murder at the age of 17. She had been the primary carer for him and his sister while their mother served a prison sentence of several years and they had continued to live with her afterwards. She believed he was unfairly convicted, although he was present when his friend had shot another young man. He was given a sentence of 15 years, two years before our interview.

Celia (homicide)

Celia's nephew shot and killed a man who was a drug dealer; she assumed her nephew had met him when he was in borstal. She said she had a very close bond to her nephew, and that he lived with her family for a while. He was convicted of manslaughter on the grounds of diminished responsibility and was detained indefinitely in a special hospital.

Christine (violent offence)

Christine's daughter was convicted of three armed robberies which she described as quite violent, involving knives and a gun in one case. She had committed these offences alone, but Christine said she was made to do it by an abusive boyfriend who controlled her heroin supply. The robberies had happened several months before the interview, and she had been convicted that week. She was sentenced to four years, which Christine said was relatively lenient and took into account the pressures she was under when she committed the offences.

Clare (sex offence)

Clare's husband was 60 when allegations of sexual abuse were made by his adult children from his first marriage. He was convicted of sexual assault and indecency. This happened several years before I interviewed Clare; she was his second wife and they had a ten-year-old son whom Clare was certain was not a victim. She supported her husband through the prison sentence, but decided to end their marriage on his release.

Debbie (homicide)

Two years before our interview Debbie's husband had killed his grandmother. Debbie had been pregnant with the youngest of her four children at the time. She said her husband was convicted of manslaughter on the grounds of diminished responsibility, and that he had mental health problems and addictions to drugs, specifically crack cocaine.

Dorothy (homicide)

Dorothy's daughter was convicted of murder and given a life sentence shortly before our interview. Dorothy thought this was very unfair. She said that her daughter had been present at a murder committed by someone else, and did not participate in the killing, but was judged to have had an equal role and given the same sentence.

Eileen (sex offence)

Eileen's husband was convicted of sexual offences against his young grandchildren. He was sentenced to four years and served two-and-a-half. Eileen was not sure of the truth of the allegations, but said she knew he was 'not a paedophile'. Her husband had been released from prison at the time of our interview.

Frances (sex offence)

Frances's husband was convicted of the rape of their 15-year-old foster-daughter, who became pregnant as a result and was removed by social services. He eventually pleaded guilty, although only after DNA tests had proved him to be the father of the baby, and was sentenced to three years and nine months.

Gill (sex offence)

Gill's husband was convicted of indecent assault against two of her nieces, her sister's children. The offences had happened at night when the nieces were staying at her house and Gill had been sleeping. Her husband was sentenced to two years and had been released at the time of our interview.

Harriet (sex offence)

Harriet's son was accused of sexual offences against his young children after his marriage ended, seven years before our interview. The police eventually decided not to pursue charges, but social services were involved and believed the allegations and he was denied access to his children as a result. Harriet believed the allegations when they first came to light, but at the time of our interview was convinced of his innocence.

Hilda (homicide)

Hilda's son was convicted of killing a care worker. The case attracted a great deal of publicity and Hilda said it would sometimes appear on the television. He was detained indefinitely in a special hospital.

Jane (violent offence)

Jane's daughter was convicted along with her daughter's husband of inflicting injuries on her 11-month-old son and hospital investigations showed he had received many previous serious injuries. Her daughter was 19 at the time and this had all happened in the year prior to the interview. She received a two year sentence.

Louise (violent offence)

Louise's daughter had been convicted of kidnap and grievous bodily harm. The victim was someone she believed was responsible for the death of her partner's teenage son from a heroin overdose. Charges related to the alleged drug dealer being kidnapped and assaulted, and a gun was thought to have been involved. Her mother thought it likely that her daughter would serve a prison sentence of several years.

Lillian (sex offence)

Lillian's son had been convicted four years prior to our interview of sexual offences against children. Lillian was unsure of the exact charges, but they related to watching pornographic films with children and taking indecent photographs. He was sentenced to ten years.

Lisa (homicide)

Lisa was unusual amongst participants in this study because she had met her partner since his imprisonment. He had been convicted of killing another boy when he was in his teens and was sentenced to detention during Her Majesty's Pleasure, and was still in prison when I interviewed Lisa despite being in his thirties. She had been with her partner for several years at the time of interview, but only ever had contact with him through prison visiting and letter writing.

Lorraine (serious drug offence)

Lorraine's daughter was arrested a year before the interview for possession with intent to supply a large amount of cocaine and heroin. Although the drugs were found in her bedroom, Lorraine thought she had been 'set up' but neither she nor Grace were willing reveal the source of the drugs because threats were made against Grace's life. She was sentenced to four years. Although the offence was not violent or sexual, I chose to include Lorraine's case as it fitted with my original criteria: the offence attracted a long prison sentence and Lorraine herself identified as a relative of someone convicted of a serious offence.

Mary (violent offence)

Mary's daughter was convicted of a violent offence when she was in her thirties. She knew very little about the details of the offence – she thought it took place at a party at her daughter's house, she knew it was violent, and that it must have been serious because her daughter was sentenced to 12 years. This happened about four years before our interview. She said she had avoided TV and newspaper coverage at her daughter's request and did not attend court.

Monica (violent offence)

Monica's daughter, who was in her mid-twenties, was arrested for attempted murder after assaulting her baby (Monica's grandson) a year-and-a-half before our interview. The charges against her would later be reduced on appeal and she would be released from prison.

Nancy (sex offence)

Nancy's husband, to whom she had been married less than two years, was convicted four months before our interview of 12 offences including the rape and sexual assault of two of his daughters, who were now adults. One of the charges related to indecent photographs of one of his daughters when she was 13 years old and this was the only charge Nancy believed to be true.

Nicola (sex offence)

Nicola's partner was convicted of sexual offences against his young niece, which included two counts of rape and three of indecent assault. He was sentenced to five years almost a year before our interview. The offences were said to have happened nine years previously, when he was twenty-one; Nicola did not know him at this time. At the time of our interview she had ended their relationship.

Pauline (homicide)

Pauline's son was convicted of the murder of a man he met in a bar and was sentenced to detention during Her Majesty's Pleasure as he was only 17 at the time. He was held in a secure special hospital and likely to remain there for some considerable time.

Penny (rape)

Penny's son had been convicted of rape and indecent assault of two women shortly before our interview. One victim was a friend and one was a woman he had met in a nightclub. He was sentenced to six years imprisonment. Penny believed there had been a miscarriage of justice and was campaigning on his behalf. She thought the women were motivated to make the allegations by the prospect of financial compensation.

Sarah (violent offence)

Sarah's mother was convicted of a violent offence against Sarah's father which left him blind, for which she received a three year prison sentence. The offence happened eight months before the interview. Her mother and father were both pensioners and both heavy drinkers, with a history of violence in their relationship, although her father was usually the victim of the assaults.

Stephanie (homicide)

Stephanie's first husband was convicted of killing a young woman whom the police said looked very much like Stephanie. This was after Stephanie had gone to live in a refuge with her three young children to escape domestic violence. He was sentenced to life imprisonment, and when I interviewed her she was concerned about his future release.

Outline of the book

Chapter 1 examines how the relatives recalled their life before they discovered the offence, and the often catastrophic process and impact of discovery. Discovery was said to be a traumatic and life-changing experience, comparable to bereavement, and its effects had to be accommodated in some fashion. Accounts of life before the transition were polarised, presenting either as *problem-identifying* (emphasising problems such as the offender's mental illness or addiction) or *normalising* (emphasising the positive aspects of life before discovery and how life was otherwise 'conventional').

Chapter 2 examines the changes that took take place in the lives of relatives after they discovered the offence. One consequence was the re-negotiation of family responsibilities and the emergence of new roles devolved largely on female relatives and revolving around the offender and his or her needs. Description centred characteristically on sequences of experience as relatives moved forward from the low point of discovery. Relatives experienced particular difficulties in supporting the offender through the criminal justice process. Some of these difficulties can be found in the literature on prisoners' families, but there were others graver still for the relatives of serious offenders who described being affected by the heinous character of the crime, their lack of prior experience of the criminal justice system, and the length of the prison sentence subsequently imposed.

The relatives I met experienced secondary stigma, being themselves subject to what I describe as a 'web of shame', constructed around kin contamination and kin culpability, and Chapter 3 examines what is at work. The relatives were contaminated by their familial *association* with the offender, sharing a common background or household; and by an alleged *genetic* connection that could provoke very primitive ideas of bad blood. They were blamed and deemed to be responsible through sins of *omission* (that is, they are supposed either to have known or to be in a position where they should have known about the likelihood of the offence and they should have stopped it), of *commission* (that is, some deed in the long-term or immediate past caused or contributed to the offending, or perhaps that they were directly involved) and of *continuation* (that is, by continuing their relationship with the offender and supporting him or her they could be deemed to be condoning the offence and responsible for maintaining their stigma). This chapter defines and describes these sources of shame and explores how shame is transmitted to relatives through their interaction with others and through powerful public, lay, and expert discourses on family responsibility.

Chapter 4 examines the accounts that relatives constructed about the offence, drawing on a literature of motivational accounts. When accounting for the offence, relatives were found to use what might be called 'actor adjustments' ('he/she really isn't that kind of person') and 'act adjustments' ('what he/she did really wasn't as bad as you might think') (Ditton 1977; Cohen 2001) to attempt to explain what had happened and to limit culpability. Four types of actor adjustment and four types of act adjustment were found to be in play and this chapter explores the different forms they took.

Relatives were not only called upon to account for the offence, but they also felt an internally- or externally-driven need to account for their *own* actions. In Chapter 3, relatives were shown to be subject to shame constructed around several dimensions and Chapter 5 looks at how relatives addressed those different dimensions in accounts about their own role. The chapter shows how relatives offered stories that were intended to deflect family blame and shame, but many people were nevertheless obliged continually to struggle with ambivalent and conflicting feelings about their personal responsibility.

Chapter 6 explores relatives' use of self-help. Many of the participants were members of Aftermath and the chapter outlines its work. Most of the participants in the research were female, as are most participants in self-help services for relatives of offenders, and some of the reasons for this lack of proportion are considered. The chapter explores what self-help groups offer their members and I suggest that they supply a 'collective narrative' for understanding experience which is a *resource* to be combined with other sources for purposes of understanding. Embedded in this collective narrative are *flexible categories* which members may deploy in a contingent way.

Note

1 Although the concept of social exclusion and how it informs Government policy has been subject to much debate. The social exclusion discourse has been said to re-frame issues that are actually to do with poverty and inequality in terms of a disconnection of individuals from mainstream values and aspirations (Gillies 2005).

Chapter 1

Discovering the offence

> I suppose that at the end of the day it's not going to be as bad as the day you first hear that it's happened. You know, is anything going to be?
>
> (Alice, son convicted of homicide)

Try to imagine as you are reading this that you receive news – from a telephone call or from someone knocking at your door – that a close relative has been arrested for a horrific offence. Imagine you were told that the person had sexually abused children, for example. How would you react? Disbelief? Shock? Horror? Panic? Your reaction might depend on a number of different factors – your relationship and history with the alleged offender, your opinion of the person conveying the news, or your own personal ability to deal with sudden distressing events. You are told of evidence for these allegations – do you believe it? Are you unsure? Does the news confirm suspicions you already had? As you read this you might be thinking 'this would never happen to me'. Does that thought reflect a sense of security and belief that none of your close kin would commit a crime? Or a belief that events like this only happen to particular kinds of families?

Perhaps the most unusual or surprising reaction would be one of indifference. It is inconceivable to most people to imagine not caring about allegations made against a close family member, and even if they had suspected, to be formally confronted with the news might still be very distressing. As we will see, relatives in this study consistently described feelings of shock and distress at finding out about the offence, despite quite polarised accounts of life with the offender before this point. The day that they first found out about the serious offence was described by relatives in this study as a life-changing turning point. The day was etched with clarity in their minds and became a new centre of gravity, a new point around which all other events were constructed; a knock on the door, a telephone call, a letter, or a conversation brought catastrophic news and suddenly changed everything. They learnt of the offence from a number of different sources, but most frequently from the police, either through a telephone call, a visit to ask questions or to ask whether they knew the whereabouts of the offender, or suddenly having their house searched, as in the case of Beverly who was woken by police looking to arrest her grandson for a violent offence involving a firearm:

> At about twelve o'clock, half-past eleven, twelve o'clock, I was in bed asleep with my boyfriend and my front door came off. And there was seven police standing over us with guns with lights on. My neighbours came out of the door and everybody was out there looking because they took us outside. And we had to stand up outside they handcuffed my boyfriend with plastic cuffs and they're searching all through the place and that. ... And then total shock and disbelief you know, just couldn't believe that [my grandson] would get himself involved in anything like that, do you know what I mean?
>
> (Beverly, grandson convicted of violent offence)

Other sources of this news included social workers, in the case of two relatives of sexual offenders, other relatives, or even the victims – one wife was sent a letter by her husband's victims which she handed over to social services. Police appeals for information often rely on someone from an offender's immediate circle coming forward and one mother in this study had recognised her relative's description in a newspaper report and notified police of her suspicions.

Gill discovered that her husband had been sexually abusing her nieces when her daughter Dawn was playing with her cousins. The cousins had told Dawn what her father had done and she ran to tell her mother:

> When she said that, it's like somebody had come up and just picked up the biggest mallet and just smacked me here and smacked me there. So I shouted for my sister and she come running up and I knew then, I knew. And I couldn't believe it, see, and she said 'do you believe them?' And I said 'of course'. First I'm going 'no, no' and then she said 'do you believe them?' and I said 'of course I believe them' and I put my arms around them and I saw [my daughter] Dawn and she was crying. Oh and all I remember, I just said to them 'oh you're brave girls for telling me' ... and I went home and confronted [my husband].
>
> (Gill, husband convicted of sex offence)

Hilda had lost contact with her son and was shocked to find out about his offence some months after it happened when it appeared on a television programme she happened to be watching:

> *R*: How did you feel when you found out?
>
> *H*: I felt sick. It was the biggest shock. I mean I've had some shocks, but I think that was the biggest. But in a way, I felt relief when [my partner] come in, because at least I could tell him as well, you know, let him have some of it.
>
> (Hilda, son convicted of homicide)

The shock of discovery

Although they found out in different ways, relatives commonly described experiencing feelings of shock, disbelief, unreality, and feeling sick. One wife said that when the police arrived to search her house she felt as if she was in a television programme, as if the events were happening to someone else. Giddens has described feelings of disembodiment and unreality as characteristic features of disruptions to 'ontological security' – an attempt to transcend danger in extreme conditions, as Bettelheim described in Nazi concentration camps (Bettelheim 1970) – but also a temporary 'splitting' reaction to disruptions experienced in difficult situations in everyday life (Giddens 1991: 59). Relatives described feelings of shock at the offence itself and at its anticipated consequences:

> You're in a situation where you've all had this terrific shock, you're having to deal with ultimately the sentences that they get, you're having to deal with actually what they've done, which is significant.
>
> (George, son convicted of homicide)

For some relatives the shock manifested in physical symptoms:

> I can actually remember physically what I felt like that day, half dead. It's like when you've got the worst dose of the flu but double-fold, it's like you just, your limbs have got no weight but they feel dead heavy, you know, I can feel how I felt but you couldn't describe how you felt. You weren't floating, they were heavy but there was nothing in them, you were just nothing, you were just hollow.
>
> (Gill, husband convicted of sex offence)

One mother described how her reaction to the shock of the police arresting her son for rape was to immediately clean out all her kitchen cupboards because she felt so defiled. The immediate consequences were described by relatives as devastating and symptoms of shock persisted for some time:

> I had sort of ten appalling days of you know, driving to prison and seeing solicitors and going to social services meetings and not being able to get there because I was snowed in, and oh blimey. I went back when I got home, I went home first to see [my husband] and [my son] and then I went over to see my Mum and I took to my bed nineteenth-century style and I went to bed and I couldn't get up, it was the most extraordinary sensation I've ever had, I was lying in bed and I couldn't move my arms and legs, they were so heavy, I stayed in bed for two days, I just couldn't move at all. I think exhaustion and shock and whatever.
>
> (Monica, daughter convicted of violent offence)

Relatives said they could not imagine how they would ever come to terms with the news: life as they knew it had been shattered and smashed to pieces. One mother at an Aftermath seminar weekend described feeling numb, and like many of those I spoke to, compared the process to bereavement: 'It's grief, a form of grieving, but you haven't got the respectability of them being dead'. This lack of respectability was important; relatives felt their grief was not legitimised because they were seen as somehow implicated and not free of blame.

What was it that relatives grieved for? There were a number of losses described: of their relationship with the offender or of free contact with him or her following imprisonment; of their hopes and dreams for the offender and what his or her life might hold – one father at an Aftermath meeting described how his hopes for his son to have a good job, a house of his own and to get married and have children were destroyed when his son was arrested for murder and subsequently given a life sentence; of other family members – in some families conflict emerged over whether to support the offender, for example, resulting in rifts and severed relationships; loss of the victim, if within the family or close circle – obvious in homicide cases, but also a result of children being moved into care or contact ceasing with grandchildren. Jane was grieving the loss of her grandson who had been removed to the care of social services and adopted with no further contact with his birth family:

> *J*: Losing my grandson. That hurts, he's out there somewhere and I can't get to him. . . . I've got a room in the house, I know it sounds morbid [crying] but it's the only way I can cope with it, it's

dedicated to Gareth. He's got clothes hanging in the wardrobe, he's got a cot, highchair, potty and toys on the floor and curtains up.

R: You think of that as his room?

J: That's Gareth's room.

(Jane, daughter convicted of violent offence)

Relationships with others might also be lost; there were many examples of relatives losing friends. There were consequential practical losses for some relatives of a job, finances, a home, and of time which was now devoted to the offender and his or her needs. One mother at an Aftermath meeting said she was unable to work because her son's conviction for murder was so devastating and as a consequence had to resign from her job and eventually lost her house.

Anne described her own experience of these losses and the experience of the numerous other families of serious offenders she had supported. Anne was also a counsellor for Cruse Bereavement Care, a national UK charity which supports the bereaved, and thought there were parallels between the two roles. She grieved for the loss of her son and for her relationship with him and for the loss of his future when he was convicted of rape:

R: Are there similarities between bereavement counselling with Cruse and counselling with Aftermath?

A: Very much so, I think it's, certainly for me it was a grieving process, even to the point that I could see a turning point after two years, which they say is the norm for grieving, you know, it takes two years. It was the same, it was two years before I started to sort of improve, because you've lost, I lost my son as I knew him, I lost my son, this is how I saw it at the time, life was never going to be the same between us again, I'd lost his future, I thought his future had gone, there was going to be no future, so very, very much the same, very much the same. Many, many times I felt that it would have been easier if he had died, because in my own mind he was dead, because everything had gone, and yet there was all the shame and the guilt and everything else that came with it, you know, so I couldn't get over it like I would if he died.

(Anne, son convicted of rape)

One Aftermath Chairperson described this as a 'living death': relatives would experience many of the emotions of bereavement, but with constant reminders of how their situation differed as they supported the offender through the criminal justice process, prison sentence and beyond.

One of the overwhelming losses described by relatives was the loss of security, of what they believed in, and a consequent loss of identity and their sense of self. Traumatic events involve a disruption of meaning, and of the framework we use to understand the world, which has been described as a 'loss of the assumptive world' (Parkes 1971; Parkes 1975). Janoff-Bulman describes the psychological impact of trauma and its aftermath as one of 'shattered assumptions' and has found similarities across different victim populations (Janoff-Bulman 1992). She argues that we all have a basic 'cognitive conservatism' and tend to discount anything that challenges how we see the world which stands us in good stead most of the time and helps us to understand the world and organise our experience. Normal change in our cognitive schema would be slow and gradual and not threaten its stability, but the change wrought by traumatic events is sudden and shattering: 'the abrupt disintegration of one's inner world' (*ibid.*: 63).

The relatives I met described the impact of finding out about the offence in similar ways. Again and again different relatives spoke of their world falling apart, of how life as they knew it had ended and how they felt their previous life experience had not prepared them for coping with something like this. The traumatic impact of finding out was partly to do with this anomie and 'ontological insecurity' (Giddens 1991) which left relatives asking why this had happened to them and what they had done to deserve it, and searching to restore a sense of meaning to their lives.

Celia had supported a large number of other relatives and likened the consequences that followed discovery of the offence to Post-Traumatic Stress Disorder (PTSD):

> That's when I got involved with the [counselling] training side of Aftermath, learning about the people that I share with, who never, ever were alcoholics, who previously had never taken drugs, who previously were not anorexic, were not bulimic, who previously were not agoraphobic and I began to realise wow, it isn't just about the offence and the offender, the effects on the families are devastating, and communication, how families are literally ripped apart because of an offence being committed. . . . And then I began to realise the effects on the family. People couldn't sleep, couldn't eat, turned to drink, turned to drugs, had no-one to talk to, in isolation, and there have been several times when I've been sharing with people on the telephone and I have began to realise that this is more than trauma, this is now what people are referring to as Post Traumatic Distress that the families suffer. I'm not saying everybody, but my experience tells me that most people, that is the severity. If I could find anything else that could allow you to see the

> impact . . . that's the thing that would come closest to my experience of other families.
>
> (Celia, nephew convicted of homicide)

The description of PTSD in the Diagnostic and Statistical Manual of the American Psychological Association (DSM-III-R) would be a familiar one to relatives:

> The essential feature of this disorder is the development of characteristic symptoms following a psychologically distressing event that is outside the normal range of human experience. . . . The stressor producing this syndrome would be markedly distressing to almost anyone, and is usually experienced with intense fear, terror and helplessness. The characteristic symptoms involve re-experiencing the traumatic event, avoidance of stimuli associated with the event or numbing of general responsiveness, and increased arousal. The diagnosis is not made if the disturbance lasts less than a month.
>
> (quoted in Janoff-Bulman 1992: 49)

A further distinction is made by Janoff-Bulman between traumatic events which are 'acts of God', and those for which a perpetrator is responsible, a distinction that is difficult for relatives of serious offenders. While a perpetrator is responsible for the offence, the relative was not the primary victim in the cases in this study (although of course this is not always so, and in some cases they were related to the victims). Apportioning blame for their circumstances was therefore not straightforward and relatives struggled with ambivalent feelings. On the one hand they wanted to care for and support the offender, and not heap blame upon him or her, but on the other some felt anger for the position they found themselves in following the offender's actions:

> And I feel that if he would have opened up to me, maybe I would have been able to help him. Maybe I could have got treatment for him. But I don't know, I don't know, I'm left in the dark about this and this is what's annoying me. This is what's making me so angry inside. I'm very angry. I'm very, very angry with him. My anger won't go away. And I think this anger must be what's really eating at me, not doing me any good whatsoever.
>
> (Lillian, son convicted of sex offence)

However, anger was not an emotion that was commonly expressed either in interviews or during fieldwork. It might be an emotion that relatives felt privately but did not feel comfortable expressing publicly, and their wish to defend the offender might have taken precedence over public expressions of anger, as Anne described:

> I suppose in a way I was always trying to protect [my son] Peter, because letting people know how I felt, they were always going to blame Peter, and I didn't want that.
>
> (Anne, son convicted of rape)

The relatives I met therefore described receiving shocking news that was difficult to absorb and had turned their lives, and the way they understood the world, upside down. The impact of finding out, how it was experienced, and what followed afterwards were ultimately all influenced by what had happened in their lives before this point.

Life before discovery

Being told that your husband has committed a sexual offence against a child or that your son has been arrested for murder is likely to be shocking and devastating to most people, but perhaps more surprising to some relatives than to others. For some the news might literally come 'out of the blue'; for others it might be part of a process of gradually becoming aware of the offender's actions. Several factors might influence this process, including the type of serious offence: sex offences against children are often carried out over a period of time, for example, whereas murder is usually a single act. With some offences, then, there may not have been a history of serious offending to know about, while with others there might have been a history of many years.

Some offences are by their nature more hidden than others. Perpetrators of child sex offences go to great pains to hide their actions, whereas some violent offences are carried out in public spaces; the son of one participant in this study, for example, was seen by several witnesses with the body of his murder victim in a busy town. The location of the offence is important: if it happens within the home or within the family it might be more difficult to hide from relatives, but easier to hide from those outside. The kin relationship to the offender and where the offender lives might make a difference; the closer the family relationship the more likely the relative is to know. Time is a further important variable. Three interviewees were not with the offender at the time of the offence: two because they were second wives and the offender had committed sex offences against his now adult children which had only recently come to light and one because she met her partner since his offence which had occurred in his teens,[1] but for which he remained imprisoned. The process of becoming aware may be quicker when the offender presents other problems, such as mental illness or addiction. Furthermore, awareness may be gendered: almost all participants in this study were female, and as Howarth and Rock point out, much offending is committed by males in public places and may not be reported to women; women who are in a position of dependence may not be able to afford to know too much; and even if they do ask questions they may not receive a reply (Howarth and Rock 2000: 65). Some offenders might behave quite differently at home. Campbell says of a prolific young offender in her study: 'This is a young man who is a glue sniffer and a petrol bomber, a burglar and a joyrider who takes tea with his mother and tidies his room' (Campbell 1993: 194).

Given this range of different factors, one would expect a variety of different experiences amongst a group of 32 interviewees and a greater number of fieldwork participants. As we have seen, they all[2] described discovery of the offence as shocking and traumatic; none said she knew about the serious offending for any length of time prior to the offender's arrest (and in the few cases where they did, the police were informed very quickly, and often by the participants in this study); none said that looking back she must have known before or must have been 'in denial', a narrative that one might expect to hear from relatives of alcoholics, for example, in 'twelve-step' groups such as AlAnon.

Most relatives were keen to stress that they had little or no experience of serious offending prior to discovery. None admitted to any criminal involvement themselves,[3] and they usually spoke about their offending relative as the only serious offender in their family. Lorraine's response was typical:

> No-one ever in my family has ever gone to prison, from aunts, uncles, cousins, grandmother, even my grandfather, father, none of them have ever, ever gone into prison.
>
> (Lorraine, daughter convicted of drug offence)

Two-thirds of relatives said that the offenders had no previous history of offending (of which they were aware); for those that did, it was usually of a more minor nature and discovery of the serious offence was still described as shocking.

It may well be true that relatives in this study genuinely knew nothing, and I had no reason to doubt their accounts of life before discovery. However, we know from the literature on families with other problems such as alcoholism or mental or physical illness that it is possible for families to sustain collective denial in the face of considerable evidence to the contrary and it is worth considering how these processes might operate in this context. As Cohen states:

> Without conscious negotiation, family members know what trouble spots to avoid, which facts are better not noticed. These collusions – mutually reinforcing denials that allow no meta-comment – work best when we are unaware of them. The resulting 'vital lie' in the family may become a literal blind spot. But the facts are too brutal to ignore. They have to be reinterpreted, using techniques like minimization, euphemism and joking: 'If the force of the facts is too brutal to ignore, then their meaning can be altered. The vital lie continues unrevealed, sheltered by the family's silence, alibis, stark denial. The collusion is maintained by directing attention away from the fearsome fact, or by repackaging its meaning in an acceptable format' (Goleman 1985).
>
> (Cohen 2001: 64)

So there may be processes occurring within families that keep acknowledgement of offending suppressed, but these processes are difficult to access through research relying on retrospective accounts. Similar processes have been found in studies of wives with mentally ill husbands (Yarrow *et al.* 1955a, 1955b) and wives of alcoholics (Wiseman 1991) who try to interpret their husband's behaviour as normal, using a variety of techniques, until a point where they can no longer do so and decide to seek help. According to Johnson, a typical pattern can be discerned from the Yarrow study of mental illness in the family and two others during that period (Rogler and Hollingshead 1965; Sampson *et al.* 1962): odd or bizarre behaviour on the part of the mentally ill family member is rationalised and accommodated by other family members until a precipitating event involving clearly unacceptable behaviour pushes the family to involve the mental health system; this is a pattern which has been confirmed by later interview studies (Hambrecht *et al.* 1994; Lincoln and McGorry 1995; Johnson 2000).

When relatives of serious offenders recalled life before discovery their accounts were polarised and presented either as *problem-identifying* (emphasising problems such as the offender's mental illness or addiction) or *normalising* (emphasising the positive aspects of life before discovery and how life was otherwise 'conventional'). Accounts of families with a mentally ill member have similarly been found to describe 'either a poor pre-morbid history or a surprisingly good one' (Johnson 2000: 128). Analysing relatives' accounts in this way is not the same as dividing relatives into deniers and non-deniers of offending behaviour prior to discovery; relatives of serious offenders who offer either account in interviews might move back and forth between partial denial and partial acknowledgement both before and after discovery. As Cohen states, denial is not a property of a personality, but rather of a situation. Although some people may use it more than others, people are not either total deniers or total non-deniers: 'People give different accounts to themselves and others; elements of partial denial and partial acknowledgement are always present; we oscillate rapidly between states' (Cohen 2001: 54). Although those offering normalising accounts were more likely to be using various denial techniques, this was not necessarily so: their lives with the offender prior to discovery may well have been more 'normal' than those who offer problem-identifying accounts; the 'offender' may well have not been guilty, as some participants claimed; and problem-identifiers might be identifying one problem while denying another.

All of the problem-identifying accounts pointed to a gradual decline in the offender, because of addiction, mental illness or other problems. Often the offence for these families was preceded by many years of trying to get help for their relative and interaction with health and social services and sometimes criminal justice agencies. Anne tried to get help from her teenage son's psychiatrist before the offence, but it was not forthcoming. She had concerns about the worrying behaviour he was exhibiting:

> He became abusive to me at home, he's never been abusive to me and he's not now, but during those 18 months he was awful. He started stealing because he'd got to fund the drugs ... he was obviously abusing solvents, he used to leave cans of butane gas in his bedroom, dozens and dozens of them. One morning I picked about 30-odd cans and put them in a bag. His behaviour was absolutely horrendous. ... He was just a totally different person ... in those 18 months he overdosed about four times. We had a terrible time with him.
>
> (Anne, son convicted of rape)

Stephanie was another relative who offered a problem-identifying account. Her case was unusual in this study because her husband had a long history of committing serious violent offences, and she was often the victim:

> *S*: Yeah, he was charged with ABH, he broke my nose, blacked my eyes, held a knife to me, threatened to throw boiling hot water over me, all sorts of injuries I've had from him.
> *R*: And this went on for a period of time?
> *S*: From the word go when we got married. From the night we got married he was violent towards me.

She had tried to get help for her husband from several sources:

> A lot of people who commit serious offences need help, and they're not getting it, because when [my husband] committed his offence, I went to everybody: doctors, psychiatrists, probation, everybody and said before the murder, 'do something else he's going to commit something serious', but nobody listened to me.
>
> (Stephanie, husband convicted of homicide)

Eventually Stephanie left her husband and sought safety in a women's refuge. He then killed a young woman who was a stranger to him and whom the police had said looked very similar to Stephanie.

Previous offences reported by those in the group that offered problem-identifying accounts included drug use (in particular heroin and crack cocaine) and stealing to support it and, in two cases, other minor offences. Only three reported previous violence from the offender, an attack against a stranger by one offender and domestic violence from two others. Even those offering problem-identifying accounts still described shock and upset at discovering the serious offence; despite being more sensitised to dealing with their relative's difficulties, they say the news was unexpected:

> I suppose because I knew he'd been in borstal I knew that he could get into trouble and was likely to end up in prison. Never did I imagine he would kill somebody, no, no.
>
> (Celia, nephew convicted of homicide)

> The offence was a complete surprise. I always thought that she would kill herself, I never, ever thought that she would turn it on anyone else, let alone a baby. There were warning signs that she was in a bad state, but traditionally that has always led to either a suicide attempt or some other wildly destructive behaviour.
>
> (Monica, daughter convicted of violent offence)

Those relatives who offered normalising accounts, on the other hand, were keen to stress how everything in their lives prior to discovery was otherwise conventional:

> *R*: What was he like just before this happened, when he was 18, 19, what was he like then?
>
> *A*: Well we didn't know any different from, he was just normal. You know, he'd been, he'd joined the TA [Territorial Army] and he'd been away at camp and he'd done everything, you know, and we just could not understand it, because he was acting normally at home. ... Because they thought maybe he was schizophrenic at

first, but from all the tests they did, he even asked the psychiatrist if he could read his notes! You could tell how normal he was.

R: So would you say his offending was a complete surprise or were there any warning signals?

A: It was, it was a bolt out of the blue. No warning signals at all. Perfectly normal teenager – wouldn't clean his room at all.

(Ada, son convicted of rape)

Relatives who offered normalising accounts stressed positive aspects of life before the offence and gave examples of how they had lived just like anyone else – the jobs they had, the things they did, their preoccupations were all 'normal'. Normalising accounts of life before the offence addressed both the offender's and their family members' culpability. Parents could convey the message that 'we did our best'; all relatives could convey the message that 'we did not know'; and normalising accounts might even help to show that the 'offender' could not possibly be guilty of the offence of which he or she has been accused or convicted. Problem-identifying accounts addressed culpability in a different way. By pointing to problems such as mental illness or substance addiction relatives were able to identify 'reasons' and so minimise their own and the offender's responsibility (these accounts will be explored in Chapters 4 and 5).

For some of those offering normalising accounts the offence itself was the precipitating event after which they recognised problems the offender had; others in this group continued to normalise after discovery of the offence, particularly those who questioned their relative's culpability. For those offering problem-identifying accounts the offence was yet another, more serious event which though perhaps unexpected in its severity confirmed their prior concerns. Of the 32 interviewees in this study, 15 offered problem-identifying accounts and 17 offered normalising accounts. Table 1 shows the distribution of these accounts.

Offence type appeared to be an important variable. In particular, problem-identifying accounts were more likely when the offence was homicide, and normalising accounts when it was a sex offence. Other variables were not significant: relatives of male offenders and female offenders were roughly divided equally between the two groups, as were non-supporting relatives. Mothers were equally likely to offer either account (8:9), but wives were more likely to offer normalising accounts (7:3) (although with low numbers it is only possible to identify possible patterns and not suggest statistical significance). An initial explanation might be that wives or partners were more likely to be sharing a household with the offender prior to discovery, and therefore might have more to gain from offering accounts which stress that everything was normal and they could not have known. However, the seven wives offering normalising accounts were from the child sex offence group, and

Table 1 Accounts of life before discovery

	Number of interviewees offering 'problem-identifying' accounts (15)	*Number of interviewees offering 'normalising' accounts (17)*
Homicide ($n=11$)	8	3
Sex offence ($n=10$)	1	9
Rape ($n=3$)	2	1
Violent offence ($n=7$)	4	3
Drugs ($n=1$)	0	1
Relatives of male offenders ($n=24$)	12	12
Relatives of female offenders ($n=8$)	3	5
Non-supporting relatives ($n=5$)	2	3
Mothers[4] ($n=17$)	8	9
Wives/partners ($n=10$)	3	7

the three offering problem-identifying accounts were from the homicide group, so the source of this difference is probably found in the offence type rather than the kin relationship.

It is important to consider *why* relatives of child sex offenders were more likely to offer normalising accounts. One reason might be the nature of the offence: sexual offences are generally secretive and offenders might go to great lengths to hide their actions from family members. It may be more difficult to pick up on signs or clues, unlike someone with a history of violent offending, for example, who might present with physical marks or offend more publicly. It is possible, therefore, that in many cases family members really did not know and that in all other ways life appeared normal. Child sexual abuse may be such an affront to relatives' world that they might experience a stronger 'urge to normalise'. One interviewee, for example, described how she had been told by her six-year-old niece that her husband had 'licked my tottie [vagina]'. She had reported this immediately to the girl's mother (the interviewee's sister) who had said that she should not worry because her daughter had been having bad dreams and that would be why she said it, and that it was best forgotten. When she was confronted with a further disclosure from her niece some time later she says she was haunted by having missed her earlier attempt to tell: 'with it being nearly two years since she said that, [finding out] nearly killed me. I could have stopped so much of that. . . . If I'd have took it on board I could have stopped it for these last how ever many months'.

Normalising accounts could partly be a response to current public opinion, that people who commit sexual offences against children are the lowest of the low, almost sub-human. For child sexual offenders more than any other offenders their offence becomes their master status, something their relatives try to resist; these attempts at resistance will be considered in Chapter 4. Relatives might also want to convey that they think their family member will not re-offend, and that he has a happy, 'normal' family life to help him achieve that aim. Relatives of sex offenders in this study felt they experienced greater blame than relatives of other serious offenders and they might therefore want to convey that they did not know, that they did not collude, that they could not have prevented it and that they are justified in continuing to offer support to the offender (see Chapters 4 and 5).

Finally, it is worth noting that being unsure of the offender's culpability might be at best uncomfortable and at worst extremely stressful for relatives, and some remain unsure after they have been told of the offence. Wiseman points out that the model provided by the study from Yarrow *et al.* (portraying wives struggling with ambivalence in the stages prior to acceptance of their husband's mental illness) did not really consider the damaging effect that this might have for the wives. In her own study, Wiseman found a 'serious psychological toll taken on the wives of alcoholics as they suspect their own sanity while being bombarded with conflicting evidence during the difficult judgement period' (Wiseman 1991: 34), something which may be similar for relatives of serious offenders struggling with ambivalent feelings and unsure what to believe about the offender's culpability, before, during and after discovery.

Discovery of the offence was therefore a transition point for relatives and a difficult stage. Life as they knew it had been destroyed, thrown into confusion, and they did not know what would replace it. All their thoughts and energies were devoted to the predicament of the offender and they needed to find ways to cope, to move forward and to find ways to adjust to what had happened.

Notes

1 This interviewee, Lisa, gave an account of life before the offence rather than life before discovery. This was based on what she understood from secondary sources rather than first-hand experience and was problem-identifying (see Table 1).

2 Except Lisa – see previous footnote. She was told about the offence some time after meeting her partner.

3 Although one interviewee was working in the sex industry as a 'stress management therapist' and was taking calls from clients throughout the interview, but she did not perceive this as criminal – she thought she was

offering a very valuable service – and she did not make reference to any other criminal involvement.

4 Other relatives have not been included in the table as a separate category because there was only one in each category: one father, one grandmother, one daughter and one aunt of a serious offender. Each of these four offered problem-identifying accounts.

Chapter 2

Life after discovery

> In every single aspect my life has been changed, you know. In effect, I feel I have a new life. That was my old life, this is my new life. It's just made me see everything in a different light, it kind of woke me up . . . life began at 40 for me, March 1998, my world as I knew it, gone.
>
> (Gill, husband convicted of sex offence)

Discovery was an important turning point in the trajectories of relatives' lives; a catastrophic interruption which, as we saw in the previous chapter, left devastation in its wake. Relatives did not remain stuck at this point, however, and their lives continued to change and develop. For interviewees in this study the length of time since finding out about the offence varied, ranging from just a few months to more than 15 years. Observation and fieldwork conversations took place over several years, and I remained in contact with some relatives once the research had ended. Over time it was possible to see different processes at work as relatives tried to assimilate the changes wrought by discovery and find ways to cope.

Relatives' descriptions centred characteristically on sequences of experience and four broad stages appeared to be significant: *initial impact stage; early coping stage; accommodation*; and *moving on.* Broadly, participants made some progress from the initial shock of discovery to a point where they were beginning to cope, progressing to a point where they had further adjusted to the changes in their lives, and finally for some relatives to a point where they were able to consider the whole matter to be in the past, though they were in the minority among participants in this study. Within each stage there were a number of different processes occurring which are summarised in Figure 1. Prus has shown

Stages	Processes within each stage
Initial impact	External events: passage of time; criminal justice process; marking significant anniversaries
⇩	
Early coping	Intrapersonal processes: emotional development; developing coping strategies; rebuilding sense of meaning; developing new perspectives; narrative reconstruction of self and identity
⇩	
Accommodation	
⇩	
Moving on	Interpersonal processess: changes in relationships within and outside the family; finding support (and rejection); organisational membership

Figure 1 Life after discovery

how conceptual development can be maximised in social research by focusing on 'generic social processes' (Prus 1994). By abstracting these processes from the specific context in which they occur, comparisons can be made with other contexts where participants face similar problems. This enables qualitative researchers to generalise about processes rather than populations; similar processes to those I found might operate in other social contexts when individuals are coping with analogous traumatic experiences.

Three broad types of intertwined processes emerged from relatives' accounts: *external events, intrapersonal processes* and *interpersonal processes.* First, some relatives marked time according to external events and particularly the criminal justice process, which was predominantly so for those who could see an end to a prison sentence. Gill's husband was sentenced to two years; for her, life began again as they slowly repaired their family life on his release. Others such as Celia, Hilda and Pauline, had relatives held indefinitely in special hospitals. They could not plan for their relative's release, but marked time according to significant anniversaries and described how they had changed in their ability to cope and in their relationships with others. Secondly, there were internal, intrapersonal processes as relatives themselves changed as they adjusted to what had happened and developed coping strategies, rebuilding a sense of meaning and a sense of self and identity. This chapter examines some of the adjustments relatives had to make, and Chapters 4 and 5 look at relatives' attempts to make sense of events. Finally, there were changes in relationships within and outside the family as relatives found both support and rejection. The stigmatisation which was the source of this rejection is examined in Chapter 3. Coming together with others to collectively manage their problems was important for many participants and will be discussed further in Chapter 6.

The framework has been constructed for the purpose of summarising the experience of many relatives; a typology such as this risks underplaying individual variation, for example in the time frame for progression through the stages or in the greater relevance for individual relatives of some processes rather than others. The stages in Figure 1 are therefore broadly conceived and may disguise the many smaller stages through which relatives passed and the different emotions relatives experienced in each stage: this is not an attempt to impose a rigid framework on relatives' experience or suggest that they all reacted in the same way to events. Real people have different reactions to events and these processes and stages have been loosely framed to allow for that individual variation, while simultaneously mapping the different kinds of progress made by relatives from the point of discovery. Progress through the stages might not be straightforward or linear. Some participants, for example, had reached a stage of accommodation and were offering support to other relatives when they were 'knocked back' by events such as renewed publicity of the offence or a family rift which left them needing a higher level of support.

An attempt to impose a more rigid framework was found at one Aftermath seminar weekend. A speaker who was a community psychiatric nurse showed the audience a 'grief wheel' which she suggested captured their experience, with the stages of *disbelief, guilt, anger, acceptance* and *normal functioning*. This provoked a strong reaction from some audience members who were not happy with the idea of this emotional cycle being imposed on their experience, and two commented: 'As a mother of a child who has committed murder you never fully accept it – you never get to the end of that wheel!' and 'I'm still in that anger stage and that's after 19 years'. The reaction of these relatives was not unfounded. There have been a number of 'stage' theories of dying and bereavement, examples of which include Averill's *shock, despair* and *recovery* (Averill 1968); Kubler-Ross's *denial, anger, bargaining, depression* and *acceptance* (commonly applied to bereavement, though originally intended also to apply to adjustment to one's own death) (Kubler-Ross 1969); and Parkes's *numbness, pining, depression* and *recovery* (Parkes 1972); for a review of theories of bereavement as a career see Small (2001) and Rock (1998a, Chapter 3). These stage theories have been criticised for being prescriptive (Samarel 1995) and for suggesting 'a fixed endpoint for mourning' (Corr *et al.* 1997). In relation to Kubler-Ross, Samarel has suggested that 'some health care professionals have abused the theory by attempting to force patients to move from one stage to the next according to an imposed schedule' (Samarel 1995: 94) and in relation to

Parkes's theory, Walter has argued that it has been reduced and over-simplified by some of those working with the bereaved into a form of 'clinical lore' with prescriptive, fixed stages through which all must pass (Walter 1999).

The stages in Figure 1, then, are not intended to capture single emotions or to be prescriptive or suggest a fixed endpoint (as we will see, some relatives felt able to 'move on', but they were in the minority among those I met). The first stage relatives described was one of *Initial impact* immediately following discovery where life was in disarray and the all-consuming changes were very difficult to manage. Nancy's husband had only recently been imprisoned at the time of the interview and she described how she felt:

> [My life has] just been turned upside down. I feel as though I'm in a void. I've lost my husband; I can't grieve for him because he's alive. I have contact with him but my life's been put on hold. It's as though you were in a tunnel and there's no light. When this happened all my friends, my personal friends, didn't want to know me.
>
> (Nancy, husband convicted of sex offence)

Anne's son had been convicted of rape several years before we met. She described how she felt during this first stage:

> *R*: What about when it happened? What was the effect on your life then?
>
> *A*: Oh God, I wouldn't go, I wouldn't go to the village, I wouldn't go, if I had to do anything out the front [of the house] I'd just keep my head down, if anybody walked past. It's debilitating, it's the only way I can describe it, just going through the motions. I wished at that time, I'm a coward, if there had been a painless way of committing suicide I'd have done it. You just can't see any way out, can't see how anything can get any better for you, it's just too much to bear . . .
>
> *R*: How long did that go on for, feeling like that?
>
> *A*: Probably two or three years. Probably two years before I started to feel a little better . . . I feel such a lot better; you really do put it behind you.
>
> (Anne, son convicted of rape)

Anne was one of several interviewees who spoke of contemplating suicide. A letter to the Aftermath newsletter in March 1998 stated: 'I felt like committing suicide several times, but [my Aftermath supporter] was there to help me . . . I'm sure I would be dead right now without her help and support.' Others described suffering depression and other mental health problems and seeking medical treatment:

> I'd never been to the doctor for years but I did, I was in rather a bad state and she put me on some anti-depressants. And I couldn't seem to stop crying wherever I went. I'd be walking down the street and then I would, people would look at me because I was just so emotional, you know, I just, it was dreadful. It was, you know, I'd go to the prison and then I'd leave there and go home and I couldn't even cook a meal because I thought 'how can I eat, how can I eat this food when he's in there, shut up in isolation?'
>
> (Lillian, son convicted of sex offence)

Following the analogy of bereavement used by many relatives, this was a period of intense mourning and visible grief. Relatives at this stage had experienced a shattering of their world and their very identity, but had not yet had the chance to absorb this new knowledge. An important part of coping was beginning to make some sense of their predicament, integrating what had happened into their inner world and their self-narratives. The work that relatives did to repair identities and restore a sense of meaning will be examined in the following chapters.

Harriet described her feelings at this initial stage. Drawing on her own experience and her experience of supporting other Aftermath members, she felt this period lasted even longer:

> It was just a nightmare time, I couldn't believe it was happening. . . . you actually feel you're going to go mad; the brain cannot take this degree of trauma. It will either explode or I shall go mad . . . They say it takes two years with a bereavement, I would say it takes four [years] before the family starts to come to terms and pick up their lives a little bit and start to live for themselves, and not just one hundred per cent for the person inside [prison].
>
> (Harriet, son accused of sex offence)

Most interviewees described difficulties in finding the right kind of support to help them through this difficult stage. The first source of support for some relatives was other family members, and there were examples of participants receiving help with transport to prison visits or with money. However, where participants did receive support they felt they could not lean too heavily and some mentioned concerns with not expressing their feelings openly to other family members for fear of upsetting them. Some relatives turned to friends for support, but had to deal with the problem of if, when, and how to tell, and risked rejection when they did (see Chapter 3). Some participants described support from their religious faith; one mother thought the support from her priest had been the most important she received. However, this support was not always forthcoming: one man at an Aftermath meeting talked in some detail about how he had felt rejected by his religion when his brother was convicted of murder and an interviewee recounted feeling that people in church were staring at her when her husband was convicted of murder. Some relatives used Aftermath or other prisoners' families organisations, although not all had found Aftermath at this early stage. Those who did emphasised the importance of the telephone support they received and some participants who acted as supporters to relatives at this time described receiving desperate telephone calls in the early hours of the morning from relatives who did not know where else to turn.

After a period of time, relatives enter a new stage of *Early coping*. This is not to suggest their difficulties are over, rather that they begin to realise they are managing better and can see some 'light at the end of the tunnel'. For Monica, this was when the criminal justice process was resolved, which took several months:

> I don't think there was a particular turning point, although having said that I think once it was dealt with, once we knew what was going to happen, but it was just slowly, slowly, slowly, things got a bit better.
>
> (Monica, daughter convicted of violent offence)

As we have seen, Anne thought it took two or three years to feel that she was coping; Harriet suggested it took four.

The next stage is one of *Accommodation* where relatives continued to attempt to make sense of events and to develop strategies for coping. In terms of external events, a prison sentence might end or relatives might settle into a pattern of regular prison visiting and supporting the offender and assimilate this into their lives. Again, this is not to say their difficulties are over, and despite accommodating to their circumstances many still find those circumstances distressing, particularly when faced with painful reminders. Accommodation is not the same as acceptance (one of the suggested stages of mourning in the grief wheel example above); relatives often stressed they could never accept what the offender had done, nor fully accept their own resulting circumstances.

At this stage some relatives reach a point where they feel able to offer help to others, an important principle of most self-help groups and for many participants in this study the medium through which this was made possible. As relatives said, it was unlikely they would meet another relative of a serious offender in their daily lives, or certainly one of whom they would be aware; a serious offender in the family would not be a topic of casual chit-chat. However, some participants were asked to offer support to others in a similar situation outside the self-help setting – one mother was asked to do so by her priest, for example. The role of Aftermath members who were 'supporters' to other members typically involved telephone and face-to-face support, and being the first point of contact when the member had particular problems. During fieldwork I listened to discussions between Aftermath members about the difficulty of placing a fixed time limit on when members would be ready to become supporters. Aftermath as an organisation thought that a period of time should pass from discovery of the offence before members would be able to offer help to others, but recognised that there would be individual variation in how long this should be. This problem is not specific to relatives of serious offenders; one interviewee had been involved with Compassionate Friends which asked for a three-and-a-half year gap from the death of a child before its members could support others and another had been involved with the adoption charity NORCAP which, she explained, specified that members must be one year post-reunion before they can support other adoptees: 'so things have had a chance to settle'.

Helping others also happens more informally within the self-help setting, for example through conversations in groups or informal gatherings, and in the case of Aftermath at 'lunches' (see Chapter 6). Gill described how helping new members had made her realise how far she had progressed:

R: What do you get from the lunches?

G: First and foremost I feel like they're part of my family. And when new people come in, it's so great and so terrible at the same time to see people in the state that you were, back down the line. It gives you such a push to say 'yes, you were there, look how you've come on, you can go further'. And it also, when you get talking to people, you feel sometimes that you've helped them by saying to them, 'yes here was I, two or three years ago', and I think it helps them, although not in the first stages, because nobody can really help you, you just need to be able to have somebody there.

(Gill, husband convicted of sex offence)

Helping others might also help relatives to view their own suffering as having a purpose, which can be an important strategy for coping with a traumatic experience (Janoff-Bulman 1992).

Moving on might have a different meaning to individual relatives. On an emotional level, many of the participants who had discovered the offence some years previously had moved on to a point where they said they were coping, where the offender and his or her needs were no longer their main preoccupation, and where they felt more 'at peace'. As Anne said in the quotation above 'I feel such a lot better, you really do put it behind you'. However, relatives did not describe moving back to life as it had been before the offence. Their life, and they themselves, had been changed forever. Those with relatives serving indeterminate sentences in special hospitals or prisons were not able to move on in a physical sense, particularly if they continued to support the offender and to devote time to this undertaking. Many relatives said they thought these events and their repercussions would always remain part of their lives; as one said: 'you're never free of it'.

Even when relatives felt they had moved on, they would occasionally be reminded and taken back to past feelings. Sometimes reminders were found in the minutiae of daily life. One uncle, for example, said he could not watch violent television programmes or films after his nephew was convicted of a killing. Language could also hold vivid reminders:

> I couldn't watch the television or read anything, and I still hate the word 'rape'. I hate it, I find it very difficult to say even when it's rape in a field! You know, I can't call it that, I say 'look at that lovely yellow stuff over there!' I can't bring myself sometimes to say the word.
>
> (Anne, son convicted of rape)

> Very often I hear mothers shouting at the children, 'if you don't come here and do as I tell you I'll bloody well kill you!' And do they really mean it? Do they know what they're saying when they say that?
>
> (Celia, nephew convicted of homicide)

Several interviewees and fieldwork participants talked about significant anniversaries when memories came flooding back, even many years later. Celia described how there were many anniversaries that were still important to her even eight years after the offence, and to others she had supported in Aftermath:

> So you have the anniversary of the killing, the anniversary of the first court, you have the anniversary of the Crown Court, you have the anniversary of the sentencing.
>
> (Celia, nephew convicted of homicide)

Moving on might happen for some families after a prison sentence has been served. Once families no longer need to deal with any aspect of the criminal justice process, they might feel the worst is over. Others may feel that the repercussions remain long after the prison sentence and continue to need support and/or want to help others. Repercussions are likely to be ongoing for those related to lifers or to sex offenders who might be subject to further restrictions on release from prison; several interviewees were preoccupied with the restrictions that would follow the offender being placed on the sex offenders' register and how these would affect their lives. Further difficulties might be experienced on release such as re-grouping as a family, re-negotiating family responsibilities, and the lack of accessible support. Families might also be affected by employment problems, particularly likely when a serious offender is released from prison, or other problems because of the seriousness of the offence, such as whether a sex offender can return to the same area. In the long-term, relatives worried what they would tell children as they grew up, and some interviewees even mentioned concern over what to tell future grandchildren.

For some relatives there was a final stage of moving on to the point where being a relative of a serious offender was no longer the main focus of their lives. In Clare's case this was because her relationship with her husband had ended when he was released from a prison sentence for sexual offences. She had begun a new relationship, and although she remained an active member of Aftermath for some years, when I interviewed her she was contemplating leaving the organisation and did so shortly after. She explained her reasons for wanting to leave:

> I feel I've come to a point in my life where I want to move on. And I find that still going to Aftermath, still going to the lunches . . . I find that it keeps regurgitating everything. And I think up to a certain point that's helpful as part of the therapeutic process you're going through. But I think I might have got to the stage now where I'm thinking that's not helpful to me anymore. I want to move on, I want to be able to leave some of that behind me now. I don't want to keep regurgitating, and with the best will in the world, just by being involved in it, you can't help but keep doing that.
>
> (Clare, husband convicted of sex offence)

I stayed in touch with some participants once the research had ended, and heard other stories of relatives moving on. Changes in external events often lead to changes in their lives – one mother, for example, described how her son had been released from prison and had since married and had children, and her life now centred on her role as a grandmother rather than as a mother of a serious offender – and her visits were now to her son and his new family rather than to the prison.

Increased responsibilities after discovery

When a serious offence is discovered, everyday family arrangements are thrown into disarray. In the families of those I interviewed, this forced a re-negotiation of family responsibilities and life became more emphatically organised around the offender and his or her needs. New caring relationships were established, with one relative usually taking the lead in supporting the offender (and sometimes other family members) through the criminal justice process and imprisonment. In all the families in this study who were supporting an offender, the primary supporter was a female relative and usually a wife or mother. In interviews and through fieldwork I repeatedly found women who had put their own needs to one side to meet the needs of the offender and other family members. Although it is difficult to assess the role of men in families without directly interviewing them, from the descriptions given by the women I interviewed and spoke to during fieldwork most men were not involved to anything like the same extent. These women sometimes had help with particular tasks from other family members and from friends, but were primary supporters in the sense that they were the first port of call, taking overall responsibility, and in most cases doing considerably more than anyone else.

Other studies have found that where there are choices to be made about caring, rather than a caring trajectory that is largely by default (such as caring for an ageing spouse) women are more likely than men to take it on. Decisions are made on the basis of kinship obligations which are strongly gendered in our society (Arber and Gilbert 1989; Finch 1989; Qureshi and Walker 1989). Finch (1989) has shown how kin relationships are re-negotiated at points of disruption and suggests reasons why women are more likely to be responsible for caring for dependent family members and for running households and to play a more active role in family life than men: women have different access to resources, particularly sources of money; in the domestic division of labour men and women are given different responsibilities; and men and women's lives are often organised differently so that women are more likely to be able to offer the time and domestic labour involved in caring for others. This leads to a 'built-in tendency for caring responsibilities to fall on women' (Finch 1989: 53).

Although Finch was writing in 1989, gendered patterns in the division of labour continue today. There have been some changes – figures for the last decade show a fall in the rates of economic activity for men and a rise in the rates for women – but striking gendered divisions remain. In Spring 2003, 84 per cent of men were economically active, compared with 73 per cent of women (National Statistics 2004a). Over nine out of ten people who are economically inactive in order to look after the family or home are women; having a dependent child is the main reason women give to explain this inactivity (Weir 2002). Women are still much more likely than men to work part-time. Nearly 40 per cent of women with dependent children work part-time, as do 23 per cent of those without children; compared with only 4 per cent of men with dependent children and 9 per cent of those without (National Statistics 2004b). Women still spend more time than men on domestic chores. In the UK in 2000/1 women spent on average over 2 hours 30 minutes each day doing housework, cooking, washing up, cleaning and ironing; this was 1 hour 30 minutes more than men (National Statistics 2004c).

Caring for a relative is often narrowly perceived to mean physical care within the home but can encompass much more, particularly during times of adversity which bring additional problems that need to be managed. Horowitz has made a distinction between four broad categories of family care-giving activities: personal care and domestic tasks; emotional support; mediation with formal organisations; and financial assistance (Horowitz 1985). Brody adds another form of care, invariably provided by the family, of response and dependability in emergencies and other kinds of special need that do not occur on a daily basis (Brody 2004). These authors are writing about the care of the elderly; relatives of serious offenders do not usually provide physical care – and may have very little physical contact if the offender is imprisoned – but it is useful to conceptualise family care-giving in this way as it shows the breadth of possible kinds of caring.

Once an offender has been arrested, there is likely to be a need for practical support and emotional support throughout the criminal justice process. Practical support might include liaising with solicitors, dealing with the police during the investigation, attending court, fending off the media, and prison visiting. For mothers of offenders, organising one's life around the needs of an adult child might mean reverting to an earlier state of affairs. One interviewee, for example, organised her life around her son who was in his fifties and serving a prison sentence for sex offences, visiting him every two weeks, shopping for items he needed and also sending him money, writing regularly and generally being his first point of contact for any difficulties. She also cared for his son, her grandson, who was a young adult and who lived with her. Wives described organising their life around the needs of the offender, again visiting, shopping and sending in money, but also writing regularly and waiting in the home for phone calls from the offender in prison. One interviewee described how she would send a letter every day, which she would start writing before she went to bed and finish when she got up in the morning. This helped her to feel that she was sharing her life with her partner and that he was with her throughout the day.

Many women described being the emotional lynch-pin in the family and a source of emotional support for the offender and other relatives. Angela described supporting her family when her husband was accused of child sex offences. She felt she had to be strong and hide her own emotions from her sons who depended on her:

> I had to sort of keep going, I had to keep the family together because one of the things that I felt was that's why this was done, to break my family up, and that wasn't going to happen. There was no way [the women who made the allegations] were going to split my family, because that's what they wanted to achieve and they didn't. So it was important that I kept going. If I hadn't kept going then everybody else wouldn't. And everybody looks to mum, 'mum'll do it. Me mum's alright, me mum's alright so we'll be alright because me mum's alright'. And I think that's in any situation, any sort of, you know, any sort of stress the family goes under, if your mother can cope then you know, then you're alright.
>
> (Angela, husband accused of sex offence)

In the period of emotional upheaval following discovery the main supporting relative may be leant on by the offender and by other relatives as they attempt to absorb what has happened. This is not to suggest, however, that all supporting relatives react to discovery with a show of strength. As we have seen, feelings of shock and trauma were described and many felt as if their world had fallen apart. Some relatives even had to seek psychiatric treatment at this point and many described their desperation for support or their relief when they found it.

However, a significant number of the women in this study had considerable caring responsibilities and had to find ways to manage. Twenty-one interviewees described family responsibilities that occupied much of their time. Sixteen of them had adult children and described the support they gave them; ten had children under the age of 16, and six were single parents. Fourteen had grandchildren, and in some cases were their primary carers. In addition, supportive relationships were described with partners, nieces and nephews, and with elderly parents. The phrase 'women in the middle' has been used by Brody to describe women caught between multiple competing demands on their time and energy (husbands, children, parents and work) 'and often in the middle emotionally between elderly parents on the one hand and husbands and children on the other'. The negative consequences of this position have consistently been documented in research findings – on their own mental and physical health, family well-being, vocational activities and other aspects of their lives (Brody 2004). The women in this study were also 'women in the middle', caught between competing demands and often in the middle emotionally between the offender and other family members. Being so placed can take its toll and, in three families in this study, supporting mothers had become estranged from their other adult children through conflict over their dedication to supporting their offending offspring.

The criminal justice process

New responsibilities can revolve around dealing with the various stages of the criminal justice process. It is important to look at the whole criminal justice process, rather than just focus on the effects of imprisonment on the family; relatives are often very involved with each stage of the investigation, which in some cases can take years to process from discovery to sentencing. If a relative is held in custody from the point of arrest, a supporting relative can be their link to the outside world – a source of practical supplies, emotional support, and ability to bear news or relay messages. Relatives might be in contact with the police at the point of arrest or during the investigation and might be interviewed or have their house searched. A number of relatives commented on having to clean up the mess after their house was searched at a time when they themselves were shocked and distressed. The offender might need different kinds of support as the police investigation develops and relatives might need to liaise with legal representatives who will also be an important source of information about likely outcomes.

Relatives reported mixed experiences with the police, some of which were very negative, but even relatives who recounted negative experiences often spoke of particular officers who had treated them well. Angela's husband was eventually cleared of alleged sex offences against his (now adult) nieces at Crown Court. Angela had experience with the police as the relative of a victim of sexual abuse, but when she had to interact with them as the wife of the accused she felt that her treatment was strikingly different:

> *A*: [The police] were very hostile . . . the policewoman they sent to interview me was quite arrogant. She had the attitude that [the abuse] had to come out. But it didn't happen, so how could it come out? The policeman in charge of the case, the way he conducted himself at the trial was horrendous. He just stood laughing and joking with the witnesses. I was actually attacked in the court foyer on the Monday by one of the [alleged victims], and he stood there laughing. He stood there grinning with his arms folded, didn't go to my assistance or anything. My barrister reported him for his

conduct in the court buildings. He said that the appalling way he'd carried himself in the courts that week was noticed.

R: How do you think the police saw you?

A: As a sex abuser's wife. That's how they saw me... I always said to them, 'but he's innocent'. And they just laughed at me. You know, it weren't things they said, it was their attitude and the way they looked at me and you know, everything.

(Angela, husband accused of sex offence)

Many relatives were sympathetic to the role of the police investigating a crime, and said they understood that the police had a job to do. Some relatives, such as Monica, experienced very good treatment and understanding from the police. Overall, a lack of consistency in how the relatives were treated was reported; according to relatives in this study, much depended upon the personalities and inclinations of individual officers.

The court experience and sentencing were usually the second most significant events after discovery of the offence. Frances, for example, described how she managed to cope between discovery of the offence and the court case, but had to be admitted to a psychiatric hospital when her husband was imprisoned for a child sex offence. Many of the relatives I interviewed found court upsetting and frightening. When possible, Aftermath offered court support to families because they recognised that this could be such a difficult time. This would involve other Aftermath members who had been through a similar experience accompanying the relatives to give them emotional support and to provide information about what is likely to happen, the rituals involved, and how to avoid the press:

> On an emotional level, families can very often experience the trauma of facing the horrific gravity of the crime, alongside the complexities of the judicial system. Many families have never been inside a courtroom and find they are experiencing a system that is totally alien to them. Having an Aftermath supporter by their side means that many practical issues can be dealt with for them. This, along with the emotional support offered has proven to be invaluable.
>
> (Aftermath 2000: 4)

Some relatives were publicly identified for the first time and came into contact with the victim or the victim's associates. Others described their overriding concern for the welfare of the offender:

> At the beginning I was upset, because of [my daughter] Caroline being remanded in custody, because I was fearful for her, fearful for

> her physical survival. And it was horrible not being able to visit with her or touch her, because they have these glass screens up, and she looked so little . . . she looked so tiny and so frail, and she just looked awfully vulnerable and you didn't really feel you could look after her properly. And there were loads and loads of gutter press who were pestering me and pestering [her friends] and I got identified as her mother . . . people were looking at me simply because attention had been drawn to me, and I think I felt judged a bit, you know, because there's always this feeling that parents have done badly by children who go wrong, so I felt judged. But mainly I was just worried to death about Caroline I think.
>
> (Monica, daughter convicted of violent offence)

> We went down [to see my son after he was sentenced] and oh God it was awful, and that picture stuck with me for ages because, you do absolutely silly things when I think back on it. He'd only got trainers, you know, he was 17, hadn't got any proper shoes so he'd wanted proper shoes to wear to court and we'd bought him new clothes which is absolutely ridiculous, as though it makes any difference, so he'd borrowed a pair of [my husband's] shoes and I mean can you imagine? A seventeen year old wearing a fifty year old's shoes and I just picture, I sat next to him in the cell, and we clung to each other, and that picture, that looking down and seeing these stupid shoes on his feet as though they were going to make any difference. And I kept picturing him putting them on in his cell that morning getting dressed and putting on these ridiculous shoes because he thought that that's what he should do, wear shoes, and that picture of those shoes stuck with me for ages. I threw them out, I couldn't bear to look at them, because I could see, you know, us clinging on to each other. Those shoes.
>
> (Anne, son convicted of rape)

Some participants found themselves interacting with associates of the victim in court, and two interviewees said they were verbally abused. Most participants described feeling in shock at hearing the verdict and the sentence; several said they collapsed in court:

> After the judge said his piece and he went into his room, he came out, all I heard him turn around and say was 'four years'. I don't know what happened after that, I just was out of it, I collapsed. The next minute I think all I knew after that was them telling me 'come on', and they'd got smelling salts, and they wouldn't let me see her, by this time she's already down in the dungeon, them days, that

> day, I don't want to live no more of those days. I don't want to see no more of those days.
>
> (Lorraine, daughter convicted of drug offence)

It is important to note that sometimes a prison sentence can improve the lives of relatives. Some are primary victims of the offender such as Stephanie in this study, or may suffer other difficulties due to the offender's poor mental health or addictions for which prison can bring some relief. This is perhaps more often the case than is reflected in the sample in my study. Relatives for whom the prison sentence is an improvement are less likely to support the offender and less likely to seek help from organisations such as Aftermath, and are therefore much more difficult to access. After sentencing relatives might need to adjust to a lengthy prison sentence, to new knowledge about the offender and what happened, and possibly to changes in their views and the opinions of those around them about the offender's culpability.

Supporting a prisoner

> Speak kindly stranger when you pass the prison
> On your busy journey past its gates
> For did you know
> And then again how would you?
> There are those who live their lives
> And those who wait.
>
> (Poem by a member in Aftermath newsletter March 1998)

Supporting a relative in prison or a special hospital imposed particular demands and relatives described many of the difficulties that appear in the prisoners' families literature: financial problems, emotional difficulties, stigma stemming from imprisonment, demands on time, the struggle to maintain a relationship with the prisoner and concerns about the impact on children (e.g. In the UK see Boswell and Wedge 2001; Codd 1998; Mills 2004; Morris 1965; Shaw 1992; and in the US see Comfort 2002, 2007; Fishman 1990; Girshick 1996; Hairston 1991). Participants often described devoting time to letter writing, visiting, waiting for telephone calls and shopping for the prisoner, the needs of the prisoner becoming their primary occupation:

> My own life had to be shelved, we had to a) try and make [my son] realise there was a reason for living and b) just try and see him through this nasty mess and everything else had to just go by the board.
>
> (Penny, son convicted of rape)

Visiting a prisoner can be expensive, particularly if he or she is a long way from home. Although close relatives can claim transport costs from the Assisted Prison Visits Unit, some relatives found the processes for doing so to be complicated and often they had to find the money in advance. For those on a low income, meeting the needs of a relative in prison was particularly difficult:

> *R*: And how has all of this affected your life?
>
> *J*: I have to focus more on her. She keeps asking me to send things in. She doesn't realise I'm on income support, it's not a lot. When she does write, which is not very often any more, she asks for different stuff like slippers or knickers or bras or whatever. Stamps, writing paper, envelopes. And a visit to go and see her every fortnight, or whenever she sends me a VO [Visiting Order] . . . It takes three buses. It takes about three, three and a half hours.
>
> (Jane, daughter convicted of violent offence)

Prisoners generally earn very low wages and depend on those outside to supplement their income so they can make purchases from the prison 'canteen', and to purchase items which they are allowed to have sent in. Participants on low incomes described 'going without' in order to meet these needs or to meet the costs of visiting – one mother said she herself went without eating on visit days so she could spend the money she had on crisps and chocolate for her son. Some families particularly suffer financially if the main breadwinner is imprisoned which was the case for five wives in this study who described having to juggle finances and in two cases cope with considerable debts when their husbands were imprisoned.

Some difficulties are worse for relatives of serious offenders. Because of the seriousness of the offence, relatives had specific worries about the safety of the prisoner and some experienced difficulties when visiting. Many participants worried a great deal about the prisoner, and mentioned concerns about their mental and physical health, and in some cases concerns that they might attempt suicide. Both Monica and Jane's daughters had committed violent offences against their children. They were aware of the potential for their daughters to be victimised by others in prison should this be known. Monica said her daughter was moved onto a main location in the prison despite her protests that she was worried for her safety, and as a result her daughter wouldn't leave her cell and, Monica said, did not eat any food for a week because taking food into the cell was against prison regulations. Monica's daughter was eventually released and given psychiatric treatment, but Jane's daughter was still in prison when I met her and she continued to be concerned for her safety:

> You get more grief in prison if you've done an offence against a child, especially a baby, than you do for any other crime. If you go to prison and you're there because you've knifed somebody, if it's an adult it's bad, but they don't think, but if you go in and it slips out that you're there because you've hurt a child, a baby, then they'll all go for you, they'll all beat you up.
>
> (Jane, daughter convicted of violent offence)

Relatives of sex offenders also expressed particular concerns for the safety of the prisoner. Even if the prisoners had been deemed vulnerable because of their offence and separated from other prisoners, the status of relatives might be revealed during visits:

> *L*: You might get talking to somebody, you can't help talking to people that have got children, you might talk to the child. And then when you go in, if they say to their husband 'oh, I've been talking to that woman over there' you know, 'she's a nice lady'. And then he could turn around and say 'well you don't want to talk to her, the person she's visiting is a sex offender'. And then you feel the next time you go this person won't even acknowledge you.
>
> *R*: Is that something that's happened to you?
>
> *L*: Oh yes, yeah.
>
> *R*: Has anyone ever said anything to you?
>
> *L*: No, no, no. They never said anything. But they've said aloud about it to other prisoners. Oh you know, 'those people over there, oh they're sex offenders, they're always kept separate from the other prisoners'. And this, sometimes this is very hard to cope with you know.
>
> (Lillian, son convicted of sex offence)

> I can actually go into the visiting centre, sit at a table, chat to the people. Nobody ever says who they're visiting, what the offence is. I can go in, and as soon as they see me go over to the R section and they go over to the other section, they know I'm on protection wing. When I come out, they avoid me like the plague.
>
> (Nancy, husband convicted of sex offence)

Particular difficulties arise for relatives of serious offenders that have no prior experience of the criminal justice system, as Alice explained:

> We are like children being taught how to handle this and to cope with it, because we've never done it before, have we? So you know, you teach a child how to do something, you have to teach us as

> parents, you know, or brothers or sisters of the criminal, what to do, because we have no experience. I had no experience of prison – a little experience of the police, just everyday, you know, phone them up for the burglar alarm across the road – but no experience of what to do and how to deal with it. So somebody has to teach us, but nobody's teaching us properly are they? Because when you ring up it's as though you're expected to know how to book a visit!
>
> (Alice, son convicted of homicide)

Almost all participants had not visited a prison before. They needed to go through a process of socialisation, of learning how to do it and how to do it properly. In some instances they had been lucky enough to find Aftermath or another prisoners' families' organisation that could provide both formal and informal information. However, there are quite wide variations between prisons in visiting policies, so providing blanket information can be difficult. In 2003 a national Prisoners' Families Helpline was established, co-ordinated by Action for Prisoners' Families and two other organisations. It receives over 1200 calls each month, indicative of the demand for this kind of information from all prisoners' families. Calls 'range from simple questions about prison visiting procedures and local support agencies, through to concerns about a prisoner's welfare' (Action for Prisoners' Families 2006).

Some prisons have visitors' centres which offer a bridge between the prison and families, helping them to navigate the complex rules and regulations. Some relatives were just left to find out by trial and error, and numerous examples were given of things going wrong. Having no prior experience of prisons and prison visiting and no informal social network to tell them how to do it, relatives did not know what the visiting process would entail: what they could wear, what ID would be needed, where they would check in, how long this might take, what they could take into the prison, what the prisoner might need them to bring such as clothing or other items, how they could get money to the prisoner, what being searched might involve, where they would sit, what they and the prisoner would be allowed to do, how they should talk to the officers, how the officers would talk to them, and so on. Experienced prison visitors have learnt how to navigate these stages, although the pains of prison visiting remain. Novice visitors find they are constantly getting things wrong, which can make an already difficult situation much worse. Some of these mistakes can have seemingly devastating consequences such as a visit not taking place or the prisoner being left without money or other items.

Problems with prison visiting are particularly pertinent to families of serious offenders because they are likely to spend a great deal of time visiting prisons over the course of a long sentence; some will even be prison visitors for the rest of their lives. Although attempts have been made to improve the experience of prison visitors, for many it is harrowing and terrifying. Most relatives understood the need to search visitors, but some found the experience to be intrusive and not always handled sensitively. Visitors often felt that the punishment meted out to the prisoner was extended to them. Prisons have a difficult job balancing control and security issues on the one hand with rehabilitation and welfare concerns on the other, and this balance is played out dramatically in the visits room. One American study of women visiting prisoners described how they 'assume the peculiar status of quasi-inmates, people at once legally free and palpably bound' as they are brought within the reach of the discipline of the prison rules, regulations, searches and the submission to authority required of them (Comfort 2003: 103). Visitors are often sympathetic to security issues and many interviewees mentioned this, but also wanted to be treated with respect and dignity. Some prisons and prison officers achieve this more effectively than others. One mother asked in an interview why prisoners were not treated like families for the duration of the visit rather than families treated like prisoners – an admirable aim if security needs could also be met. During discussions with those that work in the prisoners' families arena suggestions were made about how security might be improved without further infringing on visitors, such as searching prisoners thoroughly as they leave visits and searching everyone who enters the prison, including all staff.

Relatives visiting special hospitals often found the experience easier on a practical level because they were not subject to the same level of rules and constraints and more was done to facilitate contact with families. Five interviewees were in this position. However, having a relative in a special hospital brought its own set of problems, and interviewees mentioned the indeterminate sentence length, visits being affected by the behaviour of the patient or medication side effects and their own fear of other patients:

> It's very emotional having to go to [the special hospital] anyway, it's not a nice place. [My son]'s got a nice habit of when you're sitting there he'll say 'don't look now, that bloke behind you, he got done for murdering two people'. He thinks it's funny, but it turns my stomach over.
>
> (Hilda, son convicted of homicide)

Furthermore there are only a small number of special hospitals and relatives may therefore have much further to travel. For one elderly mother in this study, her poor health combined with the distance of the hospital meant she was no longer able to visit and thought it was unlikely she would ever see her son again.

A difficulty reported by those visiting prisons and special hospitals was judging what was appropriate to talk about during visits. Visitors found themselves treading a difficult line between not talking about problems on the outside and worrying the prisoner, and trying not to over-emphasise positive news from the outside and remind the prisoner of what they had lost. As a result, they ended up treading a middle line talking about mostly 'safe' bland subjects; one mother drew parallels between this and hospital visiting. Restricting conversation to safe topics during prison visiting has been similarly reported in other studies (Action for Prisoners' Families 2003; McDermott and King 1992). This brings particular problems for those trying to maintain relationships over long periods of time – sometimes indefinitely – relying on visits, occasional telephone calls and letters as their only means of communication.

This chapter has looked at life after the traumatic, life-changing event of discovery of the offence and relatives' progression through the stages that follow as they begin to assimilate and adjust to their new status. The focus has been on how relatives constructed events and how they understood their predicament, and it is worth noting that their accounts might also serve a purpose of negating blame, of making a point about themselves as moral actors and morally distancing themselves from the offender. Why this should be necessary is the subject of the next chapter which considers how relatives of serious offenders experience stigmatisation and blame.

Chapter 3

Secondary stigma, shame and blame

> I think it's a stigma. I think that. I think people don't want to know where there's somebody in prison for a sex offence. I think that they shy away from you. They don't want to know you. They don't want to be involved. They don't want to ask you anything or be involved in any way.
>
> (Lillian, son convicted of sex offence)

> It's the support we need because we are pariahs. So no-one wants to know us in that respect. It's the stigma . . . that's the feeling you have, that you're, suddenly you're a second class citizen. You just, you know, you might as well be a tramp under Waterloo Bridge or whatever, no matter how much you tried to maintain your dignity or respect, anyone could come along and knock you down. That's how I felt. I just felt the lowest of the low and not even fit to go into church. . . . Had he just stolen something, I wouldn't have felt like that. . . . We're definitely the outcasts.
>
> (Eileen, husband convicted of sex offence)

Bringing dishonour and shame upon one's family is a notion more commonly found in the Mediterranean and the Middle East and an extensive anthropological literature describes how honour and shame are defined in these cultures. Although some of these studies have been criticised for emphasising idealised and hegemonic versions of social identities (Lindisfarne 1999) their imagery remains powerful and, in the eyes of many, familial shame remains located in these cultures, associated with closely bound extended families, and is rarely considered in other contexts. In our society, however, the ties that bind kin together are strong enough for dishonour to flow from the actions of one relative to another, and for a family to have a reputation which can be damaged by the actions of one member. When those actions comprise some of the most grave and vilified crimes in our society, the whole family can be tainted with the resulting stigma. However, this is more than just a stigma by association; the stigma of the offender does not simply 'rub off' on the relative because of their close proximity. Relatives of serious offenders have a secondary stigma based on both contamination and causal implication and in this chapter I intend to examine exactly how this operates.

The concept of stigma has transposed into popular usage and was referred to by several relatives in this study to describe their circumstances, as in the quotations from Lillian and Eileen above. It is a useful concept to help us to understand how relatives of serious offenders had been marked, how their identities were perceived as spoiled, and the consequences that followed. Applying the concept to offenders' families is not new. It is a common theme in the prisoners' families literature (although the emphasis is on stigma following imprisonment rather than the offence) and Goffman's classic study (to which all later studies of stigma refer) cites a 12-year-old daughter of an ex-convict as an example of someone thus afflicted (Goffman 1963: 43). Goffman described a stigma that stemmed from a relationship with another as a *courtesy stigma*, which he said was attached to '. . . the individual who is related through the social structure to a stigmatized individual – a relationship that leads the wider society to treat both individuals in some respects as one' (*ibid*.: 43). Being treated 'as one' with the offender is a central part of relatives' secondary stigma, but as we will see it also has other important dimensions. I will use the term secondary stigma because it is both a stigma by contagion – an extension of the offender's stigma travelling through kinship ties – and a stigma attached to the new identity the relative holds as a '*mother* of a murderer' or '*wife* of a sex offender' and the blame this new status attracts.

In his original formulation Goffman identifies three types of stigma: physical deformities, blemishes of individual character, and tribal stigma (*ibid*.: 14). Later authors have identified a range of significant dimensions, including the extent to which a stigma can be hidden, how a stigma changes over time, the degree of disruption it causes, its aesthetic qualities, what is perceived to be the origin of the stigma, the 'peril' or perceived danger to others (Jones *et al*. 1984) and the extent to which the stigma can be controlled (Crocker *et al*. 1998). The power of a stigma will be intensified if a person is thought to have some control over it (Heatherton *et al*. 2000); the relatives I met were deemed responsible in particular ways for both the origin of their secondary stigma (their offending relative's actions) and for its maintenance (their continued support for the offender).

Shame and secondary stigma

Shame is an emotion at the core of stigma. It is an emotion conveyed in a stigmatising interaction and a key emotion felt by the stigmatised. As we saw in the introduction to this book, shame has been conceptualised in a range of different ways. In trying to understand the shame experienced by relatives of serious offenders, I have found Nussbaum's analysis of shame's structure, thought-content and role in human life to be particularly useful. Nussbaum sees shame as focused on the whole self, and on a sense of personal failure (see also Lewis 1971; Lewis 1992; Tangney 1991; Nathanson 1992):

> To put things very generally, shame ... is a painful emotion responding to a sense of failure to attain some ideal state. Shame, as is generally agreed by those who analyze it, pertains to the whole self, rather than to a specific act of the self. ... In shame one feels inadequate, lacking some desired type of completeness of perfection.
>
> (Nussbaum 2004: 184)

Nussbaum describes shame as 'a permanent possibility in our lives, a daily companion' (*ibid.*: 173). It is an expression of an awareness of our own inadequacy and 'any ideal to which one holds oneself has shame as its permanent possibility' (*ibid.*: 192). Shame comes in many different forms, and Nussbaum draws on Goffman's analysis in which he shows how all deviations from normal are marked for occasions of shame, 'normal' referring to both statistical frequency and a sense of what is normative or proper (although of course the very idea of normal is a fictional construct as no-one is normal in all respects). Shame is an emotion induced by stigma, but because it 'concerns matters that lie deep' it can also be 'an emotion of self-assessment whether the world is looking on or not' (*ibid.*: 205). Shame takes the whole person as its primary object, concerning 'the overall tissue of self-identity' (Giddens 1991: 67), and can have a dehumanising tendency: '... one thing that shaming of subgroups typically expresses is a denigration of the very humanity of people being shamed' (Nussbaum 2004: 231).

Relatives of serious offenders are marked off for shaming as a group in response to a two-fold sense of failure: first, and at its most basic, it is their proximity to the failure of their offending relatives to adhere to some of society's most fundamental norms; secondly, it is their perceived failure to attain ideals of family roles and relationships and the blame they attract for their own role in events that have occurred. Because shame is also an emotion of self-assessment, relatives were vulnerable to painful feelings of failure as they searched to understand what had happened and whether any of their actions might have been contributing factors. The ideals to which they are held – of 'good mother' or 'good wife' for example – are, as we will see, pervasive and powerful in our society. Their shame can therefore be seen as partly vicarious, and partly based upon their own culpability and sense of failure, but is a painful, negative emotion, focused on their – and their family's – very identity.

For Nussbaum, then, shame is primarily a negative emotion which refers to a sense of one's own failure and to one's whole self and ultimately is 'dehumanising' (*ibid.*). She concludes that the use of shame in punishment is deeply problematic and does not accord with respect for the dignity of all citizens in a liberal society. Nussbaum disagrees with Braithwaite's contention that shaming of a certain kind can be positive and useful in controlling crime and is critical of what she sees as his failure to make a clear distinction between shame and guilt (*ibid.*: 240). Nussbaum says she is sympathetic to the proposals Braithwaite advances (that offenders should not be stigmatised or humiliated; that punishments should focus on the act and not the person; that offenders should make atonement before being forgiven), but believes they belong in the realm of guilt rather than shame. For Nussbaum, it is guilt that contains a separation between the person and the person's act, not reintegrative *shame*.

The debate between Nussbaum and Braithwaite cannot be answered by a study of relatives of serious offenders which does not focus on offenders or on responses to them, although the conceptual differences between shame and guilt are important, and I will return to them in Chapter 5. My findings do, however, raise a number of questions for Braithwaite's theory. Families of offenders appear in his theory as conduits for shame: their role is to experience and be aware of the reactions of others; to impose this shame on the offender; and to do so in a way that is reintegrative:

> The effectiveness of shaming is often enhanced by shame being directed not only at the individual offender but also at her family. . . . When a collectivity as well as an individual offender is shamed, collectivities are put on notice as to their responsibility to exercise informal control over their members, and the moralizing impact of shaming is multiplied . . . (the offender's) loved ones . . . will soon let her know that sinking deeper into the deviant role will only exacerbate the shame they are suffering on her behalf.
>
> (Braithwaite 1989: 83)

This chapter delves further into the shame that relatives suffer on an offender's behalf and raises the question of whether or not a degree of suffering is a reasonable expectation, particularly in a society where responses to serious crime are not generally reintegrative. In the current climate, the disapproval expressed to sex offenders, for example, is rarely expressed within a context of respect and love and is unlikely to sharply terminate with forgiveness, and consequently their relatives' suffering is likely to be significant and prolonged.

Most of the relatives I met experienced stigmatising shame – what Braithwaite (1989) also calls disintegrative shame – and the picture in this book is therefore perhaps more pessimistic than the one he describes. He uses as an example the reaction to a murder committed by a butcher in his home town during his childhood. He remembers his mother moralising about the incident, talking about the disgrace it had brought to the perpetrator's parents, and reflects that this shaming would have been going on in all the houses in the neighbourhood. However, he doubts 'if anyone in the neighbourhood actually confronted the family with its shame. They did not need to. The butcher's family would have known that moralizing and gossip were rife. Instead people tended to express sympathy to the family that something so terrible should have happened' (1989: 75). As we will see in this chapter, many of the relatives in this study found little sympathy from others in their communities, were directly confronted with shame, and that this shaming and moralising was more than vicarious and also constructed around the relatives' own culpability.

Reintegrative shaming is described by Braithwaite as a 'family model' because it imitates the way that effective punishment is exercised by parents: disapproval for an act is expressed within a context of love and respect and a child is not outcast for having done wrong. Braithwaite states: 'Reintegration . . . is often the job of the family and close friends; their task is a nurturant one – to show that even though the blow to reputation has been severe, the offender is forgiven and still accepted by her loved ones, and her loved ones are by her side to provide practical support in getting on with life' (*ibid.*: 87). This is partly achieved by making a separation between the offender and his or her actions, which was precisely what most relatives in this study claimed to do. However, as we will see in this chapter and later in Chapter 5, this was an account that was often not honoured. Relatives' continued support for the offender was seen as implicitly condoning the crime and was a further source of their secondary stigma.

Relatives of serious offenders, like other stigmatised groups, 'feel shame in their own eyes, and are forced to hide from the shaming gaze of others' (Nussbaum 2004: 284). Relatives were always aware of the potential to be under the shaming gaze of others, and this gaze evolved into action when friendships were ended, acquaintances crossed the road to avoid conversation, or relatives were subject to gossip, verbal abuse and in a few cases physical attack. There were five types of familial contamination and culpability which appeared to be the basis of this shaming gaze: *association* and *genetic* which are based on familial contamination, and *omission*, *commission* and *continuation* which are based on direct causality, for which relatives are blamed. These separate but interlinked dimensions of shame weave together to form an all-pervasive and all-powerful network from which relatives have little escape: even if they can avoid dimensions of blame, dimensions of contamination will always remain. I have called this network the 'web of shame' and will now consider its different dimensions.

The web of shame: kin contamination

Ideas about deviance being contagious have a long history. David Matza showed how these ideas informed what he described as more 'primitive' epidemiological models of deviance as pathology; affiliation was seen to explain the process of becoming deviant and in earlier versions of this model contagion was the method through which the affiliation process worked (Matza 1969: 101–4). Foucault pointed to our fear of the contagion of madness (Foucault 1967) and more contemporary analyses have used the idea of contagion to explain the effects of social learning on anti-social behaviour (Jones and Jones 2000), or violence being transmitted through the mechanism of criminal retaliation (Topalli *et al.* 2002). The use throughout is of course analogous: no-one is suggesting that deviance is 'caught' in the same way as an infection or disease – Matza (1969: 102) wrote that sociologists never really believed this, but just acted and wrote as if they did – but the idea that through close proximity some of the deviance (or its resulting stigma) can contaminate remains powerful. Furthermore, our fear of contamination might partly explain the strong reaction often elicited by the stigmatised as ideas of contamination and contagion to the self are at the very core of the emotion of disgust (Nussbaum 2004). The first two dimensions of the web of shame, then, refer to contamination: through their close proximity (geographical and/or genealogical) relatives of serious offenders are perceived to be tainted or polluted either through association or through a genetic or biological connection.

Association

On a basic level, relatives shamed by association are perceived to be the same as the offender by virtue of their kin relationship, to come from the same 'stock' as the offender and to therefore be tainted or contaminated by sharing a background or household:

> But it's, it's when one member of a family has committed a serious offence I think neighbours, the media, friends, often find it difficult

> to cope with this and therefore the family are treated as though they've done something wrong as well.
>
> (Lisa, partner convicted of homicide)

> Because you're a wife of a murderer or rapist of whatever you're classed in the same category as them. If you're a son or a daughter of a murderer they will paint you the same.
>
> (Stephanie, husband convicted of homicide)

This dimension can also refer to a likeness or similarity between the relative and the offender because of their close proximity:

> We come up against the prejudice and stupidity of other people, and you do get tarred with the same brush.
>
> (Nicola, partner convicted of sex offence)

> And that was one of my great fears in a sense that somehow you're tarnished with the same brush even though it had nothing to do with me.
>
> (Clare, husband convicted of sex offence)

Angela recounted the experience of someone she was supporting:

> I had a lady who went to visit in prison and she was strip-searched for drugs, because they'd had a tip-off that she was taking drugs into her husband. And she said she felt like a piece of meat on a slab. She said she felt like being herded like cattle. And she said, well actually one of the prison officers, one the officers was arrogant, enjoyed his job, and he actually said 'you're all alike'. And that's it. If you've got somebody in your family that's committed a crime, you'll be judged for that crime as well as your family member because you're related to him. Sad, but that's what happens because everybody thinks, people who it's never touched, people who's had perfect lives or near perfect lives and have never been touched by anything like it, they can sit down and say 'you're all the same' . . . they judge the whole family for it, not just the offender.
>
> (Angela, husband accused of sex offence)

Relatives of serious offenders can therefore be 'treated as though they've done something wrong as well', 'classed in the same category' and 'painted the same' as the offender, 'tarred with the same brush' and judged as 'all alike . . . all the same', and as in Goffman's courtesy stigma (Goffman 1963) treated 'as one' with the offender, simply by virtue of their association, in this case their kin relationship, with the offender. This contamination can be experienced by any member of the offender's kinship network, although the closer the kin relationship the stronger it is likely to be.

Genetic/biological

Relatives might also be shamed for an alleged genetic connection that may provoke very primitive ideas of bad blood. Relatives who mentioned genetics questioned whether this might provide an explanation for the offender's actions. Perhaps not surprisingly they were more likely to comment on this when the genetic heritage was from someone else, as in the case of two interviewees who were adoptive parents and questioned whether there might be a genetic basis to their offspring's offending, or George who identified his son's mother's side of the family as the source:

> [My son] Justin was seriously depressed when he committed his crime, really badly depressed, which is part of the gene from [his mother's side]. Because her father was really, suffered badly from a depressive illness, but Justin was really in a bad state, I'd taken him to the hospital a couple of times to sort of see if they could do anything for him, but I couldn't deal with a depressive illness then as I could now, because I know a lot more about it.
>
> (George, son convicted of homicide)

One wife of a sex offender said her son was concerned that he might inherit a propensity to sexually offend from his father, and a mother of a sex offender said her grandson had expressed similar concerns. New conceptions of an individual who is genetically 'at risk' of offending are developing as a new biology of control emerges based on genetics and neurobiology (Rose 2000); seeking explanations in biology has implications for those who are genetically related to offenders. Furthermore, a lay understanding of heredity and genetics might make even more unequivocal connections. Relatives may be judged and deemed 'all the same' because of this shared biology; it may be inferred that if they share those genes they are also 'at risk'; and in the case of parents or grandparents they might be blamed for passing on that heritage. As we will see in Chapter 4, genetic explanations can potentially mitigate the offender's responsibility, but the finality of these explanations (suggesting causes of offending that would be difficult to alter) and the extent to which they taint relatives meant they were often resisted.

Mothers particularly felt blamed for their biological connection to the offender, and often spoke of their horror that someone born of their body had committed such a heinous act. Pauline thought mothers had a particularly strong connection to their children: 'You've carried him for nine months, he's part of you, isn't he? Okay dads might have a bond but there's always that special bond between a mother and a baby.' Motherhood is central to how women are defined by others and to their self-perceptions (Phoenix *et al.* 1991: 13), and in being defined through motherhood these mothers felt they were defined through their offending sons and deemed responsible, having brought them into the world, for their very existence.

The web of shame: kin culpability

Relatives' secondary stigma is underpinned by ideas about family members having responsibility for each other's actions. Relatives have an uncertain status in relation to the offence and are caught on the cusp between victim and offender status, many claim secondary victim status, but simultaneously attract blame. The last three dimensions of the web of shame refer to this familial blame, but before examining these dimensions I will step back and consider why it is that relatives might be held accountable for the actions of other family members. Powerful discourses on family responsibilities permeate all areas of family life. The family is often represented as the guardian of morality and responsible for its members' failings; if they deviate, the family must have failed in its functions. This message has many sources. Historically, a white, middle-class nuclear family has been presented as the normative ideal in both American and UK academic discourse (Chambers 2001), politicians make morally crusading speeches about 'family values' and the media draw attention to failing families. Teenage pregnancies, lone mothers, and truanting children are just some examples of failure from 'bad families' to which our attention is drawn.

Notions of familial responsibility are reflected in the relationship between the state and the family. There is a long history of the British government being concerned with family life and making assumptions about the role of the family in legislation. Since the 1970s there has been a greater stress on 'supporting the family' and families have been encouraged to look after their members, one theme being 'strong moral disapproval of people who apparently do not acknowledge that they have certain responsibilities to their relatives' (Finch 1989: 3). This disapproval is particularly strong in the case of parents of young offenders. Provision has been made in legislation to hold parents directly responsible for crimes committed by their children, with the parental 'bind over' in the Criminal Justice Act 1991 and the 'parenting order' introduced in the Crime and Disorder Act 1998, further widened in its use in the Anti-Social Behaviour Act 2003 and set to widen yet again with proposals made in 2006 under the Government's 'Respect' agenda.

In November 2000 the courts were given powers to send parents to prison for up to three months if they allowed their children to truant and a number of mothers have been imprisoned under these powers in recent high-profile cases. The continuing assumption in these parental responsibility laws is that parents of young offenders have not accepted responsibility and that they can be forced to do so with court orders and financial penalties (Arthur 2005).

Furthermore, expert and therapeutic analyses repeatedly locate explanations for offending behaviour within the family. Studies show family factors to be important predictors of offending. Reviewing these studies, Farrington suggests that the important factors are: criminal and antisocial parents; large family size; child-rearing methods (poor supervision, poor discipline, coldness and rejection, low parental involvement with the child); abuse (sexual and physical) or neglect; and parental conflict and disrupted families (Farrington 2002: 670). Studies of sex offenders point to factors in family background such as poor parental relationships in the case of incest male-object perpetrators (Gebhard *et al.* 1965) or problems with mothers in the case of incest offenders (though apparently not other paedophiles) (Paitich and Langevin 1976), even though 'evidence on this matter is very spotty and inconclusive' (Finkelhor *et al.* 1986). Dobash *et al.* (2001) found that just over a third of men currently serving prison terms for homicide offences came from broken homes, and a quarter had a father who was violent to their mother, though as Levi and Maguire point out, these statistics show that a 'surprisingly large percentage do not appear to come from a severely dysfunctional family or personal background' (Levi and Maguire 2002: 815).

Expert knowledge that locates explanations for offending within the family filters through and informs the everyday understandings of lay people; most people in society would be aware of seeking explanations for offending behaviour within childhood experiences and family background. Expert knowledge in turn condenses common-sense reasoning and relatives are confronted with such knowledge as they, or the offender, interact with professionals. Offenders might interact with psychiatrists, doctors, probation officers, social workers, and take part in anger management or sex offender treatment programmes, all of which can have underlying messages about the source of offending behaviour. Relatives in this study felt they were constantly faced with the belief that serious offenders were 'made' by their families.

So how might familial blame be gendered? The roles of 'mother' and 'wife' are constructed around responsibility for the well-being of other family members and mothers and wives may be particularly blamed when things go wrong. Historically, motherhood and mothering have been subject to particular regulation, often targeted at working-class mothers. Informal networks were undermined as a source of knowledge as experts such as health visitors and midwives were trained to instruct mothers. In the modern era, there are numerous experts, often in disagreement, vying for the right to define 'good mothering'. Bowlby's theory of maternal deprivation (Bowlby 1981) was very influential from the 1940s and 1950s onwards, pointing to adverse consequences if the bond between mother and child and the constant presence of the mother were in any way threatened (Chambers 2001: 52–3). Neo-Freudian thought was prominent in the 1940s and 1950s, with the emphasis on looking at the family of origin in order to understand the individual (Ladd-Taylor and Umansky 1998). The legacy of these perspectives persists: good mothers create emotionally secure children and adults, and either explicitly or implicitly, bad mothers create a catalogue of different problems.

Mother-blaming has a long history. Until relatively recently psychiatric discourse blamed autism on mothers rejecting their children; schizophrenia was blamed on maternal rejection; and anorexia on troubled mother–daughter relationships. Homosexuality was blamed on over-protective or independent-minded mothers from the 1890s to the 1950s; and juvenile delinquency on working mothers (Ladd-Taylor and Umansky 1998). An analysis of 125 articles written by mental health professionals in scholarly journals found that mothers were blamed for 72 different kinds of problems in their offspring (Caplan and Hall-McCorquodale 1985) and in many of the articles the writers 'stretched ludicrously far in order to avoid blaming anyone other than the mother' (Caplan and Caplan 1994: 70). In the mental illness literature before the 1960s families were seen as causal agents; poor socialisation and communication with parents were blamed, though again mothers in particular were seen to be at fault (Caplan and Hall-McCorquodale 1985; Cohler *et al.* 1991; Cook 1988; Cook *et al.* 1997). A subsequent generation of research has questioned whether poor communication and the other symptoms observed in these families might not actually have been caused by the offspring's mental illness rather than the other way around (Cook *et al.* 1997).

One study looked at the portrayal of serial killers in popular film and academic analyses, and concluded that in both, mothers were blamed for their son's deeds:

> Academic case studies of actual serial killers read like only slightly subdued versions of the Hollywood screenplays. Here, too, mothers create sons who kill. As in the films, fathers, boyfriends, stepfathers, and lovers appear only as shadowy figures, if at all. . . . Clearly, academics and film producers are reading from the same cultural script when they seek to explain serial killers' behavior. . . .

> Whatever goes right in the child's development reflects the ability of good parents; whatever goes wrong reverts solely to the mother.
> (Epstein 1998: 259–61)

Political discourse focusing on individualistic explanations for crime has been powerful in placing responsibility for offending firmly with offenders and their families. Campbell showed how in the early 1990s mothers were particularly blamed by the British politics of the time for the riots and unrest on housing estates:

> If the New Right ventured into the estates and saw the streets captured by thin, pale boys, it did not see the menacing response by men to the abolition of work, nor the street megalomania of boys trying to be men; in short, it did not see a *masculine* response to an economic crisis – it saw instead the failure of the *mothers* to manage the men.
> (Campbell 1993: 303)

Though marriage and other intimate relationships have undergone significant changes in recent years (e.g. see Beck and Beck-Gernsheim 1995; Giddens 1992), discourses based upon traditional models of marriage and intimacy remain powerful. For example, Cheale has suggested that the promotion of new family forms centres on the growth of individual freedoms and erodes the sense of duty that binds families together in caring for each other (Cheale 1999). Chambers points out that the undercurrent here is that it is *women* who are deemed disruptive for demanding freedoms which are taken for granted for men and that female emancipation continues to be blamed for the breakdown in modern family values (Chambers 2001: 129). Women as wives have particular 'duties' and are imbued with particular responsibilities for maintaining family values and promoting 'good families', and blamed for not fulfilling them when things go wrong.

Marriage, and particularly strong marital attachment, have been found to be important in predicting male desistance from crime. As Laub and Sampson (2003: 41–6) explain, this may be because good marriages have an 'investment quality' with social bonds growing over time, so increasing the incentive to avoid crime. The effect of a good marriage takes time to appear and inhibits crime gradually. Marriage changes routine activities and less time is spent with delinquent peers; parenting responsibilities can similarly lead to changes in routine activities as more time is spent on family activities. Marriage may further lead to desistance because it generates direct social control from spouses and has emotionally sustaining features (Laub and Sampson 2003). These possible reasons for the association between marriage and desistance could also imply the inverse when a husband *does* commit crime: the marital attachment and social bond are not strong enough; the husband has little incentive not to commit crime; he is not diverted by spending time with his wife or children; the marriage is not emotionally sustaining; and the wife is not able to exert control or keep her husband on the 'straight and narrow'.

Studies of the wives of men who sexually offend against children have found that they are often blamed, particularly in the case of father–daughter incest. The father is not held totally accountable, and the mother is centrally implicated, blamed as collusive, or seen as orchestrating the abuse through her inadequacies or emotional absence (Davies and Krane 1996). Assumptions such as these have been shown to feature in the accounts of some child protection professionals such as social workers, police officers and nurses (Kelley 1990) and in the child sexual abuse literature, which 'carries a legacy of at least 25 years of blaming non-offending mothers either partially or fully for the sexual abuse of their children' (Humphreys 1994: 50).

Returning to the last three dimensions of the web of shame, we can see how this history of familial blame plays out for the relatives of serious offenders. They are subject to blame for *omission*, something they did not do; *commission*, something they did; and *continuation*, for maintaining their secondary stigma by supporting the offender or not severing their connection.

Omission

Relatives who were shamed for sins of omission were deemed blameworthy because of something they failed to do: they either knew, or should have known, about offending or the likelihood of an offence and therefore could have stopped it. This was particularly likely to be so where a household was shared, i.e. parents with children still living at home or spouses of offenders, and even more so when the offence was child sexual abuse. Problem-identifying accounts, as described in Chapter 1, might partly seek to address this dimension ('we tried to get help and it wasn't forthcoming'), as might normalising accounts ('we couldn't have known – everything before the offence was fine').

Relatives of those who offend within the family are often seen as in a better position to know about or to prevent offending. As we have seen, wives of men who sexually offend are often blamed and might be labelled 'collusive mothers' (Russell 1986). The victim of Frances's husband's crime was their teenage foster-daughter. She says she did not know of the offence until her husband was charged:

> My CPN [Community Psychiatric Nurse] had arranged to come round and see me, well the day, the day that [my husband] went

> down to the police station he was charged, she came to see me a couple of hours after he was due at the police station and she got in touch with one of the doctors at the hospital who came out to see me the next day, and his first words to me were 'Did you know it was going on and did you condone it?' And I thought if somebody of a professional nature has said that, how many other people were saying that? And whether some people thought that I knew it was going on I don't know, but I have lost a hell of a lot of friends.
>
> (Frances, husband convicted of sex offence)

Frances draws attention to the power of professionals to define and to their importance as sources of accounts (see Chapter 5). Her quotation illustrates blame for sins of omission, but the suggestion of 'condoning' sexual offending also suggests possible blame for sins of commission or collusion. Blame constructed around omission is based upon two issues: first, whether or not relatives did know (and as we have seen in Chapter 1, this is by no means straightforward) and second, if they did know why they did not act. The blame levelled here is that relatives were bystanders, and is similar to that levelled at bystanders in other circumstances outside the family often involving strangers, such as when homelessness, crimes or other kinds of misery are witnessed without action. The 'classic bystander' image is one of indifference, but as Cohen explains, the reasons can be more complex: 'Observers will not act if they do not know what to do, feel powerless and helpless themselves, don't see any reward, or fear punishment if they help' (Cohen 2001: 16).

Relatives might also blame themselves for not preventing the offending. As we saw in Chapter 1, one interviewee had not acted upon an earlier disclosure of sexual abuse from her young niece; when a later disclosure followed she said she was horrified that she could have stopped the abuse earlier. Jane's daughter and her daughter's partner were both convicted of inflicting serious physical injuries over a period of time on Jane's 11-month-old grandson. Jane said that had she known he was in danger she would have done anything she could to protect him, but still blamed herself for missing what she now thought was an earlier warning sign:

> I had [my grandson] Gareth ready to go, and as I passed him to his step-Dad he turned in to me, and held on to me like that, and screamed, and I said 'no Gareth, you've got to go now because Nanny's going to bed', and he screamed and he clung even tighter and his little fist, I'm sure that was a sign that something was happening, because he was always scared of [his step-father]. Always scared of him. I won't forgive myself for that, that's the only warning sign I had and I ignored it, I won't forgive myself ever for

> that. I feel like I've let him down [crying]. I love him dearly, but I've let him down. I should have been there to protect him, not put him back into danger.
>
> (Jane, daughter convicted of violent offence)

An unsuccessful recent attempt was made to move from moral accountability to legal accountability for omission when charges were brought against the relatives of would-be suicide bomber Omar Sharif, under new laws that put a duty on people to inform the police of an impending terrorist attack. In 2004 a jury cleared Sharif's widow of failing to alert the authorities to a terrorist attack, but did not reach a verdict on Sharif's brother and sister. They were cleared in 2005 by an Old Bailey jury who decided that they had not known of his plan and could not have prevented it; they also cleared his sister of inciting her brother to commit a terrorist act (BBC 2005).

More successful attempts at making omission legally accountable have been enacted in recent times through parental responsibility laws which have developed in order to make parents criminally liable for failing to prevent offending or adequately supervise their children. As we have seen, use of the 'parenting order' has increased in the UK. Criminal legislation to prosecute parents in the US is developing fast, with at least 36 States mandating some type of responsibility provision beyond civil liability for parents or guardians of delinquent children. California's law imposing criminal parental responsibility is one of the most stringent. Enacted in 1988 as part of the Street Terrorism and Prevention Act, the law makes it a crime when parents or guardians do not 'exercise reasonable care, supervision, protection, and control' over their children. Violation brings a misdemeanour charge and can include a fine of no more than $2,500 and a one-year prison term (Office of Juvenile Justice and Delinquency Prevention 2006). In Canada, parents are made liable under the Parental Responsibility Act 2000 for loss or damage caused by their child, unless the parent can satisfy the court that they were exercising 'reasonable supervision' over the child at the time and made 'reasonable efforts' to prevent or discourage the child from that kind of activity (Ontario Statutes 2004).

Commission

Relatives might also be blamed for something they actually did, either in the long-term past, or in the immediate past just before discovery.

(i) Long-term past

Relatives shamed for sins of commission might be blamed for having created the offender, having responsibility for the person he or she became. This is clearly particularly the case for parents:

> They always, well they do say don't they, 'oh it's the way he's been brought up. It must be something in the family. It must be his parents' fault, it must be'. You know, they do. They never seem to think that these people [the offenders] have got a life of their own and what they do is nothing to do with it, their parents or their family.
>
> (Lillian, son convicted of sex offence)

Monica described her feelings of responsibility as a mother:

> Of course there's this sort of feeling of guilt and responsibility. Not responsibility for the offence, but responsibility for her being as she is, and feeling that, you know, if you had been a better mother, if you had done things differently, if, if, if, then maybe she would be less mentally unstable or less self-destructive, just an easier person. Maybe that's true, I don't know.
>
> (Monica, daughter convicted of violent offence)

As we have seen, explanations for offending behaviour are often located within the family, and may be seen as the consequence of 'bad parenting' or 'bad mothering'. Relatives are aware of these explanations, and parents who participated in this study frequently asked 'where did we go wrong?' Mothers felt particularly blamed: notions of motherhood are constructed around both the biological bearing of children and the social construction of mothers as idealised nurturers (Davies and Krane 1996) and the mothers in this study felt blame and guilt based on nurture as well as nature, questioning their role in the upbringing of the offender and whether something in how the offender was raised could have contributed to his or her actions.

(ii) Immediate past

Relatives might also be seen as absolutely culpable because of their own actions, either by directly colluding or covering up, or actually being involved in the offending. Again, this was particularly likely to be so where a household was shared at the time of the offence and particularly likely that wives of sexual offenders were blamed in this way:

> *R*: How do you think the police saw you, as the wife of somebody who was accused of sex offences?
>
> *E*: Well, me? As far as one particular officer was concerned, I was involved.
>
> (Eileen, husband convicted of sex offence)

The role of 'wife' is partly constructed around responsibility for fulfilling the sexual side of a marriage, and wives might therefore feel responsible or be blamed (however unreasonably) for their husband's sexual activity elsewhere. A study of the excuses of 'child molesters' found 'my wife wouldn't sleep with me' to be one of those excuses (Pollock and Hashmall 1991: 57). If an offence happens within the family, the wife of an offender might be blamed for not protecting the victim. Frances questioned whether she was to blame for her husband's sexual offending:

> It's very strange actually because nobody knew it was happening to me, and I didn't know it was happening then, but yeah, I felt guilty that I didn't know it was going on, and I felt to blame. Because the way I looked at it is because it was a sexual offence, there was, there must have been something wrong with me, to make him want to go with her, if you can understand it. I don't know, I was no different to what I was when we first got married. Disability-wise, yes, I was probably worse than when we first got married, but apart from that there was no difference.
>
> (Frances, husband convicted of sex offence)

Some family members were accused of being directly involved in the offending. One grandmother in this study was accused in court of supplying the weapon used in an attempted murder, but no criminal proceedings were taken against her. It should be remembered, of course, that some relatives do collude and offend together, and one participant did have several members of her family convicted of the same serious crime. However, many participants in this study described feeling that they were suspected of colluding when they were not involved in any way.

Within social psychology there have been studies of collective responsibility, looking for example at how one might feel guilt for the actions of a member of one's in-group – though primarily defining 'in-group' on the basis of nation, ethnicity, or gender, rather than kin (see for example, Branscombe and Doosje 2004). Some studies of collective responsibility have also made the distinction between making inferences of responsibility on the basis of omission and commission. Lickel *et al.* (2003) use the distinction in a study which tests ideas about how and why people decide that members of groups are responsible for the actions of fellow group members, administering questionnaires to 113 individuals recruited at a university about the Columbine High School shootings. However, although they define omission as I do (failing to prevent the event) they take a shorter-term view of commission (encouraging or facilitating the event). I have defined commission as something a relative did either in the long- or short-term past, allowing for parents 'creating' the offender and being blamed for who the offender became, as well as colluding, covering up, or actually being involved in the offending. Thus Lickel *et al.* hypothesise (and find statistical support for) willingness to assign responsibility to the parents of the killers primarily by omission, failing to prevent the offence, and their peer group (the 'Trenchcoat Mafia') being judged as collectively responsible primarily by commission, contributing to it happening by their actions at the time. They found judgements of collective responsibility to be predicted by the degree of authority over the wrongdoer (mediated by inferences of omission) and the 'entitativity' or closeness of the group. Groups to whom the killers were closely connected were held more highly responsible (like kin or peer group) than those to whom they had weaker ties (such as neighbours or community leaders).

Although it is a very different study to the one on which this book is based (asking participants to respond to very structured questionnaires and scales and looking for statistically significant relationships and general models) Lickel *et al.*'s study provides support for the distinction between omission and commission, and suggests the importance of factors such as authority over another's actions and the interconnectedness of kin relationships to mediating how the different dimensions of the web of shame might operate. Authority cannot be the only important factor to assigning responsibility for omission, however; the ability to prevent an offence from happening might be based upon authority and control over another's actions, but an offence could also be prevented by actions which do not require authority or control such as notifying the police of allegations of offending or seeking help from mental health or other services.

Continuation

By continuing their relationship with the offender and offering the offender their support, relatives were further stigmatised and deemed responsible for the maintenance of their stigma. This dimension will be discussed in detail in Chapter 5. However, there are few paths out of secondary stigma for relatives of serious offenders. Although they could eliminate this dimension of blame by breaking contact and not supporting (and five wives in this study had chosen that path), the other dimensions which refer to the past and to their kin relationship remain.

The consequences of secondary stigma

Secondary stigma and the web of shame manifest in interactions with others. Many of those I interviewed recounted negative reactions; one of the most common was loss of friends:

> And then there was another [friend] who I had been friendly with for many years and I thought, 'oh rather, in case it's in the papers I'll ring her and I'll tell her about it', and she'd always been a very sympathetic person, but I hadn't seen her for quite a long time, but I thought in case she sees anything in the paper I'll tell her. And I rang her and I told her and she said 'Oh dear' and that was it and I never heard from her again. Now if that were me, I would have been saying 'can I help?', so obviously I didn't have a good choice of friends.
>
> (Alice, son convicted of homicide)

N: When this happened all my friends, my personal friends, didn't want to know me.
R: Really?
N: Truly. So now I've got no friends, all I've got now is colleagues and I'm just so, I am literally on my own . . . they just kept away. . . . They'd make excuses at first and they, you got to the stage where you thought 'oh this is a waste of time', so you just left it. I thought they might have come round before now but they haven't.

(Nancy, husband convicted of sex offence)

Mixed reactions were found from other people outside the family, from acquaintances and neighbours met in the street. Some relatives found support, while others were ignored:

> Not friends as I would call friends, people that I've known over the pub and that sort of thing have walked over to the other side of the road.
>
> (George, son convicted of homicide)

> Some people have crossed roads so they didn't have to speak to me and some people have crossed the road suddenly and said, 'it's not your fault, don't worry about it, I'll still talk to you'. But I suppose some people, it's like a bereavement, you don't know what to say but if you don't know what to say, you're going to keep your mouth shut and keep on going, aren't you? But I certainly found out who my true friends were.
>
> (Pauline, son convicted of homicide)

Jane experienced local children throwing eggs at her windows and tearfully described the reaction of her neighbours:

J: They just totally ignore me. They won't speak to me. You know, 'she's not worth bothering about'. It's like they're blaming me for what she's done.

R: That's terrible. Why do you think they see you as in any way to blame?

J: I don't know, I don't know. And sometimes I get people shouting abuse at me. Telling me to f-off or go and live somewhere else, but not in them words, with swear words in between.

(Jane, daughter convicted of violent offence)

Other serious consequences described by relatives included one interviewee who had her house attacked and all her windows smashed by a relative of the victim; another who had received threats against her life, a risk she took very seriously and hence was anxious that her anonymity should be totally protected in this study; a mother who was spat at in the street; another who described receiving abusive telephone calls, never tracing their source. During fieldwork I had conversations with other relatives who had suffered attacks on their houses. In some more extreme cases relatives have had to go into hiding and take on new identities, one example being the families of Jon Venables and Robert Thompson who had killed the toddler James Bulger in 1993 when they were ten years old. One set of parents were supported by Aftermath at the time of the highly publicised court case, appearing in a BBC documentary about the organisation (BBC 2, *40 Minutes*, February 1994). A further example can be found in a study of the media reporting of sex crime which described a newspaper article in which the wife of a convicted rapist told of public revenge on her and her three children aged 4, 5 and 10, which included 'men urinating through the letter box, the children being roughed up at school, her washing being slashed and receiving obscene phone calls night and day: "from the public reaction you'd think I was alongside helping him", she said' (Soothill and Walby 1991: 128).

The experience of stigmatisation and shaming may be even more powerful for those left on the outside when a relative is imprisoned. In prison, coping with daily life may take precedence over concerns about stigmatisation and prisoners can exist in an environment where offences are not discussed and their past actions not challenged. They may also be amongst other offenders where their offending is in some sense 'normalised'.[1] The wives, mothers and other close kin have to continue everyday life, often in communities where their tainted status is known. They have to live with daily examples of shaming and it is they, rather than an imprisoned offender, who must face whispering as they pass in the street, gossiping in the post office or open comments, as Stephanie described:

S: It was only when I went into the village where my Mum lived that people started taunting me, 'you murderer's wife'.

R: Just walking down the road? People you knew or people that just knew who you were?
S: People I'd grown up with. My friends that I thought were friends, school friends, didn't even speak to me.
R: Really? Right. So did you still go to the village?
S: Yeah, I never stopped because my Mum was there and that was my main priority. But as time went on people forgot, or they just didn't say anything to me, but even now I go to the village and I can see, they look at you, you know, as if to say 'oh, we know who you are'. Yeah, they do know who I am.
R: And how does that make you feel now?
S: Why am I still being punished? It's as though I've done a life sentence as well, which I honestly think I've done more of a life sentence than he has. Because he's in prison he's doing the sentence, *but it's me what gets the flak out here.*

(Stephanie, husband convicted of homicide. Emphasis added)

This state of affairs can continue for many years and in some cases for life. Secondary stigma is therefore very real in its consequences for some relatives. All relatives are aware of a web of shame and the shaming gaze of others, but some will be brought face to face with judgement and blame, bringing it into sharp relief.

Reacting to the reaction: strategies for stigma management

Disclosure and secrecy

Following discovery of the offence, adjustment must be made to the new status of 'relative of a serious offender'. Relatives' experience of secondary stigma and their strategies for managing it will depend on whether this status is known. Goffman distinguished between the *discredited* (whose stigmatised status is known) and the *discreditable* (whose status is not, but has the potential to be so). These are not absolute qualities of a person but rather qualities of interactions and 'a stigmatized individual is likely to have experience with both situations' (Goffman 1963: 14). There were some circumstances where relatives had little control over disclosing information about their status, for example if they lived in a small community where anonymity was impossible and information passed through informal networks and/or where they had been exposed by media coverage. There was some media coverage of the offence and sentencing for most participants in this study, ranging from a short article in a local paper to radio, television and newspaper coverage and nation-wide saturation. This exposure exacerbated many families' difficulties:

A: I think the media coverage was bad. I mean it weren't blown all over the papers but the headlines were you know, 'sex beast', and that's hard to handle when you look at the man that you love sat there and it's him they're talking about.

R: Was it just in the local papers?

A: Yeah. The repercussions on the kids were bad. I mean it got so bad that [my husband] Dan was worried about letting them out you know, 'don't let them go to shop, make sure you know where they are all the time' because he was scared, we were both scared that they were being picked on and they were getting abuse thrown at them in the street. The youngest one had to move schools from one side of [the city] to the next, to the other side because it got, they put in the paper that Dan had been charged for rape. And Alex went to school and came home and sort of broke down, in tears, and said that this lad had said to him 'your Dad's a rapist'.

(Angela, husband accused of sex offence)

Other relatives had a greater degree of control over what was known, and had to decide how to manage information: 'To display or not to display; to tell or not to tell; to let on or not to let on; to lie or not to lie; and in each case, to whom, how, when and where' (Goffman 1963: 57).

As Herman (1994) argues, being a 'secret deviant' is more complex than just deciding whether to disclose or conceal one's status, and studies suggest that individuals selectively conceal or disclose such information at particular times, in particular situations, and with particular people (see, for example, Bell and Weinberg 1978; Schneider and Conrad 1980; Veevers 1980; Miall 1986). In her study of ex-psychiatric patients, she found that many lived in states of emotional turmoil deciding who to tell, when to tell, and how to tell. The strategies they employed to control and manage information included *selective concealment* (the major strategy, selectively withholding discreditable information, with decisions made on the basis of whether others were safe or risky), *therapeutic disclosure* (a cathartic disclosure to trusted, supportive others in order to re-negotiate the perception of the stigma), *preventive disclosure* (in order to minimise future anticipated rejection), and *political activism* (a collective management strategy, coming together to participate in activist groups). Within each of these strategies, Herman identifies various devices used by the ex-patients. She says her findings show that ex-psychiatric patients are not passive and powerless individuals, but rather 'strategists, expert managers, and negotiators who play active (although not always successful) roles in the shaping of deviant outcomes. In other words, ex-patients are instrumental in shaping their own social fates; they attempt to elicit desired reactions through their own behaviours, through techniques of stigma management, and through the expectations and images they project' (Herman 1994: 370). As we will see, relatives of serious offenders were similarly engaged in active strategies to manage their secondary stigma and to manage the reactions of others.

In her study of how murderers' relatives managed stigma, May (2000) applies some of Herman's strategies and Glaser and Strauss's notion of open or closed 'awareness contexts' (Glaser and Strauss 1964), identifying three 'meta-strategies' of stigma management. Within closed awareness contexts the relatives in her study managed *information* (through strategies similar to those in Herman's study). Within open awareness contexts the relatives managed *space* (selectively avoiding people, contexts and spaces) and managed *self-presentation* (using 'dissention' and 'collective support'). May suggests that dissension (using particular accounting techniques about the offence) was used by those relatives who challenged the murder verdict, believing that the verdict should have been manslaughter, while collective support (in this context joining Aftermath) was used by relatives who accepted the offender's guilt and the murder verdict. Relatives of serious offenders in my study used techniques to manage space (what I have called *avoidance* below) in both open and closed awareness contexts, and as we will see in later chapters had a range of views about the offender's culpability (both Aftermath and non-Aftermath members) and used a variety of accounting techniques.

However, I did find similar methods to those described by Herman (1994) and May (2000) used by relatives in my study to manage *information* in their interactions with others. Lillian, for example, describes what Herman calls 'selective concealment' and May calls 'representation', and George describes the technique of 'preventive disclosure':

> Oh they know he's in prison, yes but they don't know what he's in prison for. I just said it was matrimonial things that had happened you know. I didn't tell them why. I just hadn't got the courage to tell them. I can't explain. I thought well I'm living amongst these people and they're quite sort of middle-class people that I just couldn't bring myself to say exactly why he was in prison you know? It's very hard, especially when they've got children of their own and grandchildren, you know? And on top of it all, at the particular time, there was so much in the papers and on television. Every time I put the television on, there was sex offenders. Every time I picked up the paper, it was about sex offenders.
>
> (Lillian, son convicted of sex offence)

> As far as my friends and associates and people like that, I've always, the jobs that I've had, I've always told the bosses and whatever else

> what's gone on, so that they wouldn't pick up a newspaper and read it and not know what's going on. I haven't done this at university because I don't need to do it any more, but I would do it if I needed to do it. I did it with the principal on my access course and with the managers that I've dealt with ever since.
>
> (George, son convicted of homicide)

The main motivation for relatives to disclose to outsiders is the stress, strain and loss of intimacy associated with secrecy; the main drive to keep it secret is risk of rejection and the serious consequences associated with being discredited. The difficulties of keeping a stigma secret have been considered by several authors (Crocker *et al.* 1998; Goffman 1963; Smart and Wegner 2000). These difficulties can be either interpersonal, affecting relationships because 'every relationship obliges the related persons to exchange an appropriate amount of intimate facts about self, as evidence of trust and mutual commitment' (Goffman 1963: 108), or intrapersonal, an internal struggle with stress, strain and anxiety (Smart and Wegner 2000):

> Well, yes, because you can't let everybody know everything. If you've got a really good friend, one of my friends knows but the others don't, it's as though I'm deceiving them all, I'm living a different life, because they say 'oh what about your ex-husband?' and I'd say 'oh he's in prison' and I can't bring myself to tell them, because I'm worried what they'll think of me.
>
> (Stephanie, husband convicted of homicide)

Stephanie had re-married and had a daughter since her ex-husband's offence. Her daughter was 15 at the time of our interview and did not know of the existence of Stephanie's ex-husband, an example of how secrecy can be sustained in families. When making decisions about disclosure, relatives must balance the difficulties of secrecy with the difficulties that might follow their status being known, and as Herman (1994) and May (2000) both suggest, decide within each separate context.

For some relatives, the strategy of secrecy is very successful; they would prefer the consequences of secrecy to what they perceive to be the possible consequences of exposure. Alice, for example, lived some distance from her son and the site of his crime, and had re-married and therefore did not share his name:

> *A*: Yes, yes . . . I don't tell anybody, this is perhaps why I don't get support, because people don't know, very few people, no-one in my estate here knows.
>
> *R*: Really?

A: No, no. My next door neighbour doesn't know, the people across, the girl who looks after my dog doesn't know . . . it isn't talked about, it just isn't discussed.
R: What do you say if somebody asks you?
A: Oh he lives away, he works, he works in the government. I tell lies. Nobody really asks me, you know, somebody said, my niece said, 'just say he's in the prison service'. Which isn't a lie.

(Alice, son convicted of homicide)

However, even those most successful at disguising their status will find it revealed in certain contexts, and in particular during involvement with the criminal justice process and prison visiting when their secondary stigma is revealed, as one elderly mother described:

L: They treat you, when you go to the prison, they treat you like dirt.
R: Do they?
L: Really like dirt, you know, and you've only got to say something that you don't like and 'oh well, that's just too bad, if you don't like it, write to the governor'. You know, it's – we're not the – we're not the people that have done wrong. We're innocent of these crimes but they treat us, we're like lepers in a way. You feel ashamed when you go in and you feel ashamed when you come out . . . you feel as much the criminal, you can't help it. You feel bad, you feel dirty, you feel unclean, you feel, you know, you just don't feel the person that you are for that time that you're there.

(Lillian, son convicted of sex offence)

Avoidance

In both open and closed awareness contexts, relatives can strategically maintain various types of physical distance, though for different reasons; in the former they might move house or stay indoors to avoid tension or disgrace while, in the latter, they might avoid intimacy with others that could lead to an 'obligation to divulge information' (Goffman 1963: 122). As we have seen, May (2000) found the strategy of 'managing space' to be used by murderers' relatives, though only in open awareness contexts where particular people and places would be avoided. Alice described Goffman's second type of avoidance; her circumstances remained secret but she kept her distance from new people she met to avoid having to reveal more:

I tend to be, although I don't sound it, more withdrawn. Because I'm afraid of, of getting in conversation, for instance, I started to go, just

> last year or so, line dancing before, when I was on my own when [my husband] Clive was retired, there was a friend who was going and I went, and then she stopped going and I thought I'm going to carry on going by myself, because it was that sort of atmosphere whereby you could go by yourself because you don't have to have a partner and people are very friendly. And I did strike up an acquaintance with quite a few people actually, and who would say 'I'll call and see you' and I'd say 'oh well', but I feel as though I've held back on these overtures . . . people constantly talk about their families and their children, and I found that difficult . . . they say you know 'our Margaret' or 'our Tracy', or 'I've been having a day out with our . . .' just in general . . . and I not only don't offer, I try to hedge around it, because I don't want anybody new in my life to ask me questions. You know, I just don't want to.
>
> (Alice, son convicted of homicide)

As May suggests, the strategies used by relatives might vary and become more selective over time (May 2000). Celia described how in the early stages she avoided contact with her neighbours because her circumstances were known:

> Then I found that if I wanted to go and hang the washing out on the line I would check to see if there was anybody out there, I've just realised as I'm talking to you, because I didn't want to talk to anybody about it at all, and so for a while although I'd go out, as soon as I heard voices either side I'd either you know, immediately come back in or go in the shed and wait or whatever, so yeah, I'd forgotten about that.
>
> (Celia, nephew convicted of homicide)

Several participants in this study moved to avoid living in a community where their status was known. Ada experienced negative reactions from neighbours after her son's conviction and as a result moved away:

> *A*: The girl next door, she was very sympathetic and helpful, and the people on the other side were absolutely the opposite, you know. One of the reasons that we left that house.
>
> *R*: What did they do or say?
>
> *A*: They didn't say a thing, they just you know, cut us dead. They'd been very friendly, but as soon as that happened it was *finito*. We still see them, they come up every Friday morning to the market here and they walk straight past us.
>
> (Ada, son convicted of rape)

Resistance

Resistance is a strategy that can be employed at several levels by relatives managing their secondary stigma. First, it is clearly easier for those who question or deny the offender's culpability to resist. Nancy was one such example:

> It went to the papers and the headline was 'sex beast sexually assaults two girls', not his daughter, two girls. And it made out that he was a serial sex beast, that was it, it said a serial sex beast over a period of years. And people were, they looked at me. I thought well I'm not putting my head down, I've not done nothing wrong. [My husband] Bill's not done anything wrong but he can't prove he's not done anything wrong. And it was them eventually that put their head down because I looked them straight in the face but it hurt. I didn't let them know how much it hurt me.
>
> (Nancy, husband convicted of sex offence)

Nancy described resisting because she said her husband had done nothing wrong – but also because she said she had done nothing wrong. This was the second level of resistance; relatives would offer accounts resisting the blame levelled at them, even when they accepted their relatives' culpability (see Chapter 5).

Resistance also operated at a third level. At the discovery of the offence, relatives lost their own and their family identity as they had seen it, but were reluctant to replace it with the alternative identity of 'mother of murderer' or 'wife of sex offender'. This was the identity that they felt others wanted to force upon them but that they did not want to adopt, though it might have become their master status in the early stages. They were fighting a totalising conception of the offender's identity (see Chapter 4) and consequently of their own identity: their relative was more than a sex offender or a murderer and they were more than a sex offender's wife or murderer's mother. This was tellingly illustrated when a documentary made during the period of fieldwork roused objections from Aftermath and a request was made to change the title from 'A Killer in the Family' to 'A Kill*ing* in the Family'. Aftermath was unhappy about the label 'killer' and was successful in changing the title before the documentary was broadcast, although it was too late for many of the TV listings magazines which printed the original version.

Resistance was likely to grow as relatives moved through the stages outlined in Chapter 2. Anne described how as she got stronger she realised her son was 'the one that matters, and if people choose to punish me for supporting my son that is their choice, I can't do anything about that. I have to do what I feel is right'. A further type of resistance was choosing to ignore the reaction of others, and this was Lorraine's response to being spat at in the street: 'I just took no notice, I thought well let them carry on because they'll have to stop soon, they can't just go around keep doing that, you know.' Lorraine's response was unusual amongst participants in this study. This might be a factor of a sample selected either through self-help group participation or self-selection responding to a leaflet: these relatives might be more affected by what has happened and less willing to ignore and the strategy might therefore be more commonly employed than reflected here. Stronger resistance might also be employed – it is not beyond the realms of possibility to imagine relatives 'hitting back' when confronted with some of the consequences of their secondary stigma – yet this was not reported. This may again be a factor of the sample; it may reflect unwillingness to report that sort of thing; or it may be that relatives felt disempowered by self-doubt or blame and were disabled by the problem of moral ambiguity, not able to present themselves as wholly righteous.

Accounts: verbal management strategies

Relatives use verbal techniques to manage their shame and stigma, constructing accounts about the offence, why it happened, the offender, and their own role, and incorporating these accounts into their self-narratives. Relatives might offer accounts of literal denial of the offence or accounts that try to improve the impression of the offender or what he or she has done. For relatives who believed the 'offender' to be innocent, there was nothing to explain other than injustice: the offence simply did not happen, or an offence did happen but their relative had no role to play in it whatsoever. However, participants who used literal denial were in the minority in this study. Most were confronted with 'tension' (Goffman 1963) that needed to be managed through accounts and events that needed to be assimilated. Relatives were called upon to offer these accounts in a variety of situations and to a variety of people; these accounts are the subject of Chapters 4 and 5.

Collective management

A self-help group such as Aftermath helps members to manage their stigma by bringing together those in similar situations for support and offering a collective narrative about their shared circumstances which also attempts to deal with the different dimensions of their stigma and shame; this collective management will be examined in Chapter 6. As we will see, this strategy for stigma management was not the same as Herman's collective strategy of 'political activism' (Herman 1994), because Aftermath was not an activist group but instead focused on helping members to cope with their predicament.

Differences between relatives of serious offenders

Although there are typical experiences of stigma among relatives of serious offenders, they do not all experience it in the same way. First, the types of shame experienced by relatives and the degree of secondary stigma depend on kin relationship and how that relationship is constructed. We have seen, for example, how mothers and wives experience particular kinds of stigma and shame. This study has focused on adult relatives of serious offenders, but the stigma of children of serious offenders illustrates this point well. Children of serious offenders do suffer secondary stigma, and children are often discussed in the literature on prisoners' families (see, for example, Boswell and Wedge 2001). However, they will not be given responsibility for the actions of adults, and hence their stigma is constructed only around contamination: they are subject to shame by association or for sharing a genetic heritage. We might also speculate that their plight attracts more funding for supporting prisoners' families and research precisely because they do not experience blame for direct causality as adult relatives do. However, this contamination might be serious in its consequences and long-lasting. Some participants expressed concerns about how having a serious offender as a parent (or grandparent) might affect children in the family in years to come. Evidence from relatives of perpetrators of offences in the Second World War suggests that stigma can be passed down the generations. There have been numerous media reports of the children and grandchildren of Quisling party members in Norway suffering exclusion, for example, and in the Netherlands self-help groups were organised for around 800 descendants of Nazi collaborators who claimed to suffer discrimination in present-day Dutch society because of their parents' past (Bar-On 1990: 241).

An important difference was the type of serious offence: what families were seen to be contaminated *by* or blamed *for* made a difference. All relatives of serious offenders might potentially experience shame on all of the dimensions described, but relatives of those who had committed sexual offences against children thought their stigma was greater:

> Sex offences, there's a stigma. There's the definite stigma of it being a sex offence. You know, I found that myself, that it was you know, like I used to get, 'that's his wife', you know, because it was a sex offence. They wouldn't have said it if he'd robbed a shop or they wouldn't have whispered behind my back, you know, if he'd, if he'd done something like a burglary or even killed somebody, you know. They wouldn't have, I wouldn't have got that attitude and that, you know, the whispering behind me back and the crossing the road

> when they saw me coming and you know, people that'd usually only just nod at me, stopped nodding at me ... a stigma that surrounds sex offenders is, you know, it evokes more of a public, you know, reaction.
>
> (Angela, husband accused of sex offence)

> *G:* I think always when it's a sex offence, the feeling of, I won't say shame because I think that applies to everybody that gets into, you know, a criminal situation, I think the shame's there for everybody but it could be a lot deeper I would say for a sex offence.
>
> *R:* In what way?
>
> *G:* Just the way people view it, you know, I think people, if somebody murdered somebody and it wasn't through a sexually motivated crime, people can accept people, but anybody who's done any kind of a sexual crime, you see it's never, to me what happened, yeah horrible, put his hands up straight away, but it went from indecent assault to all round it was rape and everything, people use their own minds. Whereas a murder is a murder. People that don't know any details build them up in their mind, somebody says 'oh it was this', they go and tell another person, and it builds up and up and up, and from being at the bottom end of a crime it ends up you know, he damned near finished them off, he's raped, beaten, you know done everything. They don't differentiate.
>
> (Gill, husband convicted of sex offence)

The community in which relatives live can be another important variable, something that is recognised by Fishman in her US study of prisoners' wives (Fishman 1990). In working-class communities, she says, arrests are not uncommon and therefore were more likely to be considered 'crisis-provoking' than stigmatising. In middle-class communities, friends were likely to be supportive but neighbours more likely to withdraw. In the main, participants in my study described living in communities that were not tolerant of criminality, and said that their friends, neighbours and other associates had little experience of offending, of which they were aware.

Relatives' experience might differ according to whether a community is close-knit or more anonymous, although the reactions of a local community cannot be straightforwardly predicted. One relative in this study came from a close-knit small community which could not be described as having tolerance for the murder her son committed. Despite this, she said she did not experience stigma:

> I've always been fortunate that we live in [name of town] and some places, some people have had to move, haven't they? Because of

> backlash and everything, but I've had none of that. I can honestly say I've had none of that at all. I'm involved in the Lifeboat ladies on the committee and on the cancer committee, I collect for the Leprosy Mission, and I do a day at the hospice, which was yesterday. Now I started doing that not long after [my son] got sentenced, probably June, and then I started there in September and I've been doing it ever since. Obviously they must know [my family name] is not a common name, but nobody's said anything.
>
> (Beryl, son convicted of homicide)

Beryl's experience comes closest to how Braithwaite describes reintegrative shaming (1989): she lived in a close-knit community and had many interdependencies; she did not experience stigmatising shaming or shaming directed at her; but she was aware of how the crime was regarded as very wrong within her community. However, among the relatives in this study, she was unusual in not experiencing any negative reactions.

Stigma is something we would expect to be worse for relatives of female serious offenders as women who offend are considered doubly deviant (Lloyd 1995). There were not enough relatives of female offenders in this study to be able to draw firm conclusions, although one mother of a female serious offender did think the consequences were worse:

> If it's a female that's done it, it's worse for the people they've left on the outside. If they keep quiet in prison, they're okay; it's just the family on the outside.
>
> (Jane, daughter convicted of violent offence)

However, if this is an area where the type of serious offence makes a considerable difference, then it might be more important than the gender of the offender. None of the eight relatives of female serious offenders who were interviewed were related to child sex offenders and in only one case was the offence murder. The rest belonged to the violent offence group and there was one serious drugs offence conviction. These relatives are still dealing with problems because of the seriousness of the offence, but it is difficult to draw direct comparisons because of this variation in types of offence. We could hypothesise that if we took relatives of male and female pairs convicted of same offence the secondary stigma would be worse for relatives of women, but this would require further research to test. Certainly, high profile cases indicate that public reaction is likely to be worse towards women accused or convicted of serious offences, see for example the highly publicised cases of Myra Hindley, Mary Bell or Rose West.

Though stigmatised, relatives of serious offenders are not a normatively separate group, but rather share prevailing norms with other members of society; this is precisely why they feel shame for the actions of the offenders which have breached some of those which are most widely held and basic. In an effort to place themselves and their loved ones within a moral order, relatives are also involved (as we all are) in stigmatising those who are 'other':

> The normal and the stigmatized are not persons but rather perspectives. These are generated in social situations during mixed contacts by virtue of the unrealized norms that are likely to play upon the encounter ... since interaction roles are involved, not concrete individuals, it should come as no surprise that in many cases he who is stigmatized in one regard nicely exhibits all the normal prejudices held towards those who are stigmatized in another regard.
>
> (Goffman 1963: 164)

Relatives of serious offenders in this study were keen to separate themselves and their loved ones from 'criminal families', professional criminals and petty, recidivist criminals who were viewed in some cases as more deserving of blame and stigma (see Chapter 5).

One important dimension of stigma is 'peril' or the perceived danger of stigma to others: 'stigma has its basis first in threat, be it symbolic or tangible' (Stangor and Crandall 2000: 80). It is perhaps an obvious point that serious offenders present a tangible threat on which their stigma is based. How, though, is the secondary stigma of relatives of serious offenders threatening to outsiders? Their threat is more symbolic and can be distinguished on several levels. First and most basically the stigma has the potential to be passed on in weaker form to those who associate with relatives of serious offenders: '... persons who acquire a degree of [courtesy] stigma in this way can themselves have connexions who acquire a little of the disease twice-removed' (Goffman 1963: 43). Secondly, relatives of serious offenders offer a threat to a 'belief in a just world' (Lerner 1980), a belief that someone's fate must be in some way deserved: 'Victims are threatening to non-victims, for they are manifestations of a malevolent universe rather than a benevolent one' (Janoff-Bulman 1992: 148).

Third, as Nussbaum has argued, stigmatising others makes us feel better about our own weaknesses: 'in shaming people as deviant, the shamers set themselves up as a "normal" class above the shamed, and thus divide society into ranks and hierarchies' (pp. 231–2). People deal with their own uncertainties and anxieties by projecting shame outwards, and this is likely to be powerful when constructed around the family:

> The family is also an area of great anxiety and lack of control. Families often contain our most intimate relationships, through which we search for the meaning of life. And yet there is much hostility, ambivalence, and anxiety involved in many, if not most, family relationships. Thus shame once again enters the picture: the roles we assign ourselves in the family, as 'the good father,' 'the good mother,' are cherished and comforting norms, and precious aspects of people's attempts to define themselves as normal, precisely because there is so much at stake when control is lost and something unexpected happens. People are typically aware of deficiency in their family roles, and thus they need all the more anxiously to shore up their purity.
>
> (Nussbaum 2004: 262)

Finally, relatives of serious offenders offer a symbolic threat to outsiders' moral world view by suggesting that their relatives are not inherently evil and that it is possible to offer them support without condoning the offence. In this way they present a kind of blurred morality which is uncomfortable and threatens the clarity of people's moral schema and our urge to categorise into good or evil.

Note

1 Although of course there are prison regimes that go to great lengths to challenge offending behaviour and some offences, such as sex offences against children, may well lead to a prisoner being stigmatised with potential serious consequences.

Chapter 4

Making sense of the offence

> He murdered his grandmother . . . he was on drugs and you know, and I think he had a bit of a mental illness . . . he had a really, not a nice upbringing and I think that's, I think part of it, you know? I don't know, I just think it was all to do with childhood and growing up and getting involved in drugs and mental illness.
>
> (Debbie, husband convicted of homicide)

> What was difficult? People judging you when they don't know the full story. And feeling that you had to explain to people. Why should I have to explain to anybody? But I felt I had to justify to everybody what was going on. Why? Do you know what I mean? They'd come in and I'd say well this is happening and this is what happened and I'd explain the lot. . . . Why should *you* justify to all the people what's happening in your life? But I thought I had to do that. So that was bad, really.
>
> (Angela, husband accused of sex offence)

When they discovered the offence, families were confronted with unusually shocking information of which they had to make sense. They tried to understand *why* their relative did what they did, the *reasons* for the offending and to formulate accounts about the offender's motivations. Trying to make sense of the offence is a crucial part of moving forward from the initial impact stage. There is an increasing emphasis in social science on how our lives are storied and on how we construct our identities through a story of the self (see, for example, Ezzy 1998; Giddens 1991; Holstein and Gubrium 2000; Randall 1995). Through this process we give coherence to our lives (Denzin 1989) and construct a consistent account of who we are. A major life-altering event cuts through this continuity and this 'biographical disruption' (Williams

1984) requires a process of narrative reconstruction of self and identity, and discovering the offence is one such event. This disruption is prolonged by relatives' experience of stigma and shame: 'Shame bears directly on self-identity because it is essentially anxiety about the adequacy of the narrative by means of which the individual sustains a coherent biography' (Giddens 1991: 65). The accounts relatives give – about the offence and about their own role – help to restore some of this coherence and are an important means for relatives to manage both their own emotional response and the exclusion and ostracism experienced in interaction with others.

Relatives' accounts of the motivation and reasons behind the crime were often tentative and searching as in the quotation from Debbie above. The motivation of relatives giving accounts about the offence might differ significantly from that of offenders who have much more invested in mitigating personal responsibility and may do it in a more calculated and categorical way to achieve personal ends. Relatives are often struggling with trying to work out what happened, piecing together information and searching around for alternative ways to view the offender and his or her actions. There may be circumstances where their accounts are deliberately calculated to achieve specific means, but they perhaps have less to gain from this than offenders. In addition, of course, they sometimes genuinely do not know the details of the offence and in some cases do not even know whether it took place; the same cannot of course be said for the offender.

There is a sociological literature about how offenders account for their own crimes, but little has been written about accounting for the crimes of others. Studies of why offenders say they committed crimes have insights that can help us to understand more about why their relatives say they did. The classic studies include C. Wright Mills's theory of 'vocabularies of motive' (Mills 1940); Sykes and Matza's 'techniques of neutralization' (Sykes and Matza 1957); Scott and Lyman's 'accounts' (1968) and Stokes and Hewitt's 'aligning actions' (1976). For a comprehensive review of the literature see Maruna and Copes (2005); my focus here will be on some of the key points relevant to understanding the accounts of relatives. Mills's seminal work focused on the inherently sociological character of motive. As the term 'vocabulary' suggests, there are only a limited number of available and acceptable motives in given situations and 'institutionally different situations have different *vocabularies of motive* appropriate to their respective behaviors' (Mills 1940: 906). Vocabularies of motive are historically and culturally specific, so certain motives will be acceptable and influential in particular societies at particular times. In the context of this study, the vocabulary available to relatives will be limited by, for example, offence type and kin relationship and how these categories are socially constructed. Motives are interesting because they tell us much about the social context in which they are given (see also Taylor 1972; Hamlin 1988; Cohen 2001) which brings into focus the theme of the previous chapter and the reasons why relatives should feel the need to neutralise or account for the offender's actions and their own role.

Mills was also interested in what accounts *do* and their relationship to action. He argued that accounts were not just formulated retrospectively, but might be given before, during or after acts and he thought that anticipating reactions to motives could operate as an effective control on behaviour. Similarly Sykes and Matza suggested that neutralisations were not just formulated after the act, but also before and could in fact make that act possible by weakening social control (Sykes and Matza 1957). This relationship between accounts and action has been much debated, but is of limited use in understanding the accounts relatives construct about the offence – by definition they cannot account until cognisant – which is often some time after it has occurred. It has more applicability, however, to understanding how relatives account for their own actions, and in particular accounting for supporting the offender (considered in the following chapter); in making decisions about supporting and constructing accounts about their motives relatives are likely to anticipate the reactions of others (Mills 1940) and the accounts they give might contribute to freeing them to pursue that course.

In their study of the techniques of neutralisation used by juvenile delinquents, Sykes and Matza suggest that their function is to realign the actor with his social group. Delinquents do not live in a separate normative world but rather share the values of conventional society, hence the need for accounts, or techniques, to neutralise the possible guilt about the act in question. When given after the act, these techniques provide the function of protecting the actor from self-blame and from blame by others by neutralising social disapproval. Sykes and Matza identified five techniques used by offenders to counter blame: *denial of responsibility*, *denial of injury*, *denial of the victim*, *condemnation of the condemners* and an *appeal to higher loyalties* (Sykes and Matza 1957). As we will see, I found examples of four of the techniques identified by Sykes and Matza in the accounts of relatives in this study. *Condemnation of the condemners* was not used to neutralise disapproval of the offence (as we will see, the range of accounts likely to be honoured in relation to serious offences is more limited). Relatives did not attempt to shift the focus of attention from the serious offence to the motives and behaviour of those who disapproved – relatives themselves, in most cases, strongly disapproved of what the offender had done. There were some accounts condemning the reaction to the offender and the family after the offence, but these were rarely condemning (for example Lillian says 'I try to explain to people that would feel against you ...') or if they were condemning, were balanced with an acknowledgement of the offence having been very wrong (see for example Gill's comments in this chapter about sex offender treatment programmes and in Chapter 5 about social services). As we saw in the previous chapter, strong resistance was unusual amongst relatives in this study who in the main were horrified by the offence and felt disempowered by self-doubt or blame.

Stokes and Hewitt defined accounts as types of 'aligning actions' necessary when there is a gap between expectations about how an individual should behave and that individual's actions. Clearly this gap is cavernous in the case of the actions of serious offenders and bridging it will by no means be straightforward, but the accounts of relatives do seek to re-align offenders, if somewhat partially, and to re-align relatives themselves. I will use the term 'accounts' to describe the motivational statements and reasons given by relatives, following Scott and Lyman's definition. They say an account is: 'a statement made by a social actor to explain unanticipated or untoward behavior – whether that behavior is his own or *that of others*, and whether the proximate cause for the statement arises from the actor himself *or from someone else*' (Scott and Lyman 1968: 46, emphasis added). Although Scott and Lyman introduce the idea of accounting for the behaviour of others it is not developed further in their work and appears to be absent from most subsequent studies of accounts. Scott and Lyman make a basic distinction between excuses and justifications in accounts: excuses attempt to diminish the actor's responsibility, justifications attempt to normalise the act. This distinction has been applied again and again in studies of the accounts of offenders, for example looking at the accounts of rapists (Scully and Marolla 1984), murderers (Ray and Simmons 1987) and paedophiles (DeYoung 1988; Hanson and Slater 1993; McCaghy 1968; Pollock and Hashmall 1991; Taylor 1972; Thomson *et al.* 1998).

Sykes and Matza's five techniques have been applied to a vast range of different types of deviance and the study has been highly cited over the years. Maruna and Copes are critical, however, of a tendency for some more recent studies to produce taxonomies of techniques without attending to some of the sociological concerns of earlier theorists: 'neutralizations have been widely recognised by criminologists but badly undertheorized' (Maruna and Copes 2005: 224).

Attempts have been made to analyse the accounts that relatives of offenders construct about the offence. Fishman (1990) found that the prisoners' wives in her study convinced themselves that their husband's offending did not matter through the device of a 'sad tale' (Goffman 1961) which attempted to rationalise deviant behaviour. Through this device they were able to focus on key events or themes to show what had gone wrong in their men's lives, and to 'reassure the women that their marriages were really worth while' (Fishman 1990: 96). In order to preserve their image of their husbands as basically 'good people' and only incidentally criminal, they used a 'vocabulary of motives' which 'explains, justifies, and answers questions about male criminality' (p. 51). The wives tried to normalise their husbands' behaviour and interpret it as reasonable, or to neutralise the negative connotations of his behaviour, using three strategies: blaming his deviant activities on outside forces ('scapegoating' or another person as the primary cause; alcoholism; or environmental factors such as unemployment or poverty); blaming the husbands (focusing on immaturity; character weakness; or mental illness) or blaming themselves – suggesting they were the cause, e.g. because they did not do enough for their husbands. Fishman's aim is to identify these themes in the wives' accounts and their role in helping the women in her study to accommodate to their circumstances. Although she refers to a 'vocabulary of motives' (p. 264) and to Scott and Lyman's study (p. 298) she does not attempt to develop a theoretical framework that integrates her findings more closely with this body of work.

In her study of murderers' relatives, May found that their accounts formed two 'clusters': those that accept the legal definition of murder and those that did not. She found differences between the 'murder accounts' (offered by three families) and the 'manslaughter accounts' (offered by four). Within the 'manslaughter' accounts, 'explanations of excuse', appealing to cultural scripts of accident and illness, and 'explanations of justification', establishing some degree of offender victimisation, were used. Interviewees in this cluster explained the legal verdict of 'murder' by characterising justice as unpredictable and blaming the jury, the judge and legal advice. By contrast, interviewees in the murder 'cluster' retained a notion of absolute culpability and absolute victimisation. They sought help from a range of organisations to try and find explanations, and all three families were involved with Aftermath. These families referred to making a separation between the person and their actions ('loving the sinner, but not the sin') and identified factors in the offenders' lives which could help explain the killings (May 1999). In my own study, I found Aftermath members with a range of views about the offender's culpability, and found that accounts about the offence were offered by all relatives (except three who retained an absolute notion of the offender's innocence rather than culpability – for these relatives the crime did not happen and there was nothing to explain) (see Table 2 on p. 105). An analytical framework is needed to capture the range of different accounts used by relatives, and one which allows for the tension between wanting the offender to take responsibility for his or her actions and wanting to mitigate that responsibility in particular ways.

This analytical framework also needs to incorporate the relatives' unique status in relation to accounts about the offence. Relatives are drawn into a pool of people who listen to the accounts of offenders and are validators – or otherwise – of these accounts. They therefore have an important role as *audiences*. However, they do not just absorb and straightforwardly reflect offenders' accounts. They will be called upon to comment on them and to give their own account of why the offence happened – and the accounts they construct may also be based on several secondary sources: relatives are therefore *commentators*. Relatives may be called to account themselves. As we have seen in the previous chapter, they may experience secondary stigma constructed around several types of shame; in this respect they are producers of accounts because they are *subjects* of those accounts and contaminated or implicated and therefore construct causal first-person narratives. This chapter considers relatives as audiences and commentators as they account for the offender's actions; the following chapter looks at the accounts offered by relatives to counter the fact that they are implicated, and how these accounts address the web of shame.

Relatives as audiences

Relatives are important audiences for offenders' accounts, and because of their closeness are well placed to judge their plausibility. As audiences, relatives listen to the primary accounts of offenders and absorb information about events and motives from numerous secondary sources, including other family, friends, criminal justice professionals, and the media. No offenders were interviewed as part of this study, but the kinds of excuses and justifications that are found in the literature on serious offenders were not straightforwardly reflected in the accounts of relatives, suggesting that relatives do not just accept what they are told by offenders. Of course, the literature does not tell us what offenders tell their families, and this might be quite different from what they tell legal or other authorities, researchers or even each other. One study of the publications of paedophile organisations, for example, found strong justifications in the form of *denial of injury*, *denial of the victim*, *condemnation of the condemners* and *appeal to higher loyalties* (DeYoung 1988). Paedophiles and other serious offenders might therefore justify their actions to each other in quite different ways: 'Preliminary research suggests that justifications of violence and deviance are most commonly used among peers, while exculpatory excuses are used when presenting one's story to strangers or outsiders (Harvey, Weber and Orbuch 1990; Toch 1993)' (Maruna and Copes 2005: 261); in this context, non-offending relatives are likely to constitute outsiders rather than peers.

Some relatives will hear quite detailed accounts from the offender; others will only have had the opportunity to speak about the offence under very restricted conditions, for example during prison visits, and yet others, like Beryl, might struggle to raise the subject or elicit any explanation at all:

> *B*: We can't think how he got involved in it. And no matter how you go round and round and round with it, you can't get an answer. It's whether he, I mean, I still don't know whether he was drunk or not, really. I just think, well one of these days we shall find out.
>
> *R*: Have you ever talked to him about it?
>
> *B*: Only to say what a stupid thing, look what a stupid thing it's all turned out to be. He doesn't really want to talk about it. Whether he will open up now, I don't know.
>
> (Beryl, son convicted of homicide)

Even those relatives that do listen to accounts from the offender are likely to use secondary sources to supplement those accounts – information gleaned from others involved, from media reports, the police, or court hearings. Families must therefore piece together *what* happened and *why* it happened, the latter usually being a long-term process, dependent upon their knowledge about the offence, their knowledge of and relationship with the offender, and their own life and experiences. Accounts given by families about the offender and the offence are therefore second-order accounts and might have parallels with a psychiatrist discussing the motivations of a patient (though the psychiatrist is unlikely to be implicated as a relative might be), or a church accounting for the action of a priest accused of child sex offences (see Thomson *et al.* 1998).

What relatives do with offenders' accounts will vary. First, the construction of a particular reality can be a joint enterprise. We have seen in Chapter 1 how family members can collude in denial of particular problems, and use techniques to repackage them (Cohen 2001; Goleman 1985) and these repackaging techniques can include the kinds of accounts described in this chapter. An example can be found in a case study of a family attributing competence to a 'severely retarded' child, suggesting that family members can construct an extreme version of reality and sustain it in the face of strong information to the contrary (Pollner and McDonald-Wikler 1985). Constructing accounts can also be a collective enterprise in the self-help context, to be considered in Chapter 6. However, relatives of offenders also make judgements about the validity of accounts – as we all do – and may challenge offenders' accounts. Braithwaite argues that a primary aim of restorative justice conferences is to challenge offenders' techniques of neutralisation (Braithwaite 1999); offenders' relatives have a key role in these conferences and their presence can make it more difficult for offenders to neutralise their actions. The relationship between offenders' accounts and relatives' accounts cannot therefore be straightforwardly predicted. Relatives might collude in denial or challenge it, and may take different positions at different times: this is a negotiated process rather than a fixed state.

Relatives as commentators

As commentators, relatives construct their own accounts about the offence, struggling to make sense of whatever information they have to formulate a coherent story:

> *C*: The question that I heard so many times [from other Aftermath members]: 'Why? Why? How can this have happened?' And I didn't know the answer to that.
> *R*: Is that mostly people at the beginning?
> *C*: Yes. But it still follows through. 'Why was it?' 'Why did this happen?' And people at various stages do that, still go back there, 'Why?' 'How?'
>
> (Celia, nephew convicted of homicide)

Family members must digest the accounts of offenders and other sources of information to construct their own accounts. This process of establishing 'what happened' from information from numerous sources has some parallels with the processes used by jurors in criminal trials (though again, without the element of causal implication) who piece together information, making inferences about motive and culpability, based upon normative understandings of what constitutes excusable or inexcusable behaviour in particular situations. One study suggests that they do so using a 'story framework' to understand the evidence (Bennett 1997).

Explaining untoward actions – offering explanations, citing reasons, contextualising – is something we all do and is part of the process of making sense of our lives. As Maruna and Copes explain: '. . . the psychological research on account making and self-attributions is clear: there is nothing pathological about neutralizing negative behaviors or contextualising one's faults in broader circumstances. Taking full responsibility for every personal failing does not make a person "normal", it makes them extraordinary (and possibly at risk of depression)' (Maruna and Copes 2005: 227). Maruna and Copes argue that using neutralisation techniques is not evidence of a criminal personality, even though excuses have been pathologised in some criminal justice policies which aim to make offenders take 'full responsibility' for their actions. Fox, for example, has shown how in the prison environment excuses are viewed as pathological. She found that accounts offered by prisoners were rejected by therapists and treatment was constructed in such a way as to decontextualise offending, so only the explanation of individual pathology remained (Fox 1999). Relatives in my study were trying to contextualise the crime by offering reasons and explanations for the offender's actions.

The extent to which relatives are called upon to give accounts will depend upon the extent to which the offence is known and the management of disclosure or secrecy outlined in the previous chapter. In that chapter we saw how relatives might be more vulnerable than imprisoned offenders to the shaming gaze of others; they might similarly be more vulnerable to the process of giving accounts. Most of those serious offenders that are caught receive prison sentences, and although they may become used to giving accounts to, for example, lawyers, the courts, psychiatrists, and probation officers, these will be called for on particular occasions, are less likely to be part of their daily life, and the frequency with which they are called to account may well diminish as a prison sentence progresses. Their relatives continue on the outside, chatting with neighbours, talking to teachers at their children's schools, listening to gossip and may even, as we have seen, be subject to direct abuse. On a daily basis they are the people in the market-place for consuming and producing accounts and may continue to be so for years after discovery.

Relatives' accounts are given on several levels: to themselves through an internal dialogue; to those within the family and their close circle; to those outside the family with whom they have informal contact; sometimes to those they meet formally, for example social workers, psychiatrists and those in the criminal justice professions; and for some eventually to self-help groups such as Aftermath; each forum has its own nuanced expectancies. The accounts analysed here were given in the somewhat artificial context of the research interview. Maruna and Copes warn that neutralisations might be produced by the situational demands of the interview and artificially created for the interviewer, particularly when the interview takes place in a prison or other correctional setting and the interviewee's 'deviant' status is clearly marked. Accounts might be produced which do not represent accounts that would be given in other circumstances (Maruna and Copes 2005: 260–1). This is a valid point. My aim has been to try to understand some of the processes by which relatives make sense of the offence and make sense of their own circumstances. To do this, it was necessary to talk to them in some detail. Interviews were mostly in relatives' own homes, took place in many cases over several hours, and were often with relatives I had known for some months or even years through fieldwork. Most interviewees knew me well and, I hope, were helped to feel comfortable talking about their situation. They perhaps had less invested than an offender in a correctional setting in concocting neutralisations for my benefit. However, the interview is an unusual situation and it is worth being cautious about the context in which relatives' accounts were elicited and the extent to which they can be generalised.

Each time an interviewee spoke about reasons for the offence it was noted in the interview transcripts, and these numerous collated reasons were then examined to look for patterns. The reasons were given in response to general questioning about why people commit offences (which invariably led to the interviewee referring to her own family circumstances), and specific questioning about why they thought the offender had committed the crime; and spontaneously emerged at other points during the interviews. Through a process of gradual coding and refining, patterns began to emerge. I found Scott and Lyman's distinction between excuses and justifications less useful for analysing the accounts of the interviewees in this study because so few of the interviewees used justifications in the pure sense of the term. The concept of justifications might be stretched to include some of their techniques – there were examples of relatives using *denial of injury* and *denial of the victim*, both of which are techniques of neutralisation appropriated by Scott and Lyman in their explanation of justifications. However, Scott and Lyman tell us that 'to justify an act is to assert its *positive* value in the face of a claim to the contrary' (Scott and Lyman 1968: 51, emphasis added), and the relatives in my study did not do this. It is possible to imagine circumstances where relatives might offer justifications, and examples can be found from relatives of those committing 'political' or 'ideological' crimes: parents of Palestinian suicide bombers who say they support their son's actions and are proud of him, or relatives of Israeli soldiers who have committed atrocities against Palestinian youths who offer denials and justifications (Cohen 2001: 157–9), for example.

When offenders offer excuses and justifications they tend to be stronger and more forceful appeals to limit or eliminate culpability: 'it wasn't my fault', 'I'm not to blame', 'I did the right thing', and so on. Relatives in this study offered excuses that were less clear and more limited and partial. Many of the relatives talked about wanting the offender to take some responsibility for his or her actions and to face up to the harm caused, and how they could not condone what the offender had done, but simultaneously used techniques to try to neutralise some of the blame attached by others. Excuses and justifications cannot accommodate this dual wish, and do not adequately capture the range of techniques used by relatives with a variety of views about the offender's culpability, and as we have seen, May was only able to apply this distinction to the 'manslaughter accounts' offered by four families (May 1999). The blame levelled at offenders, given the seriousness of the offences, was often all-encompassing and might even take the form of the offender being labelled evil, sub-human and below contempt; this is what relatives wanted to adjust. A mother during a fieldwork conversation told me she hated the fact that people thought badly of her son, she wanted them to see the good things about him. A letter in the Aftermath newsletter in June 1998 stated: 'I too am a mother who dearly loves her son . . . we love our sons and we know the good in them that no one else sees. And the bad in them breaks our hearts.' It seemed that often this most basic wish – that others would not think badly of a son, daughter, husband or other close relative – was behind attempts to adjust the impressions held by others.

The most useful distinction for the purposes of this study within the literature on accounts is between *act adjustment* and *actor adjustment* (Cohen 2001; Ditton 1977). These techniques are used by offenders to evade moral blameworthiness, and I have found them to be the techniques used by relatives in their (often partial) attempts to do this on behalf of the offender. In his study of the motivational accounts of bread salesmen who were 'part-time' criminals fiddling and stealing Ditton states:

> Adjustment may be achieved in one of two ways. Firstly, by adjustment of the *actor*, which amounts to a denial of full responsibility by psychologically excusing the self on the grounds of the denial of imputability. Secondly, through the application of various definitions, it is possible to adjust the fault component of the *act* in question as a form of circumstantial excuse.
>
> (Ditton 1977: 165)

An act adjustment is therefore a response that focuses on the *act* – in this case the serious offence – and attempts to minimise or downplay the harm caused, or to normalise it. An actor adjustment focuses on the *actor* and attempts to adjust the impression the audience might have of that actor. Both accounts tend to be apologetic, like Goffman's 'sad tales', rather than asserting the positive value of an act: they are not active justifications. This is therefore a more effective distinction to capture relatives' attempts to account for the offender's actions, firstly because adjustment is a less total and less forceful plea and secondly because it does not attempt to portray the act as positive. Table 2 shows the distribution of these strategies in the accounts of the relatives I interviewed.

We can see from this table that actor adjustments predominated in the accounts of interviewees; act adjustments were much rarer and where they were used tended to be used in conjunction with actor adjustments. This is likely to be because of the seriousness of the offences – it is clearly more difficult, for example, to adjust an act of child sexual

Table 2 Number of interviewees using actor and act adjustments[1]

	Actor adjustments	*Act adjustments*	*Both*	*Neither*
Relatives of male offenders ($n = 24$)	18	7	4	3
Relatives of female offenders ($n = 8$)	8	1	1	0
Homicide group ($n = 11$)	11	3	3	0
Sexual offence against minor ($n = 10$)	6	3	1	2
Rape ($n = 3$)	1	1	0	1
Violent ($n = 7$)	7	1	1	0
Non-supporting relatives ($n = 5$)	4	1	0	0
Believes 'offender' is innocent ($n = 7$)	3	3	2	3
Mothers[2] ($n = 17$)	14	4	3	2
Wives/partners ($n = 10$)	7	2	0	1
Total[3] ($n = 32$)	**26**	**8**	**5**	**3**

abuse than it would be to adjust an act of vandalism. Studies of the accounts of offenders have shown neutralisations to be better suited to some types of crime than others, and specifically related to the type of act that is being neutralised, a point recognised by Sykes and Matza (1957), and Mitchell and Dodder who found that neutralisations were less effective for serious offences (Mitchell and Dodder 1980) (cited in Maruna and Copes 2005). Actor adjustments are more readily available to relatives of serious offenders and more likely to be honoured. Claims for mitigated responsibility because of some of these factors (under the influence of alcohol or drugs, emotional problems, etc.) often appear in excuse accounts offered by serious offenders (see, for example, Ray and Simmons 1987 on murderers' accounts; Scully and Marolla 1984 on rapists' accounts).

Relatives from the violent offence or homicide groups were more likely to offer actor adjustments, as were those from the child sex offence group. For the child sex offence group, however, these were of a more limited range (see below). All relatives of female offenders offered actor adjustments; only one offered an act adjustment, and this was used in conjunction with an actor adjustment. Neither of these strategies are exclusive; although it is useful to analyse them separately, some relatives used them simultaneously.

Seven out of 32 interviewees believed the 'offender' to be innocent, and three of these did not use any form of adjustment. Four said they believed the offender was innocent, but were less categorical and still offered adjustments. In one case a wife believed her husband was falsely accused of sex offences by his (now adult) children, but told me she accepted he had taken pictures which were 'a bit naughty' of one of his daughters; he was convicted of indecent assault and charges relating to the photographs. A grandmother believed her grandson had not committed the crime of attempted murder, although he had been there when his co-accused fired the gun. One mother believed her daughter to be wrongly convicted of murder; she had been at the scene, but had not committed the act. In another case, a mother believed her daughter had been wrongly convicted of serious drugs offences; she too had been 'set up' and found with a very large quantity of drugs which were not hers, but was unable to reveal this to the police because threats had been made against her daughter's life, and her daughter consequently served a long prison sentence.

There were three further relatives who stated that they did not know whether or not their family member was guilty, and continued to state this even when questioned further;[4] each of these used adjustments. One mother said she did not know whether or not her son had committed murder; one wife said she did not know whether her husband had committed sexual offences against their grandchildren (although she said she knew he was 'not a paedophile'); and one mother said she did know that injuries had been inflicted on her grandson by either her daughter or her daughter's partner, but was not sure of the extent of her daughter's involvement. In each of these three cases the convicted offenders continued to protest their innocence. In the remaining cases, relatives recognised some wrongdoing while attempting to adjust the impression the listener[5] might have about the offender. The forms that their actor and act adjustments took are summarised in Figure 2.

Actor adjustment (he or she is not the kind of person that does things like this)

Actor adjustments predominated in relatives' accounts and took four main forms: *denial of responsibility* (Sykes and Matza 1957), *resisting totalising identity*, *balance* and *separating the act from the actor*.

Denial of (full) responsibility

Denial of responsibility has been found to be the 'master theme' (Cohen 2001) in the accounts of offenders, and was similarly prominent in relatives' accounts where it took eight non-exclusive forms (see Figure 2). Relatives of homicide perpetrators and violent offenders were likely to point to *mental illness*, or *drugs or alcohol* as reasons for the offence but relatives of sex offenders used more limited denials and did not describe an addiction to alcohol or drugs or long-term problem which might contradict their attempts to normalise. Lillian was the exception in this

Actor adjustment	Act adjustment
1. Denial of (full) responsibility: • Drugs or alcohol • Mental illness • Hereditary/genetic • Sad tale as denial of responsibility • Led astray • Accident/no intention • Immaturity • Anger/emotions out of control	**1. Denial of the victim**
2. Resisting totalising identity[6]	**2. Denial of injury**
3. Balance (a) backwards (b) sideways	**3. Normalising the act**
4. Separating the act from the actor	**4. Comparative adjustment**

Figure 2 Act and actor adjustments in the accounts of relatives

group and pointed to her son's alcohol use and previous drug addiction, along with other actor adjustments (and in Chapter 1 was the only relative from this group to offer a problem-identifying account):

> He's never had a problem with drink, this only happened about a year before he went in prison. . . . I found all the empty bottles . . . and now he's really worried that when he comes out that he mustn't never go near drink again because that's what led him into all this.
>
> (Lillian, son convicted of sex offence)

McCaghy found that sex offenders used being under the influence of alcohol as an effective method of 'deviance disavowal' (McCaghy 1968), substituting drinking as a more acceptable form of deviance. Denying full responsibility because the offender was under the influence of alcohol is a cause that is easier to remedy than conquering an addiction and hence a more effective actor adjustment for relatives wanting to downplay the risk of future offending, and the more limited range of techniques used by relatives of sex offenders also fits with their more frequent use of normalising accounts of life before discovery. Other relatives in the homicide and violent offence groups cited addiction to drugs or alcohol and several interviewees pointed to heroin or crack cocaine addiction as a cause.

For some of those I interviewed, *mental illness* was a reason for the crime, a broad category encompassing different kinds of poor mental health such as depression, post-natal depression and schizophrenia. For some relatives, this was the key explanation for why the offence took place. Had the offender not been mentally ill, it would not have happened; hence personal responsibility was mitigated to a degree because illness was the cause:

> I think that [my daughter] did it because she was mentally unwell in some sense or other and that that mental unwell-ness stemmed from a complex mixture of her history, and post-natal depression and possible psychosis, although I don't know enough about that, and something in her personality that causes her to have periodic, I don't even know how to describe them, almost like, yeah, she goes, it's like she goes mad. She has these patches where she just loses it completely and something has to give. And whereas before it's always been turned inwards, on that occasion, tragically, it was directed at her baby.
>
> (Monica, daughter convicted of violent offence)

A further way to adjust the impression held of the actor is to point to a *genetic* or *biological* cause. If an offender is a victim of their genes, they might be seen as somehow less responsible for their actions. In their search for a reason or cause some relatives wondered whether there might be a genetic explanation. Lillian, an elderly mother of a sex offender, pointed to a history of sexual offending in her family:

> *L*: Although it's not my fault, I feel, I feel somehow responsible. It's silly really, for me to be carrying that around with me because it's not my fault what my son's done but I do feel bad about it.
>
> *R*: Why do you think you feel responsible?
>
> *L*: I don't know. Well the thing is when I was young, when I was 17, not quite, the [Second World] War was on. And my mother's boyfriend, who was an American, my mother used to bring him and his friend to the flat ... They were in the medical corps. Well one night one of them gave me something to drink which I found afterwards that it was pure alcohol from the hospital where they were stationed in Victoria. And one of these men raped me and so consequently I didn't know it at the time until I was over three months pregnant, I was pregnant. So that was my son. And when I was young, I was also sexually abused by two of my uncles. And so somehow I told my son when he was old enough to know, that, about his father but I never ever told him that I was sexually assaulted. But I did tell him that as time went by and somehow in my mind I thought, I wonder if this has triggered off anything in him or whether anything of his father's come out in him. ... You

> know, is it something in our family? Is it something on my mother's side with my, her brothers that were? Is it something that's hereditary? I don't know.
>
> (Lillian, son convicted of sex offence)

Lillian went on to explain how her eldest grandson was most affected by his father's offences and worried about a genetic link: 'he was worried that he might turn out like that. He said to his mother "do you think when I'm older, I might have these feelings, whatever Dad's done?".' Harriet also pointed to genetics as a possible explanation: if the cause was nature rather than nurture, relatives, and particularly parents, might be less implicated:

> *H*: A lot of people will say 'well I blame the parents', you know, 'if you'd brought him up properly, this wouldn't have happened'.
>
> *R*: What do you think about that?
>
> *H*: I think there are many, many factors. It may be one of the factors. I believe in our genetic make-up and there's not an awful lot one can do about it.
>
> (Harriet, son accused of sex offence)

However, this was not a frequently offered account, which may be for two reasons. First, 'mitigating evidence such as genetic predisposition is . . . a two-edged sword, which may diminish blameworthiness for the crime at the same time as it indicates the probability that the criminal may be dangerous in the future and is beyond redemption' (Rose 2000: 14). Second, as we have seen in the previous chapter, it is an explanation which might contaminate those relatives who share a genetic heritage.

A *'sad tale'* (Goffman 1961) was offered by some relatives as an actor adjustment. Scott and Lyman use this 'sad tale' (*ibid.*) as a justification, but that is not the sense in which it is offered here. Instead, a series of events are described that lead to the individual being less responsible for his or her offence because so many awful things happened to him or her (not that a series of events led to an offence being committed and that to do so was somehow right or reasonable under those circumstances). Goffman says: 'if the facts of a person's past and present are extremely dismal, then the best he can do is show that he is not responsible for what has become of him' (*ibid.*: 140). So it is an actor adjustment, and an attempt to mitigate full responsibility. Relatives described the offender's family background, abuse that might have been suffered and various other traumatic events, losses and hardships in the life of the offender. Gill pointed to abuse her husband suffered as a child, but was keen to point out that she was not offering this as an excuse for his crimes:

> I think there are reasons [for serious offences]. Not excuses, there are reasons and mitigating factors, definitely. A lot's to do with what happens to you. Especially men, I've found, don't get a chance, some through their upbringing don't get a chance to talk out things. I can only give [my husband] as an example. He was ten years older than his brother and sister, he had a Dad who in his own way is lovely but is an out and out bully, really an out and out bully, and also I mean I'd been married, when this happened I'd been married for 23 years, and I'd talked about abuse because I'd got a daughter and I was aware you know not just what was going on in my own house but I was aware that things happened, you think you're aware, you think oh that will never happen to me, but anyway that's another part of the story. But 23 years, and it wasn't until all this came out, it wasn't straight away, a couple of days later, and I finally got to find out what had happened to him as a ten year old [sexually abused by a family friend]. And the first thing I said, it made me so mad, why the bloody hell, if it happened to you, you must have known what they were going through! Why?
>
> (Gill, husband convicted of sex offence)

A denial of full responsibility in the form of a 'sad tale' was a common account form; relatives were keen for the offence and the offender to be understood in the broader context of events.

Some relatives thought the offender had been *led astray* by another. Louise believed her daughter's male friend had been primarily responsible for the kidnap and grievous bodily harm for which she was convicted, but he had fled the country and escaped prosecution. Beryl's son was convicted of murder. She blamed his co-accused, a woman with whom he was having an affair, though this was not an explanation accepted by the court:

> *R*: And do you now understand why [your son] committed that crime?
>
> *B*: No. Only that she'd got him round her little finger really ... he hadn't any friends here. And so he used to go in [the local pub], you see, and then he started working in the bar. And that's why I think really, it was companionship I suppose, and it was somebody of his age group, and er she sort of got him woven into her web, really. I've tried and tried, but I can't work it out why. And how she sort of, I mean, his solicitor said did she give you any drugs? He said no. But the sort of person she was. ... Could have been sex, I don't know. In her own way she was attractive, there's no two ways about it. Why she had to pick on my son, I don't know.
>
> (Beryl, son convicted of homicide)

For Christine, her daughter's offences of serious and violent armed robberies were explained by the influence of her violent partner upon whom her daughter was dependent for her heroin supply. Without his influence, she said, the offences would never have happened:

> *C*: She was given four years prison sentence, but they did take into consideration the person she was with when she done these robberies. He used to beat her to make her do them, because he used to wait until she was withdrawing and then tell her what she's got to do because otherwise he wouldn't supply her with what she needed.
> *R*: So she was pretty desperate when that happened?
> *C*: Oh yeah. She told the probation officer that right up to the very last minute when she was actually in the shop she was thinking of ways of getting out of it, but knew that if she came out with nothing she would get a good hiding.
>
> (Christine, daughter convicted of violent offence)

A further actor adjustment is that the crime was an *accident* or that there was a lack of intention on the part of the offender. Lisa described how, as a teenage boy, her partner had lashed out at another young boy after an altercation which involved comments about his sexuality:

> To me it was an accident, it was the mores of the time. . . . I mean to me if he said 'I had a pet cat and I set it alight' then that would mean far more to me because it was something he'd done deliberately and cruelly and this was just a horrible accident.
>
> (Lisa, partner convicted of homicide)

Removing intention by defining a killing as an accident is important as murder is defined as the unlawful killing of another human being with the intention to kill or cause grievous bodily harm. Intention is therefore a requirement for the definition of murder, although the concept of intention has itself been the subject of much legal scrutiny and debate (see, for example, Lacey 1993; Malle and Nelson 2003).

One way to attempt to adjust the impression held of the actor is to point to his or her young age or *immaturity* as mitigation. Although Dorothy's daughter was an adult at the time of the offence, Dorothy thought she was less responsible for her actions because she lacked maturity:

> There's a difference in someone who's academically very bright, which my daughter is, but there is the other part of the brain just like a child. You've got to understand, you've got to know her,

> you've got to see her, everybody loves her. . . . She's unique in a way that even in here [in prison] she's accepted. . . . She wanted to be a child with the others. She wanted to be one of the teenagers with [her children] instead of growing up.
>
> (Dorothy, daughter convicted of homicide)

Pauline was struggling to understand the causes of her son's offence and the only explanation she could find was that the offence was caused by *anger*. Her son was detained indefinitely in a special hospital and although she later referred to her son as 'poorly', the professional diagnosis she sought was not forthcoming:

> *R*: So the main difficulties or problems that you've had to cope with over the past years since it happened are with the hospital not telling you anything?
>
> *P*: They never tell you a word. They never even say your son was progressing or regressing, digressing or whatever -gressing. They just don't tell you nothing. In all the years I've had one visit from a social worker from [the special hospital] who's now left. There's absolutely nothing. No feedback from a doctor saying well he's suffering from this, that or other or he's suffering from nothing. He hasn't even got a label. He's not schizophrenic, he's not on no medication. It were just pure out and out anger. That's all.
>
> (Pauline, son convicted of homicide)

Anger here is represented as an alien thing, not part of the core self of the offender, and as an explanation in its own right. Using these eight broad forms of adjustment enables relatives to claim mitigation for the offender and suggest that he or she was not fully responsible, by contextualising what happened and pointing to different reasons outside of the offender's control.

Resisting totalising identity

Relatives are fighting for the offender to be viewed as more than a serious offender, as more than a killer or sex offender. There are two levels at which this resistance operates. First, there are those relatives who question the full culpability of the offender and therefore straightforwardly resist defining him or her in these terms:

> You see this is what used to get to me with [a prominent member of Aftermath in its early years]. She used to say 'well, you're a mother, yes, but you're the mother of a murderer', and I used to cringe. I used to think that's um, I don't class myself as that really,

at all, because he was involved, yes, but he wasn't the one that er committed the er, he was involved and then he stood back and she did the rest.

(Beryl, son convicted of homicide)

R: What I'm thinking of with regard to your own self-image, you've told me that people have thrown at you the expression that you're a mother of a killer before, have you ever seen yourself as that, and has that had any consequences if you have?

B: I don't see Justin as a killer. Um, I always perhaps euphemistically use the term Justin and Sarah came to blows, and as a result of which the girl died. Or I've sometimes sort of said, you know, 'Justin unfortunately took his girlfriend's life'. I find it difficult to say 'Justin killed his girlfriend', I would never say 'my son is a killer'. I mean Pauline and I will say 'oh of course, we're killer's mothers, aren't we?' But we're making a joke of it, if you can make a joke of it, but we're joking at ourselves, you know. But no, I don't see Justin as a killer.

(Beatrice, son convicted of homicide)

Secondly, there are those who accept the offender's culpability, but still do not want to define them solely in those terms. These relatives resist the application of the label 'sex offender' or 'murderer' to their particular family member. Gill repeats an account offered by her husband. He felt that staff running the sex offender treatment programme in which he participated in prison wanted to impose the totalising identity of 'sex offender' which he wanted to resist:

He couldn't see the point of the exercise. I really feel that in some fields like that [sex offender treatment programmes] there are people getting some gratification, I firmly believe that.[7] I wanted to know what happened to the tapes, because they were taping them, and he challenged what they were saying to him, because they were like brainwashing them as well, to say that they were sex offenders, and he said to me then after a while, he said 'they're undoing everything I've done by reading and going into myself', he said 'I'm not a sex offender', he said 'I'm somebody that has committed sexual offences', he says 'but I'm not a sex offender'. He said they were telling him that he'd got to say [exact details of the offences] all the time, they weren't allowed to refer to 'it' as 'it', they'd got to say.

(Gill, husband convicted of sex offence)

Finally, *separating the act from the actor*, our fourth actor adjustment, is also an attempt to resist a totalising identity, though one that needs separate consideration (see below).

Balance – backwards and sideways

A common actor adjustment technique used by relatives was the attempt to introduce balance in the impression held of the offender. Good qualities, acts or events are held up to show that the offender is 'not all bad'. Klockars described this 'metaphoric ledger' as a technique used by professional fences in his study (Klockars 1974) and Ditton showed how recalling occasions when they chose not to fiddle their customers allowed bread salesmen in his study to do the same (Ditton 1977). However, in this context the balance technique holds up qualities or actions to adjust the impression held of the actor – not of the act. The seriousness of the offence means it is too weighty to be balanced. A homicide offence cannot be balanced by showing that the offender was nice to the victim at other times; good qualities in the offender can be pointed to, however, to try to show he has a positive side.

Some of the balancing accounts of relatives in this study were backwards in direction, showing the good side of the offender prior to the offence, while others were sideways in direction, showing the offender's current positive qualities. Lorraine's description of her daughter is an example of the former:

> She's always been a soft, quiet natured person, she took on her Dad's side like that. ... As a child she was very forward, educationally she was very forward. ... I've still got reports from Grace from nursery, how she's, as little as she was all those years ago, she's a star pupil, she was always helping all the children when they fell down, she's helped to feed the other little ones, you know, very loving towards all the children and caring towards everybody, very mannerable, very polite. ... Very clean, even when she was little, she was very, very clean and as she got older she was growing up into a nice young girl. All those school reports from primary to secondary school, she was always in all the activities that was going, whether it was games, school plays, Christmas activities, she was involved in everything like that, she was always in and out of libraries, she was kept occupied.
>
> (Lorraine, daughter convicted of drug offence)

Sideways balance accounts focus on current good qualities to be taken into consideration. Beverly and Christine both drew attention to similar virtues:

> When I went to the prison [my grandson] asked the officer if he could show me his room which he did. And I said 'my goodness', I said 'I can't get over how nice and clean this place is'. And the man said to me, the officer said 'it's down to you' he said, 'because he

> cleans the room'. He said 'he's a very tidy boy isn't he?' I said 'he is. He's very fussy. He's always been like that'. Yeah, he's always been like that. But they said, you know, they said 'you've taught him well because he can cook and what have you' . . . because he ain't a bad boy, really on his own. He's as nice as pie, because I never had no trouble with him, as I said.
>
> (Beverly, grandson convicted of violent offence)

> And if you hear [my daughter] talking now, she's always been polite, always been, always respected her elders, you know, she talks to somebody who's older than her, she knows how to talk to them. She's always been like that.
>
> (Christine, daughter convicted of violent offence)

Most interviewees and fieldwork participants pointed to some good qualities in the offender they were supporting. Some, like Beverly and Christine, pointed to specific qualities. Others, like Debbie, just wanted me to know that the offender was not a bad person:

> But I know that [my husband's] not a bad person, I just know he's a very sad, hurting, sick person and . . . he's just not a nasty person, there's nothing, just that horrible thing [the offence] but when you look beyond that you see that he just wasn't well, you know, it was just not, and I feel sorry for him because I think that he got a really raw deal in life. You know, and I really believe that.
>
> (Debbie, husband convicted of homicide)

In fact, much of the time spent with interviewees would be taken up with their descriptions of the offender and his or her life before and after the offence, often offering positive descriptions and personal anecdotes to balance the stark fact of the serious offence. Before, after and during interviews, relatives would often show me photographs of the offender, and if they were parents they would talk about the offender's childhood and show me photographs from that time. Balancing accounts were therefore an important part of time spent informally with interviewees, in addition to being given during interviews. I also heard balancing accounts from many fieldwork participants during informal conversations at Aftermath meetings and seminar weekends. They would sometimes show me photographs and describe the offender's good qualities and tell me 'If you met him, you would like him'.

Separating the act from the actor

This technique deals with both the act and the actor, but is technically an actor adjustment: it asks the audience to look at the actor in isolation from the act. Relatives say that they can still love and support the offender without condoning what he or she has done: it is possible to 'hate the sin but love the sinner'. It is a technique necessary precisely because all the other act and actor adjustments are so partial. If relatives were offering more total excuses or justifications they would be less likely to need it. Relatives say it is possible to make a separation between the behaviour/actions of the offender and their character/person. Because this technique is such a significant part of how relatives account for continuing to support the offender it will be dealt with in more detail in the following chapter.

Act adjustment (he or she did it, but it's not as bad as you might think)

This less common form of adjustment took four main forms: *denial of injury*, *denial of the victim* (both of which are techniques of neutralisation from Sykes and Matza (1957), *normalising the act*, and *comparative adjustment*.

Denial of injury

Relatives using this technique sought to minimise the injury caused. Two attempts to do so came from Ada and Nancy. Ada accepted her son's claim that he did not commit 'rape':

> *R*: And was he convicted for three offences of rape?
> *A*: Yes, yeah. He said he never raped them, it was attempted rape, but because it was three [offences] he got five years for each . . .
> *R*: Has it ever affected how you felt about your son, the fact that he's been convicted of the three rapes?
> *A*: No, no. Because he said he never raped, he never got, you know, he just attacked. But er, no, I've never thought about it like that.
>
> (Ada, son convicted of rape)

Nancy's husband was convicted of sex offences against his now adult children. She showed me photographs during her interview which formed part of the court papers. She accepted her husband had taken these photographs but sought to minimise their seriousness:

> *N*: Now when Bill took these photographs of his daughter, she wanted to be a model and he didn't want –
> *R*: [Looking through court papers Nancy has given me] Why are these in here, these pictures?

N: Well he was giving them, they are, some of them are rude, I mean but when he took these photographs, his wife was in the room at the same time.
R: Really?
N: I mean they are, some of them, but he said he felt as though he was going to take the photographs the way [his daughter] wanted them taken. You see some of them are, they said at the time that he took these for his own personal pleasure.
R: Right, and she wanted to be a model did she?
N: Yeah. . . . Because I mean the girls did model for them, it was the photography club. He's got his degree in photography, my husband. But some of them are what you call a little bit naughty, but I mean if you were taking them for a portfolio, but you know, there is one or two which I thought were a bit naughtier, something like that [shows me photograph of child posed seductively wearing little clothing].
R: Yeah. How old was she at the time?
N: I think she was 13 at the time. Yeah. But I'd never seen these photographs in the house because when we moved, I moved my flat, I moved Bill's flat and I actually saw, looked at every photograph Bill had because to be truthful, I tossed a few out of his ex-wives.
R: So what, was he actually, was there a charge relating to these photographs?
N: Yes, he was found guilty on them. Yes.

(Nancy, husband convicted of sex offence)

It is difficult to minimise the injury caused by serious offences, especially those which are sexual or violent, which may explain why this technique was rarely used by participants in this study.

Denial of the victim

This was another technique that rarely appeared in relatives' accounts, again probably because of the seriousness of the offences and the harm caused. Both Alice and Celia were related to offenders who had killed individuals with criminal histories who were known to the police for drug offences. They both described being offered denial of the victim accounts by police officers:

> A man was killed [by my nephew], he was a drug dealer, and when I was giving my statement the WPC said 'if it's any consolation he's done society a favour', and for a very brief moment I thought yeah, yeah of course he has! And I was so disgusted with myself; I said

> to myself how can you say that? Somebody is dead. This man who we were told has got children and a wife, he's got a mother and a father.
>
> (Celia, nephew convicted of homicide)

> And so the police even said at the time 'Don't quote me, but, he's done society a favour'.
>
> (Alice, son convicted of homicide)

Interestingly, neither was willing to accept these accounts at face value. As Celia explained, she was initially tempted but realised it was not acceptable; Alice was unsure of her son's guilt and although she spent some time describing what the police had told her about the victim of the crime, was not prepared to justify the offence in this way.

Frances attributed some of the blame for her husband's sexual offending to his victim, their foster daughter, despite the fact she was only 15. Frances discovered the offences because the girl became pregnant and DNA tests proved her husband to be the father. She also partly attributed her husband's actions to his wish to have children which she said she could not fulfil. However, the mitigation offered by this act adjustment was not strong enough for her; she left her husband when he was sentenced because she could not live with what he had done:

> *R*: What's your understanding now of why he did what he did?
>
> *F*: Um, 'she offered it to me I couldn't say no'. You know, and quite honestly, as everybody says, how many men would say no? But, you know, he shouldn't have done it, she was under age.
>
> *R*: How did you come to that understanding?
>
> *F*: What, that he shouldn't have done it?
>
> *R*: No, the understanding of *why* he did it, is it something you've had to think through a lot, or?
>
> *F*: He always wanted children. Always wanted children. And er, I was not in a position to, because I'd had a hysterectomy, you know, so there was no way I could have children, um. I'm not saying that's *the* reason, but I do believe that that is some of the reason.
>
> (Frances, husband convicted of sex offence)

Beatrice's son was convicted of manslaughter after he killed his girlfriend in an altercation. She says she blamed the victim and in fact saw her son as a victim:

> *B*: I see Justin as a victim.
>
> *R*: You do? A victim of?

B: Of the victim.
R: A victim of?
B: A victim of the victim. [A psychiatrist] from the early days of Aftermath, he said 'very often, Beatrice, we find that the offender is the victim's victim', and he said 'I think this is true in [your son] Justin's case'.

(Beatrice, son convicted of homicide)

This account invokes ideas of victim precipitation which have stimulated much debate in criminology (see, for example, Fattah 1991), but perhaps leans more towards victim-blaming, for which victim precipitation studies have been criticised (Walklate 1989).

Betty was unusual among the interviewees in this study because her view was that her brother, who was in his fifties, was totally devoid of any blame despite his victim being; she thought, around 15, and, as she said in the quotation below, they had been having a relationship for several years. Her account was more total, and the only one that came close to being a full justification. For Betty the blame lay clearly with the victim who she felt was not a victim at all:

B: He was convicted of indecent assault.
R: Do you feel comfortable telling me a bit about what happened?
B: I don't really know that much about that. I do know that it was a boyfriend who had cost him in the region of about £30,000. He took him on trips on Concorde, he travelled all over the world, bought him cars, bought him motorbikes and for several years he was perfectly happy with that situation and then when he asked to borrow some more money from my brother my brother refused, he suddenly decided that he'd been indecently assaulted. That's why I say, 'they don't go into the whole case, they don't go into the whole story'. I mean as far as I'm concerned that's a rent boy, he's a pimp, and he should never have been entitled to bring the case in the first place. And he's been had for drugs; he's been kicked out of his job for moneys lost, he's a thoroughbred criminal.

(Betty, brother convicted of sex offence)

Normalising the act

This was another strategy that was rarely used by participants in this study, which may again be explained by the seriousness of the offences. George suggested that anyone could kill given the right circumstances:

Well I've always said that anybody could commit a serious offence, could kill, if the situation was right. I think, I've certainly been

> placed in a position where I could have killed somebody, you know, [when I was] quite young, so I think it's the time and the place.
>
> (George, son convicted of homicide)

Ada was one interviewee who had accepted a normalising account which she said was offered to her by her GP. I found this account somewhat surprising – her son had been convicted of three separate rapes of strangers – but my reaction perhaps demonstrates how difficult it is to construct acceptable normalising accounts about such serious offences:

> I went to the doctor myself one day when we were down here in [local city], and the doctor asked me how my son was and I said 'how do you know about my son?' And he said 'the police came and I had to give details', he said 'don't worry', he says 'a lot of young boys do that, make that offence', he said 'it's quite common'. I said 'oh I didn't know', he says 'no', he says, 'it's part of growing up'. He says 'some are caught and some aren't' . . . the doctor thought that it was a common thing; quite a few teenage boys go through it, part of growing up.
>
> (Ada, son convicted of rape)

Comparative adjustment

Drawing comparisons between ourselves and others is a characteristic of social life. Relatives in this study were trying to absorb and understand the fact of the serious offence, and their accounts often revealed their own ranking of offence seriousness, placing the act hierarchically in relation to others; the status of a particular act was therefore defined in its relationship to other acts, on both a broad level (murder is worse than sex offences) and a specific level (the crime committed by her son was worse than the crime committed by mine). Social psychologists have pointed to this tendency to make comparisons with others. Festinger has suggested that comparisons are usually made with those who have performed better (Festinger 1954), while Wills suggests that 'downward comparisons' with those in worse circumstances are usually made when we ourselves are experiencing negative emotions and feeling vulnerable (Wills 1981). Janoff-Bulman has highlighted the important emotionally palliative effect of 'comparing ourselves with people whose outcomes are not as good as our own' (Janoff-Bulman 1992: 119).

Comparative adjustment was a commonly used technique, although a single shared understanding of levels of offence seriousness amongst relatives did not exist. So, for example, Mary thought drug offences were worse than her daughter's violent offence:

M: It must be difficult though if you have had a son who, alright, if he wants to take drugs, that's his lookout, but I don't think I could tolerate any sons or daughters who sold the drugs, supplied them, no.
R: You couldn't?
M: No. Well think how that spreads out, no. We'd have too many Leah Betts[8] on our hands, wouldn't we? No, I'd find that difficult to forget because you've damaged so many people's lives.
(Mary, daughter convicted of violent offence)

Hilda thought sexual offences against children were worse than murder, the offence for which her son had been convicted:

H: When I got the first newsletter from Aftermath I read it and I read it again and I said to [my partner] Victor 'no, this isn't me', so he said 'let me read it', he said 'oh'. That was concerning children and I thought 'oh no', and then after a while you start thinking literally about what he's done and you think 'well, there but for the grace of God go I'. That could be my son here instead of being in there for murder.
R: So you were thinking it must be different for people whose relatives committed sexual offences against children? You felt that was quite different?
H: Yes, yeah.
R: Does it feel worse to you?
H: Yes, absolutely. It's ridiculous because my son took that young boy's life, but to me, anything interfering with children, to me it's sickening. . . . That is just my personal feeling.
R: So you think if your son had done something like that it would have been much harder to understand for you?
H: I think I would have killed him myself.
(Hilda, son convicted of homicide)

However, comparisons were not always downwards. Lillian and Harriet's sons were both accused of sexual offences against children and they both thought sexual offences were worse:

I mean I think murder's bad but I think sexual things like that, rape and stuff like that, I think are far worse than even murder myself, you know.
(Lillian, son convicted of sex offence)

Even now I think sexual abuse, and I mean real sexual abuse, is in some way more horrible than rape or murder. That people can do

> these things to little children. ... I find it quite horrendous, quite sickening. And although I feel like that, I couldn't feel that my son was a monster, even if he had done it.
>
> (Harriet, son accused of sex offence)

This hierarchical ranking therefore often operated as a straightforward *placement* rather than adjustment of an act, part of the struggle to absorb and make sense of what has happened, but was also used to adjust the impressions of others when the acts to which comparison was made were worse:

> There are worse crimes than the one that my son was found guilty of, then there are, aren't there? The killing of children, of defenceless old age pensioners, there's killing people slowly ... I mean if my son was, had been accused of killing a child, I really don't think I would have gone to visit him.
>
> (Alice, son convicted of homicide)

A study of ex-offenders found that they used similar comparison techniques, comparing themselves to 'real criminals' who they deemed worse in terms of the crimes they were prepared to commit and because of their use of drugs or their mental health, thereby differentiating themselves as not 'true' criminals (Maruna 2001).

Opportunities to draw comparisons occurred in the context of self-help groups and prison visiting when relatives came into contact with other relatives of offenders, or when high-profile cases were reported in the media. George described drawing comparisons within Aftermath and was aware that this might be an adjustment technique on his part:

> I think sometimes that you, even though people are talking to you about the crimes that their relatives have committed, I felt that I was being sympathetic to them, rather than them being sympathetic to me. I heard things that they said and I thought well I'm not like that, it's not just a question of say killing somebody or whatever else, there were horrible side effects some of them had. A particular chap had robbed an old man and actually buggered him at the same time, and that to me is totally offensive ... but when somebody tells you that sort of thing you sort of recoil from it, but then I think well you need my sympathy; I don't need yours so much. I don't know whether I minimise Justin's crime to a level, and maximise theirs, I don't know whether that's a way of expressing it, because in a way that's the way I felt about it.
>
> (George, son convicted of homicide)

Sometimes these comparative accounts were a response to attempts by outsiders to impose uniform definitions on offence categories. This was particularly the case with relatives of sex offenders who felt that all sex offenders were subject to the same narrow construction which allowed for no gradation of seriousness. Attempts to adjust the acts were often met with strenuous resistance – to say that one sex offence against a child was not as bad as another was to suggest it was somehow 'better'. Relatives of sex offenders faced rigid constructions of the category 'sex offender' on many occasions, but some of these constructions mattered more than others, particularly when they as family members were implicated.

Act and actor adjustments are therefore used by relatives to account for the offence and to attempt to alter the impression held of the offender. As relatives of serious offenders they care what people think of the offender and what he or she has done, but they are balancing this, in most cases, with recognition of the harm caused by the serious offence and a wish for the offender to take responsibility for his or her actions. As we have seen, relatives are players in offenders' and others' accounts of the offence, and may be causally implicated: the following chapter looks at how relatives account for their own actions and how they address this implication and it considers the purposes accounts serve and what they actually *do*.

Notes

1 No statistical inference can be drawn these figures, which only illustrate the distribution of act and actor adjustments in relatives' accounts.
2 Other relatives have not been included as a separate kinship group in the table because there was only one in each category: one father, one sister, one grandmother, one daughter and one aunt of a serious offender.
3 Row totals will not equal the number of interviewees as multiple answers were possible.
4 It should be noted that this is what these interviewees stated to me, and I had no reason to disbelieve it. It must be very difficult, however, for some relatives of those who persist in declaring their innocence to take a stand against this and say they believe in their guilt. It is possible, therefore, that some relatives maintain a public stance of 'not knowing' out of loyalty to the offender that is different from what they privately believe.
5 In the case of the interviews the listener was obviously me, but relatives also knew about the possibility of some of their comments appearing in later publications, and therefore reaching wider audiences (though they would be anonymous). Relatives might be called upon to give motivational accounts in a variety of circumstances, but many of these circumstances will not be amenable to direct observation.
6 I am grateful to Stan Cohen for this term.

7 This is perhaps the comment that comes closest to Sykes and Matza's (1957) neutralisation technique of *condemnation of the condemners*, making an issue of the wrongfulness of others, but in this account and in her later accounts about social services (see Chapter 5) Gill was not making the wrongfulness of professionals into *the* issue. Throughout her interview she stressed the harm caused by her husband's sexual offending and how horrified she was by what he had done.

8 Leah Betts died in November 1995 after taking ecstasy at her 18th birthday party. The case received a considerable publicity and media attention.

Chapter 5

Relatives' own accounts

> I think there's always this suggestion that the parents are to blame. From that point of view, you feel guilt, without a doubt. That's it, because this, again maybe at the initial time you think, is it my fault? Is it my fault, I brought him up this way? And that kind of thing. But I think you come to terms with that, and logic tells you at the end of the day his mother and I aren't influencing him any more, once he became a teenager then he went off and did his own thing.
>
> (George, son convicted of homicide)

> I would stand by her, no matter what. I'm not going to say I will agree with what she done, but I will not throw her away, I will not turn my back on her, no way; I will still be there. . . . You've got to, because if you don't, who is? Who is? You know. I stand by my kids, each and every one of them.
>
> (Lorraine, daughter convicted of drug offence)

This chapter examines the different accounts relatives gave where they themselves were the subjects, accounts that addressed the dimensions of kin contamination and kin culpability in the web of shame. These accounts, however, did not straightforwardly resist shame: relatives of serious offenders are aware on a more general level of political, media and lay discourses of family responsibility and of being under the shaming gaze of others, and many struggled with an ongoing tension between internalising and resisting shame. As we saw in Chapter 3, shame is an emotion at the core of stigma, a painful emotion constructed around a failure to attain an ideal state. Relatives of serious offenders as a group are marked off for shaming in response to their proximity to the failure of their offending relatives to adhere to some of society's most fundamental norms; because of their perceived failure to attain ideals of family roles and relationships; and because of their own possible culpability in events that have occurred. And as we saw, stigmatised groups 'feel shame in their own eyes, and are forced to hide from the shaming gaze of others' (Nussbaum 2004: 284).

Relatives were shamed in their own eyes and were vulnerable to painful feelings of failure and low self-worth. Sarah explained how she felt when her mother was arrested for a serious violent assault against her father which left him blind:

> I felt incredibly vulnerable and fairly low self-esteem and it was also, you know, why is all this happening to me when other people seem to glide through life, nothing touches them? I almost felt alienated from people because they didn't know what was going on in my life, they didn't know what was going on in my head and I couldn't socialise because you know, that was, it was in my mind all the time. And I couldn't just engage in trivial chit-chat. So yeah, I did feel a breed apart and I still do to a certain extent . . . I still feel a little alienated but I'm gradually getting some enthusiasm for life back and some self-esteem. I mean I've never really been, been one for sort of dressing up and putting loads of make-up on and stuff but there was a point where I just didn't care what I looked like, what I put on, it didn't matter. But that's beginning to go.
>
> (Sarah, mother convicted of violent offence)

Many of those I interviewed expressed feelings of guilt. I am sympathetic to the idea that while shame refers to the whole self, or a trait of feature of a person, guilt takes an act, rather than the whole person, as its primary object (Nussbaum 2004) and this accords with how relatives in this study struggled with a sense of personal responsibility for what they had or had not done which could be distinguished from a more pervasive sense of shame. However, this is not necessarily a straightforward distinction. First, it may be an easier distinction to make for shame which is partly vicarious and therefore partly stimulated by the actions of another for which one is not directly responsible. Secondly, although it is possible to distinguish conceptually between the two emotions, it may be that they are difficult to disentangle in how they are experienced in reality, particularly in the context of criminal offending. Harris (2001) has found empirical evidence for the distinction to be mixed. In his own study of the shame-related emotions experienced by drink-driving offenders, he did not find the expected differences between shame and guilt and instead a single factor of 'Shame–Guilt' emerged which was defined by having done wrong, concern about having hurt others, feeling ashamed of both oneself and one's act, feeling anger at oneself, and loss of honour among family and friends, and was associated with remorse for one's actions (*ibid.*). As Braithwaite and Braithwaite (co-authors in the same volume) state, the Shame–Guilt factor suggests 'that distinctions between shame and guilt in earlier studies may be conditional on the context or methodology employed' (Braithwaite and Braithwaite 2001: 7).

As we will see, the sense of personal responsibility felt by relatives in this study was often diffuse rather than attached to a single specific action, and was intertwined with a sense of shame. The two emotions can, however, be distinguished in this context. Relatives could feel a sense of shame without feeling guilt, if it was based upon kin contamination and they did not feel they personally had done anything wrong. They would not, however, feel guilt without feeling some measure of shame, as Braithwaite and Braithwaite suggest in relation to offenders: 'a person cannot experience guilt about a criminal wrong without this spilling over into feeling ashamed of oneself as a person' (*ibid.*: 9) In an analysis of the two emotions from a psychoanalytic perspective Carveth similarly argues:

> While it is true that no one can feel guilt about the damage one has done or wished to do to others without simultaneously feeling ashamed of the fact that one is the sort of person who has done or wished to do such damage, the reverse does not follow. It is possible to experience shame without guilt – that is, to be so self-obsessed that one loses sight of the object altogether except as a mirror or audience or resource for the self. In this sense, while it may be incorrect to say that guilt is a more mature emotion than shame – in that mature people continue to experience both – it is certainly true that the person who can experience guilt is more mature than the person who can experience only shame. In such a mature person, despite shame for the self, concern for the object (i.e., guilt) is maintained.
>
> (Carveth 2001)

Relatives might therefore potentially feel shame without guilt either if they do not perceive themselves as in any way responsible and as far as they are concerned are only vicariously experiencing shame, or because they have 'lost sight' of aspects for which they might otherwise feel responsible (though Carveth's points about maturity have limited applicability when the emotions stem from offences committed by someone else).

Many relatives in this study questioned whether any of their actions might have contributed to what happened. In some accounts, the guilt was attached to a very specific act, while in others it was more diffuse and referred to family circumstances or relationships over many years.

Eileen felt guilt when her husband was convicted of sexual offences against their grandchildren, guilt that was more abstractly focused on responsibility for the very creation of her offspring:

> Because I'll tell you what I kept saying to [my daughter]: 'What sort of mother have I been?' You look at yourself. 'What have I done to you children? Why, what have I been lacking in that this has happened? Why? Why? I wish I'd never given birth to you. I wish you'd never been born. I really wish, it's my fault, I shouldn't have married, I shouldn't have had children' and I was like that for a long, long time . . . because for a hell of a long time, I felt you know, I'd somehow, it was all my fault for *having* the children.
>
> (Eileen, husband convicted of sex offence)

Penny expressed similar guilt when her son was arrested for rape:

> *P*: Emotionally it just broke my heart really. I felt guilty, I felt as guilty as [my son].
> *R*: Why did you feel guilty?
> *P*: Because I'd given birth to him. And, I know a person is responsible for his own actions . . . but it was like I was partly responsible for what happened.
>
> (Penny, son convicted of rape)

Debbie also expressed feeling a diffuse sense of responsibility for her husband having killed his grandmother:

> *R*: Can you say any more about that, about why you say you felt responsible?
> *D*: Because it's somebody you loved and somebody you had something to do with, you know . . . you feel like, I know you ain't got no control over what they done, but because you loved them, because you shared a bit of time with them or you shared your life with them and because they're part of you in some way, you do feel, it's just, you feel responsible. Do you know what I mean? It's just hard to explain but you feel responsible.
>
> (Debbie, husband convicted of homicide)

Like relatives' accounts of the offence, relatives' accounts of their own actions were often partial, questioning, tentative and searching. A number of factors contributed to whether – and how – they internalised shame and guilt. Time appeared to be an important influence. As we saw in Chapter 2, most relatives gave accounts of life after discovery gradually improving and moving forward, and part of this process seemed to be a decline in self-blame. Pauline described how she blamed herself in the early days:

> Yeah, originally I hated myself for letting it happen and then I thought: you didn't let it happen. You didn't tell him to go out and do that. You didn't make him poorly. You didn't do this, that, and the other and then you go, 'well maybe if I'd have done that'. But you can't.
>
> (Pauline, son convicted of homicide)

Relatives' willingness to self-blame varied according to the different dimensions of the web of shame. The most strongly resisted dimensions were the first, that relatives were somehow contaminated by their association with the offender, and the fifth, that relatives were to blame for the continuation of their secondary stigma by supporting the offender. Relatives wrestled more with whether they could have done something to prevent the offence or whether they might have been in some way responsible, and a number expressed mixed feelings about a possible genetic explanation for offending. The type of offence and its particular characteristics were also significant – whether it happened in or away from the home, whether it was sexual, or violent, whether the victim was within the family, and so on. We saw in Chapter 3 how the web of shame can depend upon kin relationship, with mothers and wives being particularly affected, and this dimension was important to the ways in which relatives expressed feelings of guilt and what they felt guilty about. Whether self-blame continues, and to what degree, will further depend on personal factors including the individual characteristics and resources of relatives and the history of their relationship with the offender. Finally, self-blame might depend on the support relatives receive and, as the next chapter will show, reducing self-blame was part of the project of Aftermath.

One study has attempted to test a model that distinguishes between vicarious shame and guilt and could be generally applicable, not tied to specific social associations or types of wrongdoing. Lickel *et al.* (2005) recruited undergraduate students and asked them to recall instances when they felt vicariously ashamed or guilty for another's wrongdoing, asking them to describe instances with friends, family and their ethnic group. They found vicarious guilt to be predicted by one's perceived interdependence with the wrongdoer, the belief that one had some control over the event, and the desire to repair the wrongdoing. Vicarious shame, on the other hand, was predicted by sharing a social identity with the wrongdoer, a threat to one's self-image, and a motivation to distance from the event. People felt guilty when they had a highly interdependent association with the wrongdoer and felt they should have been able to control his or her actions, and felt shame when they had a shared social identity with the wrongdoer and saw his or her actions as reflecting badly on themselves. Vicarious guilt in this model as applied to my study would be guilt for the serious offence itself. So, for example, the wife of a sex offender who did not respond to an earlier disclosure from her niece felt guilt because had she done so, she could have stopped her husband. She therefore felt vicarious guilt because she felt partly responsible for not controlling his behaviour. However, as we have seen, guilt has also been expressed by relatives in this study for more broadly contributing factors – giving birth to the offender, the way the offender was raised, particular instances in the offender's childhood – in these examples guilt is expressed for actions for which the relative is the proximal agent, would therefore be more than vicarious, and would not necessarily depend on feeling that they should have been able to control the offender's actions.

Lickel *et al.* define 'interpersonal interdependence' as the degree to which individuals have high levels of social interaction, joint goals, shared norms of behaviour, the opportunity for shared communication and influence over one another's thoughts and actions, and give business partners, sports team-mates and close friends as examples. My study would suggest that in the context of having a close kin relationship to a serious offender, all of these criteria would not be necessary for feelings of guilt as it involves more than just control over another's actions and the connections within kin relationships are more complex and interwoven. Their description of vicarious shame as rooted in shared social identity and threat to self-image accords more closely with my analysis.

If their model was applied to my 'web of shame', then vicarious shame might be associated with kin contamination and vicarious guilt with kin culpability. However, this again is not straightforward. Taking the example of kin contamination on the basis of a genetic or biological connection, a relative might feel shame because they share this connection, but might also feel guilt for the biological creation of a child (as we have seen, often expressed) or for passing on 'faulty' genes or 'bad blood'. Conversely, relatives might well feel guilt for omission or commission, attached to specific acts they did or did not do, but might also feel shame for these dimensions – as we have seen, shame responds to a sense of failure to attain an ideal state and refers to the whole self, and relatives might feel shame for their own perceived failure as mothers or wives.

Lickel *et al.* also found a desire to repair the wrongdoing in vicarious guilt and a desire to distance oneself in vicarious shame. The wrongdoing in serious offending is perhaps too grave to easily repair (though this would not preclude having the desire to do so), and though relatives might have wanted to run away and escape, ultimately for most of those

I met these feelings were overpowered by the strength of family ties. Their distancing was achieved through accounting techniques such as 'hate the sin but love the sinner' which allowed relatives to distance from the offence without physically doing so. Lickel *et al.*'s study is useful in trying to understand how vicarious guilt and shame might operate and how the two emotions can be distinguished, but the web of shame for relatives of serious offenders is perhaps more complex than their model allows. They do recognise that in some cases people might feel both shame and guilt, having both interdependence and a shared identity with the wrongdoer, and give the example of parents of a high school student who takes a gun to school and kills several classmates who: 'might feel guilty because they should have known about and been able to prevent their child's behavior, whereas they might feel ashamed because they fear that their own "flesh and blood" is morally flawed' (2005: 148). I agree with Lickel *et al.* that even in these instances where shame and guilt co-occur, they are separable as two different emotions; but I would suggest that they are interwoven in complex ways and cannot necessarily be straightforwardly distinguished on the basis of dimensions such as behavioural control.

Self-blame might serve a particular purpose for relatives. In Fishman's study of prisoners' wives, eight of the women used the strategy of blaming themselves to explain, justify or make their husband's behaviour more acceptable, a strategy their husbands encouraged. In doing so they were able to reduce their husbands' responsibility, so making their marriages more bearable and helping them to continue to support their husbands (Fishman 1990). Self-blame has been identified by Janoff-Bulman as a coping strategy for survivors of trauma, motivated, she suggests, by the need to integrate the traumatic experience and re-build a viable assumptive world. Self-blaming helps to answer the question 'why me?' and restore a sense of meaning. However, Janoff-Bulman stresses the importance of differentiating between survivors' and observers' reactions because their motivations and implications are quite different:

> Thus, if I belittle myself, this does not give another person the right to belittle me. Consider the different implications of an individual's own statement, 'I can't believe how stupid I am!' and the reaction of another person, 'I can't believe how stupid you are!' The self-statement might reflect a desire to motivate oneself to do better; the other statement is likely to be an outright condemnation. Most assuredly, the meaning of the two is unlikely to be the same. What we say about ourselves means something very different from what it would when said by another.
>
> (Janoff-Bulman 1992: 123–4)

Using self-blame and internalising guilt as a coping strategy are not the same as accepting the fairness of being stigmatised, first because blaming oneself might be quite different to being blamed by another, and secondly because stigma and shame have the whole person as the primary object and do not separate the actor from the act. As we have seen, Braithwaite argues that *reintegrative* shame makes this separation, while for Nussbaum it is guilt that does so: 'guilt contains within itself a separation between the person and the person's act, and is thus fully compatible with respect for the dignity of the person' (Nussbaum 2004: 233). Feelings of guilt and self-blame attached to a wrongdoing may therefore not be as destructive as painful and all-pervasive feelings of criticism and failure targeted at the self.

Accounting for kin contamination

Association

Relatives were at pains to separate themselves from the criminal actions of the offender by stressing two points: that they did not condone the act (part of 'hating the sin but loving the sinner') and that they were not criminal families. A frequently expressed view was that there was another type of offender – a 'hardened criminal', professional criminal, or recidivist petty criminal – with a family that might also be criminal, or at least condoning crime. This was what many relatives in this study wanted to be distinguished from – and resisted shame for being 'all the same'.

As relatives of *serious* offenders, they saw themselves in a different category, first because they thought serious offences were more likely to be single offences rather than repeat recidivist offences:

> I've always thought it's not a way of life, serious offending isn't a way of life, whereas inverted commas 'petty criminals', it is a way of life and it's almost an occupational hazard going to prison and yeah, whereas serious offences are usually 'one-offs' in the family.
>
> (Anne, son convicted of rape)

Second, this was because they were not 'criminal families' – an offender in the family was a new experience for them and was devastating in a way it was not for relatives who were more accustomed:

> *R*: What were your impressions of the other families prison visiting?
> *B*: Well I remember one because this is what my friend said about career criminals and career criminal families and second and third generation, and some of them are. I was waiting to see [my son], I was in one prison years ago, this was in the early days, and there

> was this little Scots bloke, cocky little bloke, and he greeted the prison officers and he was walking up and down and he said 'alright?', he said 'if it's not me in here it's my lad'. And another woman who I knew well was f'ing this and f'ing that and she said 'it's fucking thirty years I've been coming here to see my father and now him, and if it's not him it's our Anthony and if it's not our Anthony it's . . .' you know, she was a career prison visitor. She'd been doing it for thirty years.
>
> (Beatrice, son convicted of homicide)

> It's stupid because it's awful what [my son's] done, but I don't think of us as a criminal-type family. And I hear that such a lot when I talk to people on the phone too [as an Aftermath supporter], so I'm not, I know I'm not the only one.
>
> (Anne, son convicted of rape)

Thirdly, relatives sought to distance themselves from the families of 'professional' criminals:

> *A*: The thing is like you don't get somebody like Ronnie Biggs[1] [coming to Aftermath for help], his family, or you know . . .
>
> *R*: You don't get professional criminals' families coming to you?
>
> *A*: . . . coming to you for help because they've got the support within their criminal network. I know that's being judgmental, but they have. I've never had anybody ring up who has you know, the likes of people who are in and out of prison all the time.
>
> *R*: Really?
>
> *A*: Never. Because it's more often than not, 99 per cent of the cases that I have had, it's something that's happened once. It's just happened, that's it. And it's hit the family like a brick wall falling down on them. You know, I've not had people that are in and out of prison all the time because it's a way of life for them. And it's a sad thing to say but it's a way of life. You know, they know the system, they know it inside out; they know how to work it.
>
> *R*: And where, so where would they get support do you think? Where would the families, people like that get support?
>
> *A*: I think it becomes a way of life. And they, like I said, they know the system, and they know how to work the system. You know, they know about prisons inside out, they know about visiting. They don't need any advice. You know, they know how to do it. Not like the Aftermath families that come and they're devastated about what's going on. They've never been to a prison in their life before. They don't even know what to expect and that's the difference.
>
> (Angela, husband accused of sex offence)

It is interesting to note that this marking of certain types of offenders and their families as 'other' and as morally inferior is an inverted form of that which occurs in prisons. Many prisoners do not want to mix with certain categories of offenders, in particular sex offenders, and the same can be true of their relatives – as we saw in Chapter 2 some of the relatives of sex offenders that I interviewed reported difficulties when visiting prisons once their status was revealed. At the same time, relatives of serious offenders are seeking to separate themselves from relatives of 'real' criminals, despite the fact that these 'real' criminals might have committed less serious offences.

Genetic

As we saw in the previous chapter, many relatives resisted genetic explanations for offending. These explanations point to the very essence of an offender, suggest the offender may not be treatable, and further contaminate those who share a genetic heritage. Clare's husband was convicted of sex offences, and although he was someone to whom she was clearly not genetically related, they had a son who might be considered 'at risk' of offending if a genetic explanation was accepted:

> I would hate to think that sexual offending is genetic, that you're born if you like, to be an offender. I still think the environment and what you learn as you grow up, what is done to you in a sense and what happens to you within society will have a bearing on how you turn out and obviously the choices you make.
>
> (Clare, husband convicted of sex offence)

Some relatives questioned whether genetics or biology might have a role to play, but most relatives in this study stressed that they had no family history of serious offending; it is possible that less resistance to these explanations might be found amongst those who do.

Accounting for kin culpability

Omission

Many relatives questioned whether they could or should have done something to prevent the offence. This is well illustrated by Frances's comments which show her struggle with self-blame for not protecting her foster-daughter. Despite this, she also resisted taking responsibility for her husband's actions and made the decision to divorce her husband when he was sent to prison:

F: I think people were horrified, the fact that the victim was also a foster child, really, because she was placed into our care for safekeeping, and that's, I think that's how I found it so hard, she was placed in my care for safekeeping and I didn't keep her safe.

R: OK, so if you could summarise it, how do you think the police saw you?

F: Probably the same way as I thought of myself. Because I felt very gullible. Very stupid. Very guilty.

(Frances, husband convicted of sex offence)

Stephanie felt she was in some way to blame because she had refused her husband's request to leave the women's refuge in which she was living to go out and meet him on the night he had committed the offence:

R: Did you have anything to do with the victim's family? Were they in the newspapers or anything like that?

S: They did a big write-up. I would have loved to have seen them. I would want to say to them you know, how sorry I am, I do feel guilty, it was my fault, I'll always blame myself, if I'd have gone out that night and met him it might have never happened, but then it could have been me [that he killed].

(Stephanie, husband convicted of homicide)

Commission

Parents commonly struggled with the idea that something they did in the past might have contributed to the offenders' actions. As we saw in Chapter 3, discourses of family responsibility often focus powerfully on the parental role and many relatives, such as Anne and Alice, were aware that they might be implicated:

R: There are lots of ideas about why people commit serious offences, what are your own views about that?

A: That's a hard one, I don't know. Textbook, I know all about why people commit offences, and that's hard for me now I'm doing this diploma [in counselling], because everything I read about child abuse and psychological disturbance and I think, 'Oh God, I've convinced myself I'm not to blame and here I am reading that I possibly am'. I really, really don't know. I've heard on one hand that it might have affected him because he'd got a strict stepfather, and I read on the other hand, I've just been doing another assignment, and I've read that I could have been too lenient with him, giving him everything he wanted. Now, my daughters say that's more than likely to be the one, he was never, he was always the apple of my eye, always, he was special, I always told him he

> was special, and when he was a baby he was brought up to think he was special. I never punished him for anything because he made life difficult if I did, so it was easier to let him have what he wanted, so therefore I think he's grown up thinking he can have whatever he wants. I know I'm talking about it from our position, for other people I don't know. I don't know, I don't know.
>
> (Anne, son convicted of rape)

> I'm a bit mixed up, really. Part of [my son's] defence [in court], which I find offensive, was his, you know, his background. . . . I mean I've read some of it, and it is, but I think it's the, I hope it's just the solicitors or the lawyers going and picking up the background. Because he didn't have a worse background than me, and I didn't go out and do anything like this.
>
> (Alice, son convicted of homicide)

Many parents, like Beryl, questioned whether something they had done had contributed to the offender's actions:

> You wonder where you've gone wrong. And it goes over and over and you think why did it happen? Is it something I've done? Or something, um, you think very deeply about things.
>
> (Beryl, son convicted of homicide)

Blaming the family of origin might be a strategy used by the offender to reduce his or her own responsibility, or a routine part of mitigation offered by defence counsel. As with Alice's son, this formed part of Monica's daughter's legal defence, but was a claim Monica resisted:

> *M*: I mean [my daughter's] view is that it was my fault which is always a bit hard to deal with. Well she says two things, first of all she reckons that I was such a terrible mother it was impossible for her to be a good mother in her turn because she hadn't had good mothering herself, and second of all she was very, very angry with me for not going back to [her home] that night [of the offence] . . . I find it very hard to deal with, you know because I feel as if I spent many years of my life doing everything I can to help her and support her and she clearly doesn't feel that I have, or that I haven't done it well enough or often enough or what have you . . . certainly one of the reports that went before the court referred to my daughter's conviction that I was to blame for what happened.
>
> *R*: Was that quite a surprise to you?
>
> *M*: No. Not really, no. I think she sometimes has quite a lot of difficulty taking responsibility for her own actions.
>
> (Monica, daughter convicted of violent offence)

Accounts that blame the family can also be part of a 'sad tale', an actor adjustment which might be offered by the offender as well as by relatives. This form of actor adjustment was clearly more available to wives and partners who had not been part of the offender's early life:

> I think in [my husband's] case it was the family, he'd been brought up, his Dad was an alcoholic, his brothers were all in and out of prison, so I think that had an effect, and then when he moved in with me and my Mum and Dad he sort of had a stable life, but then when we had to go out on our own, the responsibility, it all changed, so yeah, I think his family life had a lot to do with it.
>
> (Stephanie, husband convicted of homicide)

Some relatives questioned whether something they did immediately prior to the offence had contributed to its occurrence. Beryl said she blamed herself because her son had come to stay with her to help her care for her sick husband prior to committing a murder in her local area. She gave the actor adjustment tale, outlined in the previous chapter, of denial of responsibility because her son was led astray and her account shows how relatives' self-blaming can be another form of this act adjustment – if others are to blame (including oneself) the offender's responsibility can be minimised:

> *B*: He knew what I had to do for his father [who needs constant home care], and this is why I, well, I do blame myself really. If we hadn't been in that situation he wouldn't have been here.
> *R*: If you hadn't been in which situation?
> *B*: Well he came to help me with his father really. He came back down here, I think his divorce had gone through, I don't know. And so he decided he'd come back here, so he came home really. And if his Dad had never had a stroke and all these things go through your mind, you see. He wouldn't have been here. She'd have involved somebody else.
> *R*: She would have involved somebody else?
> *B*: Mmm. And the people in the town agree, people knew what was going on, but we didn't, that they were having an affair.
>
> (Beryl, son convicted of homicide)

Beverly was one of the few relatives who had been directly accused of taking part in the offence, although according to her description, this accusation was only made during the court hearing and no proceedings were taken against her. She flatly denied any involvement:

B: When we was in court, [my grandson's co-defendant's] QC said that I supplied two sawn-off shotguns to [my grandson and his co-defendant]. And the judge's summing up was, to the jury, 'don't let's forget that it was the grandmother that supplied two sawn-off shotguns' and I was gobsmacked. 'What are you trying to say? That I, it was me and him that went and done it?' Do you know what I mean?

R: And the judge said that in his summing up as well?

B: Yeah. And when I said to the police about it about it they said 'there is nothing you can do about it.'

(Beverly, grandson convicted of violent offence)

Most relatives resisted the idea that they had actively done anything prior to the offence to cause it. The above quotations provide an interesting contrast with the findings of studies of the motivational accounts of offenders which show stronger resistance, in the form of justifications or excuses, to the blame that is levelled at them. Relatives in this study, in contrast, offered accounts that questioned their own role while at the same time resisting taking responsibility for the actions of another. This resistance is summarised by Celia:

> It's so important to hang on to the dignity, because I did not commit this offence, and I don't believe that my family and myself should be judged, and that is very often what happens.

Celia explained that it had taken time for her to reach this point:

R: And how did you feel seeing all of this newspaper coverage at the time [of the offence]?

C: I felt guilty, I felt as if I was part of it. And that's when I say to you, I now realise that I'm not responsible.

(Celia, nephew convicted of homicide)

Continuation

The final dimension of the web of shame is continuation – relatives were blamed for continuing their stigma because they chose to support the offender. It seems somewhat contradictory that relatives should have to account for supporting each other when discourses of family responsibilities are so strong, but it is necessary because the serious offences are such forceful breaches of prevailing norms. Those relatives who chose to support the offender strongly resisted blame for continuation and offered accounts of their decision:

> I mean I try to explain that, to people that would feel against you, that it's your own child. If you can't stand by them, who can? It comes with the job of having a child. You don't have a child and just abandon it somewhere in life, no matter how old they are, there's always got to be, there will always be a bit of support if you're a decent enough parent. And I feel that no matter what he'd done, I'd still support him and if it was my last penny, I'd still send it to him.
>
> (Lillian, son convicted of sex offence)

The process of accounting for continuing to support the offender has a logical order (see Figure 3). It starts with a division between those relatives (few in number in this study) who say they support the 'offender' because he or she simply did not commit the offence and is literally not guilty, and those who acknowledge that the offender did commit a crime or is in some way culpable (as we have seen, this was not necessarily a fixed state and some relatives wavered between belief in innocence or guilt or were unsure; a justification for supporting the offender will only be needed if they believe in their culpability to some

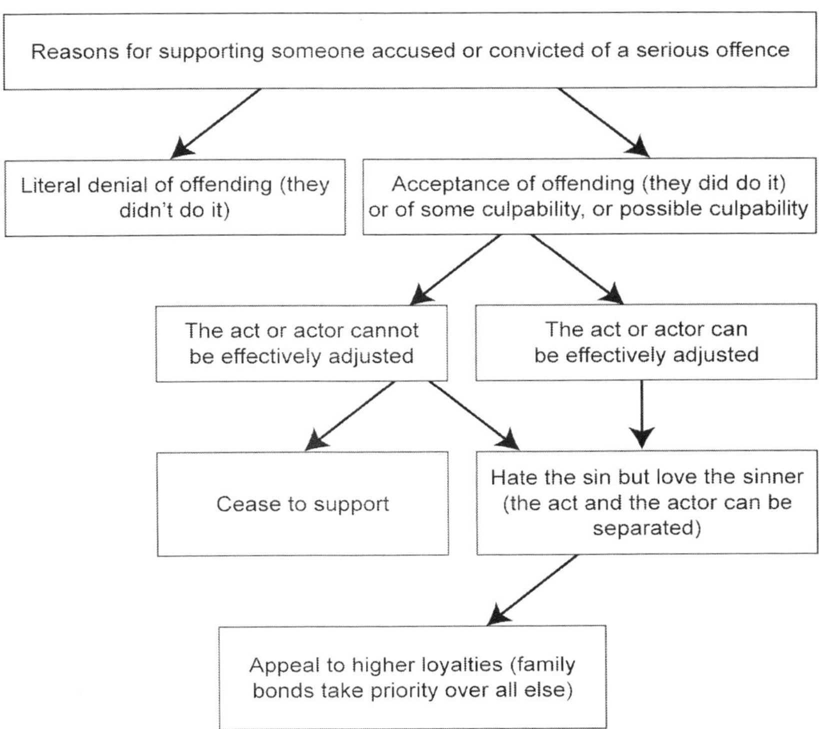

Figure 3 Justifying support

degree). If relatives do accept the offender's guilt, they will then further divide into those relatives who can offer acceptable mitigation in the form of act or actor adjustments as described in the previous chapter, and those who cannot. Those who cannot (because they cannot find act or actor adjustments that they themselves can honour or that others will honour) might cease to support, or alternatively might use further techniques to justify their support. If these adjustments are effective, relatives are able to offer an account for their ongoing support that is likely to be honoured. As we saw in the previous chapter, act and actor adjustments are necessarily partial pleas that do not usually attempt to excuse the offender totally or justify the act as right or reasonable, and a degree of responsibility for the crime can remain with the offender. Further justifications for supporting the offender can therefore also be used in addition to successful act and actor adjustments to shore up relatives' case for supporting.

Out of 32 interviewees, only five had ceased to support the offender, all of whom were wives or partners of male offenders: Frances, Nicola and Clare from the sex offender group and Debbie and Stephanie from the homicide group. One had left her husband just before the time of the offence; three left their husbands during the prison sentence; and one after his release. Three no longer had any contact with their former partner, one had contact in relation to the care of their child, and one said she continued to support the offender, and maintained contact, but considered her relationship to be over and no longer visited him in prison. It is interesting that these women felt the need to account for their decision to leave the offender, and perhaps demonstrates the strength in our society of the alternative account of family loyalties and marriage vows. These women were all Aftermath members, and in the minority within Aftermath as non-supporting relatives, which probably also contributed to their feeling obliged to account for their actions (although continuing to support the offender was not part of Aftermath's mandate). All five offered accounts explaining their decision not to support. Frances expressed feelings of guilt for not supporting her husband when he was found guilty of sexual offences against their foster daughter:

> I think I feel guilty when I meet up with other Aftermath members because not many of them, they're all supporting their particular [family] member that's committed [an offence]. No, I've not met any, I've not met up with any that have you know, divorced them and things like that. The only ones that I've met are sticking with their family, and that's why I feel guilty.

She felt the need to account for her decision not to support her husband:

> I didn't fall out of love with him. I divorced him because of what had occurred, I couldn't live with him knowing that he'd done that, I'd never have been able to have trusted him again, every time, you know if he'd come back, every time he'd left the house I would have thought oh my God, what's he doing?
>
> (Frances, husband convicted of sex offence)

Clare explained why she decided to leave her husband when he was released from prison. She explained that she could not justify or excuse her husband's actions because his sexual offences against his (now adult) children had gone on for so many years:

> I think again the separation of the prison sentence gives you time to reflect . . . I began to change and had my doubts . . . [the abuse] was over a period of some years, actually. I think it was the final straw for me in a sense of trying to come to terms with what he'd done and that's the bit I suppose that finally I found I couldn't live with it, if truth be known. I think it happened, we think at least, when now again I went through it with him, we worked out that it happened over about a period of seven years, if not longer . . . I think that's really what got to me in the end. I think [if it happens] once, it's easier to make a justification or excuse, isn't it? One could almost accept perhaps a one-off, one shouldn't I know but one, it's easier for the brain to get your head around isn't it? But somebody said 'oh well, I came home drunk' or 'I don't know it just happened' – but it did go on for as long as it did. However much I tried to justify that to myself, at the end of the day that's what I think I found hard.
>
> (Clare, husband convicted of sex offence)

All five of those who had chosen not to support talked at length about having been profoundly affected by their experiences, were all Aftermath members, and continued to perceive themselves as relatives of serious offenders at the time that I met them. For those relatives who could offer acceptable act or actor adjustments, and for those who could not but were continuing to support, two further techniques were available through which relatives could justify continuing a relationship with someone who had committed a serious offence: *hate the sin but love the sinner* and *appeal to higher loyalties.*

Justifying support: 'hate the sin but love the sinner'

This account attempts a separation between the act and the actor – a claim to 'hate the sin but love the sinner' – and in so doing to support the offender without condoning his or her actions. This is an actor adjustment because relatives ask the audience to look at the actor in isolation from his or her acts, but the technique has a dual purpose: in addition to wanting to improve the impression held by others of the offender, it also enables relatives to deflect blame that might be levelled at them for supporting. As we saw in the previous chapter it is also an attempt to resist a totalising identity, to prevent the serious crime defining the offender's master status, and following Nussbaum's distinction, might be seen as a claim for the offender's guilt and respect for his or her dignity while rejecting whole-person focused shame.

Prior to conducting interviews, I had heard the expression 'hate the sin but love the sinner' used by members at Aftermath meetings and it was an expression that formed an important part of Aftermath's collective narrative. All interviewees were asked directly whether it was a distinction that they found relevant, and for most of those who believed in the offender's culpability it was. One participant disliked the expression because of its religious connotations, but most identified with it in some way, both Aftermath members and non-Aftermath members. For some participants, this reflected the way they would deal with errant behaviour from any family member, and particularly with children:

> It always reminds me of when my daughter was little and did all sorts of vile things and she used to say as I deprived her of her pocket money or her television, 'Oh you're a nasty mummy, you hate me' and I used to say 'I don't hate you, I hate what you do', and to me there's a very clear dividing line there because I'm sure it becomes very difficult in some cases, if for example you have a woman whose husband has sexually abused their granddaughter, that must be really difficult to take, but you can still continue to love them as a person even though you hate what they did.
>
> (Lisa, partner convicted of homicide)

> Going back to my social work training and how you, you always try and say to parents who have problems with children, you know, 'it's not the child that's bad, it's the behaviour'. And if you like I used that analogy with [my son] when I was trying to explain to him what was wrong with what his father had done and I would say to him, again, separate the behaviour from the person, doesn't mean that the person who's done something wrong is all bad. I suppose that's what I was trying to say. But the behaviour was obviously wrong and very damaging. But it doesn't mean that the person's all bad.
>
> (Clare, husband convicted of sex offence)

Clare's description of using this adjustment with her son also shows how family members might construct accounts for each other, a trait that may be gendered. Other studies have found, for example, that women are more likely than men to take on the role of 'relationship historian' and observe, document and analyse major events in relationships (Orbuch 1997: 469); it may be that women take a more prominent role in families in accounting for untoward events.

A study of Catholic priests accused of paedophilia found that the Church offered accounts which involved making a separation between the character and behaviour of the priest (Thomson *et al.* 1998). This is important because 'stigma for both [the priest and the church] is reduced if conduct rather than moral essence is at issue. The Church is less culpable for failing to detect behavioral disorders than for failing to recognize low moral character, and priests can be treated for specific disorders but not for flawed moral essence' (*ibid.*: 185). Relatives of serious offenders might themselves be less culpable for failing to detect behavioural disorders, and less contaminated and culpable if the focus is on the offender's actions rather than his or her nature. Relatives could more easily defend supporting the offender if conduct is at issue; behaviour can be changed unlike inherently bad or evil character.

Making this separation between the act and the actor allowed relatives to continue to see the offender as a good person while disapproving of his or her actions. This is akin to Braithwaite's model of reintegrative shaming where the act is disapproved of, but the actor is not outcast. Braithwaite's description of reintegrative shaming depends upon this separation:

> It is shaming which labels the act as evil while striving to preserve the identity of the offender as essentially good. It is directed at signifying evil deeds rather than evil persons in the Christian tradition of 'hate the sin and love the sinner'.
>
> (Braithwaite 1989: 101)

It is precisely this that relatives attempted to do and as Braithwaite states, 'the best place to see reintegrative shaming at work is in loving families' (*ibid.*: 56). However, in more recent work Braithwaite has been less categorical about this separation:

> What we had thought we wanted offenders to feel was shame about what they had done, but not shame about themselves. Now we think this may have been a normative error. If a man rapes a child or is repeatedly convicted for serious assaults, is it enough for him to feel that he has done a bad act(s) but that there is nothing wrong

> with him as a person? It would seem more morally satisfactory for him to feel that he has done a bad act and therefore feels he must change the kind of person he is in some important ways (while still on the whole believing he is basically a good person). That is, we do not want the rapist to believe he is an irretrievably evil person; but we do want aspects of the self to be transformed . . . So long as this [shame] does not go so far as to involve a total rejection of self, this now seems to us morally appropriate, at least for serious crimes.
>
> (Braithwaite and Braithwaite 2001: 9)

This seems quite reasonable, and I would expect many of the relatives I met to agree if they were to read this quotation. The offender is allowed to believe he is still basically a good person, but that he or she must change. Many relatives spoke of wanting the offender to change – and being proud in some cases when he had – and this change might well include change in the kind of person he was. It is difficult to know, however, how much shame an offender ought to have; whether it is possible, with offences that cause such harm, to elicit shame that does not involve a total rejection of the self; and exactly what relatives might do to engender a reasonable measure of shame.

Retaining a concept of the offender as basically good and not irretrievably evil, and therefore worthy of support, seemed to be the primary concern of relatives. This was signified by the idea of separating behaviour and character, but in reality it may be that the two are much harder to untangle. We are in many ways constituted by what we do, and how we see ourselves and how others see us are tied up with our actions and how we live our lives. Certainly attempts to make a separation between the actor and the act did not always receive wide acceptance from those with whom relatives come into contact, who assumed instead that supporting the actor must signal support for the act. Celia and Harriet explained:

> I do not condone in any way, shape or form what [my nephew] Owen did, then again I know Owen, I know there is another part to Owen that other people could not be aware of, so in that sense it is separating out the deed from the person and the way the person's behaved, and I think that's where you start taking into account their history, life experiences, getting involved in drugs with Owen, whatever. So yes, I don't condone what he did at all, and I think that that is one of the things that people, some people seem to believe that because you can still visit, that because you're doing that you must agree with what he's done, that he or she has done, that you are condoning it, they find it hard to appreciate, because most

> people would say 'lock them up and throw away the key, they deserve everything they get', and they think that families should also take that stance, and some families do, and for their own reasons, but that hasn't been the way for many, many people that I know, that's not the case.
>
> (Celia, nephew convicted of homicide)

> Certainly I think people feel that the relatives, if they haven't turned on the wrongdoer, are condoning what they have done . . . I certainly am very reticent who I tell about Aftermath or where I'm going because I don't think people would understand.
>
> (Harriet, son accused of sex offence)

As we have seen in Chapter 3, relatives experienced blame because of the unacceptability, in many circles, of this account and were blamed for continuation; their continued support for the offender was construed as implicit support for his or her actions and their secondary stigma was therefore maintained.

Justifying support: appeal to higher loyalties

A final account offered by supporting relatives was an *appeal to higher loyalties* (Sykes and Matza 1957), in this case holding up family bonds to counter real or perceived criticism of their support. 'She's my daughter and I'd support her no matter what she'd done', 'he's still my son', and similar statements were recounted numerous times during fieldwork and interviews. This account might be offered in conjunction with successful actor or act adjustments or as a final account when all others have failed. Wives might hold up marriage vows and affirm their sacredness. Eileen felt pressure to separate from her husband when he was convicted of sexual offences against their grandchildren, and offered an account expressing the strength of her belief in marriage to counter this pressure:

> I don't believe in divorce. I'm not Catholic, I just don't believe you should get married in the first place unless you're absolutely certain and that you're strong enough to bear whatever it brings. You know, everything, married life is sacred to me and I spent hours talking to my children [before they married], that this was a sacred vow, that if they didn't think they could maintain, then they should get married in a registry office. . . . And so I can't, now social workers thought I was a quack you see. And in fact I called my vicar who happens to be one of the most down to earth people, and I said 'look, they're driving me mad to divorce him and I can't. I don't

> want to and I can't'. And he said 'no, stick to your guns, tell 'em' and I did. I said [in court] 'I know you all think it's ridiculous, but I love my husband as much as I did the day I married him, I want to be married to him and I've made a sacred oath and I'm not going to break it. It's as sacred as the oath I took when I walked in this box, I don't make sacred oaths everyday of my life. . . . You have no right', and the judge, he was wonderful, he said 'no one's got the right to try to force you to divorce'; I said 'well I have had pressure from social services and even my own solicitor'. And so as I said, it's been difficult for me.
>
> (Eileen, husband convicted of sex offence)

In a conversation, one mother used the expression 'blood is thicker than water' and said, like many of the mothers I met, that she could not walk away from a child born of her body. Lorraine referred to this bond:

> I will help my daughter; she'll always need my help until I'm taken off this earth, no matter how old she is. Same as like my other two [children], they'll still need my help and support until I'm taken off this earth. I will still try to do my best to fight for them, like a mother should. . . . I mean even if she was involved or did do it, you know, I'd still love her, I couldn't hate her. I couldn't hate her and I could never turn my back on her, because I'm her mother. . . . A mother can't stop loving her children, because that bond is there from the day she conceived. Oh fathers come and go, fathers, they plant the seed and they go anyway, you see, but the mother can't. She can't go and leave it, no, no, no.
>
> (Lorraine, daughter convicted of drug offence)

So a competing account was offered, and as Sykes and Matza stated, an *appeal to higher loyalties* does not offer an account of new oppositional values, but rather one that attempts to re-align the family with conventional society. The competing account of unbreakable family bonds and family loyalty is a powerful one in conventional society. However, despite the power of this account, it is not enough to simply support unconditionally when someone has committed a serious offence, and hence this account was usually offered by relatives in this study in conjunction with the separation of act and actor to show that they were not condoning the offence. It is perhaps worth noting that if relatives were themselves primary victims, these accounting strategies might have negative consequences. One study has suggested that religious beliefs such as 'hate the sin but love the sinner' might engender a tolerance for domestic abuse and a resistance to seek help (Burris and Jackson 1999).

What are the purposes or functions of accounts – what do they *do*?

The accounts relatives construct about the offence and about their own actions serve several purposes: they are a strategy for the management of stigma; they help to mend fractured relationships and damaged identities; and they are part of the process of making sense of events and moving life forward from the low point of discovering the offence. A primary purpose of accounts is to reduce exclusion and ostracism and to try to protect oneself from stigma and shame: 'Neutralizations are dynamic cognitive processes and . . . autobiographical accounts used to protect a person's self-concept from a deep-seated sense of personal shame' (Maruna and Copes 2005: 269). They may also be biographical accounts, as in the accounts relatives give about the offender's actions, and may serve to protect both the self-concept and the concept held of another. As we saw at the beginning of Chapter 4, early work on the motivational accounts of offenders stressed how they realign the account-giver with his or her social group following a perceived breach of norms, and relatives in this study sought to realign the offender through act and actor adjustments and to realign themselves through accounts about their own actions.

Telling one's story can be therapeutic and some authors have focused on the positive functions of confiding accounts to others in coping with major life events (e.g. Harvey *et al.* 1991). Accounts perform important functions for protecting the self of the account-giver and his or her self-esteem. Many authors in the wider study of narrative in the social sciences have focused on how we tell stories about our lives and the production of identity through this process of storytelling (Ezzy 1998; Giddens 1991; Holstein and Gubrium 2000; Randall 1995). Narratives can mend identities that have been damaged (Lindemann Nelson 2001) and Sykes and Matza (1957) pointed to the role of neutralisations in helping to protect an offender's self-image. For relatives of offenders, accounts can help to protect their own and their family's identity in the face of damaging contrary evidence, helping to create or preserve the identity of 'good person', 'good mother', or 'good family'. Viewing identity as narratively constituted assumes the production of a coherent, consistent 'story', while much of the work on the motivational accounts of offenders assumes fragmentation and a contingent 'story' which will be told in different ways to different audiences (Cohen 2001; Goffman 1956). However, the two need not be contradictory and can exist simultaneously. Mills (1940) suggested that vocabularies of motive actually became part of the self. Though presented differently at different times, these accounts are themselves components of a self-narrative. That self-narrative need not be rigid and monolithic, but rather flowing, evolving and flexible, stretching to allow changes across time and place.

As we have seen in previous chapters, relatives of serious offenders had to manage changes in relationships within and outside the family, which in some more extreme cases led to relationships being severed. Accounts have an important role in helping to mend fractured relationships, repairing and maintaining social interaction (McLaughlin *et al.* 1992; Semin and Manstead 1983). Accounts can be powerful tools for changing the opinions of others, and studies have found that individuals are willing to assign character traits and form impressions of others based upon accounts presented (Orbuch 1997; Orbuch *et al.* 1992).

Explaining actions to others helps us to make sense of events and experiences and to organise meaning. Through their accounts relatives try to make sense of why the offender did what he or she did; how this came to occur in their family; their current circumstances; and their plans for the future. Maruna found that the ex-offenders in his study needed a 'coherent and credible self-story to explain (to themselves and others) how their checkered pasts could have led to their new, reformed identities' (Maruna 2001: 7–8). In much the same way relatives in this study needed a coherent self-story (and a coherent story about the offender and the family) through which they could construct a positive identity and attempt to explain how their current circumstances had arisen. Doing so contributed to relatives moving forward from the initial impact stage, learning to cope with and accommodate to their situation. Finally, in focusing on the functions of accounts, it is important to recognise that though they can be deliberate strategies, the processes through which accounts are constructed may not be wholly conscious. A psychoanalytic understanding of accounts would focus on the role of defence mechanisms in protecting the integrity of the ego, processes that occur outside of conscious thought (Maruna and Copes 2005). Relatives' accounts form part of their coping processes and these processes might have unconscious aspects, rather than being deliberately calculated to achieve specific means.

The power to define

Some accounts have more currency than others, some account-givers are better positioned to have their accounts honoured, and the consequences of accounts from some quarters can be more serious. The power to define can be important when accounts of the offence are constructed, and some sources of accounts may be more powerful than others. Those labelled mentally ill, for example, can benefit from reconstructing their past to give an account acceptable to psychiatrists (Scott and Lyman 1968) and it has been suggested that if offenders are consistently offered psychiatric and legal accounts with currency they are likely to adopt them to explain their behaviour (Cressey 1962). In the case of offenders, the legal system has the ultimate power to define and accounts with currency are vital (see, for example, Taylor 1972 on the relative acceptability of the motivational accounts of sexual offenders to magistrates). Relatives in this study were subject to powerful definitions locating explanations for offending within the family, from criminal justice agencies, mental health professionals and, in the case of those with children in the family, from social services.

Most relatives did not describe contact with probation services, and where they did it was often very limited. Anne had more detailed discussions, possibly due to the younger age of her son, and was confronted with an account that focused on the family:

> I hated my husband when this happened, I hated him, I wanted him to die, because he was strict, because he tried to control [my son] because he said he could see how he was going, I hated him for it because he used to hit him and I put all the blame on him, I really wanted him to die. And then blaming myself, even the probation officer had told me that if [his step-father] used to hit him, [my son's] offence was caused because he was blaming me for letting him do that. That's lovely to hear that, a probation officer telling you that. I blamed myself for leaving his father, if I hadn't had left his father this wouldn't have happened, he'd have grown up with both of us. And I suppose that's where counselling helped me, although those feelings are still there, I still think 'well yeah, I can't say that things wouldn't be different, but that's the past and I can't do anything about that, I can only try and change the future . . .' But the conclusion I've come to in my own mind is okay [my husband] might have to own up to something because of the way he treated him, but I can't take responsibility for that. He never hit him when I was here, apparently it was only if I was at work, so [my husband] has got to cope with those feelings, those aren't mine, you know. His Dad didn't see him very often, wasn't a very good father, so that's his responsibility, I can only be responsible for what I did or didn't do . . . then I think 'good grief, look at all the families in the country that are one-parent families or broken homes, my father used to hit me more than [my husband] hit [my son], far more, you know, and I didn't offend!'
>
> (Anne, son convicted of rape)

In Chapter 3 we saw how wives of men who sexually offend are often centrally implicated, blamed as collusive, or seen as orchestrating the abuse through her inadequacies or emotional absence (Davies and Krane 1996) and that assumptions such as these have been found to feature in the accounts of some child protection professionals such as social workers, police officers and nurses (Kelley 1990). Social services became involved in the lives of several families with children following discovery of the offence and relatives of offenders described particular difficulties, centring on how they felt they were perceived as a family and disputes about whether children in their immediate or extended family were 'at risk'.

Relatives thought that social workers had a rigid conception of a sex offender: that he would always re-offend, that he would do so at any opportunity, that if guilty of a more minor sexual offence he would always progress to more serious ones, and that he would be indiscriminate in choosing victims. In addition, all sexual offences against children were treated as belonging to the same category; relatives thought there ought to be a better understanding of different levels of offence seriousness. This construction of the offender did not fit with the beliefs of relatives who did not think their own children were at risk, did not think it likely the offender would re-offend and in two particular cases thought that, although serious, offences against children involving masturbation and watching pornographic videos did not belong to the same category as the rape of a child.

Clare was a social worker when her husband's now adult children from his former marriage told her in a letter they had been sexually abused by their father as children, something she says she immediately reported to social services and then co-operated with their plan to confront her husband along with the police. She was aware of the professional construction of sex offenders and their relatives and found it difficult to be on the receiving end of these perceptions:

> And being a social worker in child protection, of course, I'd been trained to believe that once a perpetrator, always a perpetrator. And I had a ten-year-old son. So my initial thought was obviously for my own son, to make sure that he was okay. . . . I would say that professionally as far as Social Services are concerned, and I'm not sure about the other services like Health and Education, particularly with Social Services I think yes, they saw a stereotype of some families. . . . I don't like a lot of the terminology that is used and I know it's professional terminology, but I suppose because I know what the connotation actually means, you know, when you actually see it written in a document it has such awful connotations. And although you understand that therefore you are an innocent party, somehow it just, just the terminology that's used, that you are a 'non-protecting parent'. You know, all these labels that are put on

> you. Although I could argue very strongly about the reasons why I did what I did, they can actually wipe that to one side because professionally they know and whatever you say doesn't seem to bend their view. There's no balance and that's what I found frustrating about the system . . . I definitely felt I wasn't listened to because again I was either colluding or I was being a 'non-protecting parent'. And it can make you feel very demoralised, literally because yeah, assumptions are made about you because you are actually standing by a sexual offender basically. They're not interested in what you're saying your reasons are, they're only interested because research tells them this, and therefore you're colluding with the abuse. . . . And I suppose I was shocked at that, especially, I suppose I thought that people would believe what I said because I thought I was, I had integrity as a social worker, I'd built up integrity over a number a years. And I suppose naively I thought they would believe me. But then you suddenly realise that nobody believes anything you say.
>
> (Clare, husband convicted of sex offence)

Gill's husband had committed sexual offences against her nieces, but Gill said she was certain he had not abused their daughter. When he was released from prison, she said she was threatened with her daughter being taken into local authority care if her husband returned to live with them. He did return to live with them, and her daughter was eventually removed from the 'at risk' register, but only after a considerable battle:

> *G*: In the end [social services] wanted to come into my house, to our house, and watch us as a family going about our everyday business, like having our tea to see how we reacted as a family, and they really thought they were coming in to do that. Because all along I'd gone along with everything they said, everything they told me that [my husband] was saying and doing, I was believing them, more fool me. And I just woke up one day and I thought 'they want to come in and watch us? What do they think we are, bloody chimps?' I said 'for what purpose?' And they said 'to watch you, you know, going about your tea normally'. I said 'how can we do that if there's somebody sat watching us?' She said 'you won't know I'm there', I said, you know, 'you can't do that', I said 'I'm not a bloody moron', I said 'no'. And they got really, really stroppy with me then, and plus they also said, matter-of-factly, 'and we shall be coming to talk to you, sitting down and discussing yours and your husband's sex life, your marriage, but mainly your sex life'. I said 'you will, will you? No!' And they were really annoyed about that.

R: How do you think they saw you as a family?
G: I think they'd got it down like as [my husband], I'd be sat in one room, [my daughter] could be there and I could turn my head and he'd jump on her, assault her, and I'd look back and he's done it. That's how stupid they are.
R: So they really thought he'd abused her?
G: Oh yeah, or that he was going to if he hadn't. That he was going to. Or any child walking past, he would grab them, fumble and then stop.
R: And they didn't think you'd been part of it, but they thought it had been going on right under your nose?
G: Oh yes, it was actually said to me, actually said. I said 'I'm here to look after [my daughter]'. 'But you didn't stop anything happening before.' You see I was so shell-shocked, I wasn't aware before. If I'd have been aware it wouldn't have, as soon as I'm aware it stops, right? As soon as I'm properly aware. But no, I couldn't understand that mentality. Alright, they must deal with a lot of subnormal people, but I felt that's how I was being labelled, as somebody, I was actively, openly told that I was under [my husband's] spell.

(Gill, husband convicted of sex offence)

Nicola had planned for her partner to live with her and her son after his release from a five year prison sentence for child sex offences. She said social services had made it clear that this would not be possible. She had to go through complicated procedures to get clearance for her ten-year-old son to visit her partner in prison with her. Eventually arrangements were made, but social services then sent a letter telling her that she should not take her son to visit and inviting her to a meeting where their recommendation was repeated. She said she decided to end the relationship with her partner because of this:

> Let's just say social services made me feel the most inadequate thing in the world . . . they made a very thinly veiled threat which was 'we would advise that you don't take your son to [name of prison]', so I though 'alright'.
>
> (Nicola, partner convicted of sex offence)

In these circumstances social workers clearly have a tough job, and it is they who would be the first target for blame should they make the wrong decision; the accounts presented here are necessarily one-sided and do not reflect the difficulties social workers face evaluating often complex information and weighing evidence in these cases.

There are particular agencies, therefore, that make it their professional business to define the causes of offending and the circumstances of relatives of offenders, and have considerable power to impose these definitions. The acceptability or otherwise of accounts in this context can influence enormously important life events – if a relative can offer an account with currency it may mean that they can keep their child or have their husband living back at home. It is important, however, not to view relatives of offenders as passive recipients of accounts; they do not simply absorb and repeat the accounts they are offered, but rather digest these accounts and use them as resources in the formulation of their own accounts. Even where accounts are offered by those with the power to impose they are often resisted: neither Alice nor Celia were prepared to accept the justifications offered to them by police officers; Anne partially resisted the account offered by a probation officer; and Gill and Clare both described battling against the accounts offered by social workers. Elements of the web of shame were resisted by relatives, although for many the struggle with ambivalent and conflicting feelings about their personal responsibility continued. This struggle is played out collectively in the self-help context which is examined in the next chapter.

Note

1 One of the members of the gang responsible for the notorious Great Train Robbery in 1963, who subsequently spent 35 years on the run, returning to the UK in 2001.

Chapter 6

Self-help for families of serious offenders

> There's people [in Aftermath] in the same boat. They know exactly what's hitting your heart, what you're thinking, what you're feeling, how you feel and it's just amazing to have somebody there that knows exactly.
>
> (Pauline, son convicted of homicide)

The evolution of the self-help movement is very much a phenomenon of modern times and seeking support from a self-help group for a specific problem can be placed in the wider context of the growth of the self-help movement in contemporary society. The exact number of participants in self-help cannot be known because many groups and organisations do not keep membership records so estimates must be relied upon, but the scale and diversity of provision is vast. One such estimate is that 40 per cent of the US population participate in self-help (Wuthnow 1994). The second half of the twentieth century saw an enormous proliferation of self-help groups in both the US and the UK. The organisation Alcoholics Anonymous alone claims an estimated two million members worldwide and a presence in 180 countries (Alcoholics Anonymous 2006).

The breakdown of the family and other support networks which were characteristic of more traditional societies might explain the rise of alternative support such as self-help groups, but does not explain the specificity of the numerous groups that have arisen for each illness or social issue. For this is it is necessary to understand the broad societal changes that have 'modified the way and means by which people learn how to handle illness, death, birth, divorce, disease, and other life experiences' (Borkman 1999: 51–2). Giddens's theory of the reflexive project of the self in late modernity (see Giddens 1991), a time of a multiplicity of choices and of specific expertise to address problems, can help us to understand how 'individuals can reflexively reconstitute their selves within an experiential-peer community. Groups and their members appropriate professional knowledge of their predicament and interpret it to fit their day to day lives' (Borkman 1999: 62).

Finding specific expertise and knowledge is more difficult when the problem to be addressed is one that tends to be hidden and rarely discussed. Consider, for example, a person dealing with a much more common problem such the break-down of a marriage. As Giddens explains, there are a number of technical and popular writings on the subject, writings which are part of the reflexivity of modernity as they organise and alter the aspects of life they report on. Help might also be sought from other 'expert' sources – Relate, divorce mediation, or counselling, for example. As Giddens says, knowledge about 'what is going on' in the social arena of marriage and divorce is widely available and is not incidental to what is going on but constitutive of it (Giddens 1991: 14). However, for relatives of serious offenders there are no books, technical or popular, that deal with their particular predicament and how it affects them. Instead, any expert knowledge they do encounter is likely to define them as part of the problem (recall the earlier discussions of individualistic family-based explanations for crime) rather than comment on the difficulties they must manage or suggest strategies for doing so. In this context, what Borkman calls the 'experiential-peer' community of a self-help group becomes even more important to helping relatives find a way of understanding their predicament, integrating events, and restoring coherency to their self-narratives.

The focus of this chapter is on relatives' use of self-help, and particularly on Aftermath, the main site of fieldwork and the source of 26 interviewees in this study. There are a number of self-help groups for prisoners' families across the UK operating under the 'umbrella' organisation Action for Prisoners Families. However, at the time of my research Aftermath was the only national organisation specifically catering for relatives of *serious* offenders, and today no national organisation exists to meet their needs. Organisations for prisoners' families do not exclude relatives of serious offenders, and might count some among their membership, but they tend to provide information and practical support while Aftermath had a very important role in helping relatives to cope with the devastating impact of the offence. Six interviewees were not Aftermath members, but most of these still used other forms of self-help. Three used other prisoners' families organisations (two of whom received a great deal of support and attended self-help meetings), one used Families Anonymous, an organisation for relatives of drug users, and one used an organisation that supported ex-forces. Only one had not used any self-help organisation, and she received regular support from a psychiatric unit.

Through membership of a self-help organisation, relatives of serious offenders were able to form connections with other relatives of serious offenders to gain support and to collectively manage the problems they faced. Exploring the role of self-help draws together some of the themes from previous chapters: through self-help relatives found support in getting through the early traumatic stages and the criminal justice process and found ways to manage the changes in their lives; it provided collective tools for the management of stigma and shame; and it provided what I have called a 'collective narrative', a way of understanding relatives' predicament, which relatives used in constructing accounts about the offence, their own role, and their current circumstances.

Aftermath

Aftermath was a self-help organisation for the families of serious offenders set up in 1988 (see Howarth and Rock 2000 for a detailed analysis of the organisation). It had difficulty gaining recognition and legitimacy and relied on funding from charitable sources which was often not sufficient, itself a revealing indication of the moral and social marginality of its membership. It almost reached the point of closure several times due to financial crises, and finally did so in April 2005.

Between 1988 and 2001 (the period for which Aftermath collated and made available these statistics) Aftermath had 1285 families in its membership, with 200–300 active at any one time. The main categories of offences of which their relatives were accused or convicted included murder and manslaughter (40 per cent), sexual offences against a minor (20 per cent), rape (11.5 per cent), sexual offences against an adult (5 per cent) and attempted murder (2 per cent). Other offences included attempted rape (around 1 per cent) and an 'Other' category which made up around 20 per cent of the membership and according to Aftermath referred to 'Drugs, Armed Robbery, Fraud, GBH, Arson, Burglary'.

Aftermath was set up when its founder became aware of the need to support relatives of serious offenders through her volunteer work supporting victims of crime. At this time Aftermath was described as 'a loving family network' (a description that would continue) and members were linked by telephone and through meetings. A programme of individual counselling was offered to offenders and their relatives and in Aftermath's early years ex-offenders would offer support and information to members by talking to families about their experiences and the offences. In 1996, a new Chairperson took over the running of Aftermath after disputes about the purpose and direction of the organisation and he would remain in post until 2000. Under his leadership the organisation came to focus more squarely on the relatives of offenders, and although ex-offenders were made welcome, support to families became the primary focus and was offered solely by other relatives of serious offenders.

When I arrived in 1997, Aftermath had begun a period of implementing more formal, written procedures: a policy manual that outlined what it did as an organisation; accreditation from the British Association of Counselling; and a formal training programme for counsellors, distinguishing between telephone supporters, who were at an earlier stage, and counsellors who had received more training. During this period stronger links were forged with Action for Prisoners' Families (then known as the Federation of Prisoners' Families Support Groups) which in turn had an important role liaising with government. Stronger links were also forged with statutory agencies, and Aftermath began to receive more referrals from probation and police officers. Aftermath was moving towards a form of rational–legal authority (see Howarth and Rock 2000) and gaining greater legitimacy and respectability.

Aftermath continued in this form until 2000 when the Chairperson departed, again following a dispute about the role and purpose of the organisation. Disputes that led eventually to resignations were often very hurtful to those involved because so much of Aftermath and their role in it was invested in their self-identity, and there were several examples of members leaving under these circumstances. The role and purpose of Aftermath had been a long-standing tension within the organisation. During the period of my research there was much debate about the desirability of increasing professionalisation, including ongoing discussions about whether support should come from a familial network offering 'tea and sympathy' or a more formalised network of counsellors. There was a great deal of discussion, for example, over whether Aftermath counsellors or supporters had to be relatives of serious offenders, or whether this support could be offered by others and whether 'lunches' should be held in members' homes or in more neutral locations such as church halls.

A non-Aftermath member took the role of Chairperson from 2000–2002, coming to the position from his work with other charities and voluntary organisations. The organisation's administrator since its inception came to take on a more senior role in the management of the organisation as the Service Development Manager and another administrator was employed. In 2002 the role of Chair was taken over by a female Aftermath member who was a long-standing committee member and a former social worker and she remained in that role, supported by the committee, until Aftermath's closure.

Aftermath's difficulty in attracting funds derived from several sources. As a voluntary organisation they relied primarily on members or committee members to write funding applications, and though they had been successful on some occasions, success relied upon the skills, time and availability of members to perform this very time-consuming role. Their efforts to raise funds might also have been hindered by the shamed and tainted status of their membership. One member's attempt to raise money for the organisation suggested they were not seen as a worthy cause:

> Well its very salutary for me because when I ran a playgroup I used to do market stalls, charity market stalls, and we'd put up a couple of homemade cakes and a couple of old second hand books, and oh we'd coin it, a hundred quid easily, so I said to [Aftermath's administrator], 'oh I'll do a market stall, wonderful, hundred pound no problem', and I made about forty pound, and I was distraught, and it's because your charity has to have a banner that says what you are and what you do and when people realised what it was for, when they could see it wasn't for little children or cuddly animals, they didn't want to know, they just walked away, and I found that very hurtful.
>
> (Lisa, partner convicted of homicide)

The difficulties they had might also reflect a general reluctance to donate money to those associated with crime in any capacity. Rock found that self-help groups for relatives of homicide victims also struggled to find funding because of this reluctance on the part of potential donors: 'It is as if the pariah identity of the victim wards them off' (Rock 1998a: 167).

My fieldwork with Aftermath took place over a period of several years. The lunches I attended were held in church halls or community rooms and despite the rather anonymous locations, the atmosphere was warm and welcoming and had a homely and familial quality with the sharing of tea, coffee, and food that each member had brought. Members spent most of their time talking in pairs or smaller groups, catching up on news or sharing particular difficulties. As the members, who were mostly women, stood or sat around chatting, it was not unusual to see someone upset and crying or to hear bawdy laughter and joking. At some point during the afternoon the larger group would come together to discuss any current important Aftermath issues and any other issues those present wanted to raise. Sometimes this would involve personal or distressing problems people were contending with, but only if volunteered. The meetings did not have a formalised structure or rigid timetable and although they talked about the changes in their lives, members did not routinely tell their own 'stories' or give testimonies to the group.

Some of the members knew each other very well and were friends who had regular contact, but there were usually also newcomers who were made to feel welcome and accepted because of their shared bond. There was a strong emphasis on Aftermath meetings being a safe place where members would be accepted and not judged; separating the act from the actor was a fundamental part of their collective narrative. This welcome was extended to ex-offenders who sometimes attended Aftermath events with their families. Aftermath had a policy of not including children at lunches, unless by prior arrangement, to make sure their path did not cross with ex-offenders. I reflected in my fieldnotes that it must have been unusual for men who had sexually offended against children to find such a level of acceptance among a predominantly female group. Although not particularly hierarchical, it was clear that some of those present at lunches were more established members and perhaps further down the line than others. Some would have official roles in the organisation as committee members or supporters and might be meeting other members that they supported by telephone at the lunch.

Members also had the opportunity to meet at Aftermath's AGM and at other one-off events. These meetings tended to be more about addressing the business of the organisation or focused on particular practical issues and were less about emotional support, although at any of these occasions between meetings pairs or small groups of members might be huddled together discussing more personal matters. Annual seminar weekends were residential events that took place over three days. At times they felt like conferences, with the focus on practical information and different sessions with speakers from prisons or voluntary organisations; sometimes they were more like a support group with particular members feeling upset – emotions ran particularly high on the few occasions when invited members stood before the audience and told their 'story' (this was the only event where this happened and the members had been pre-booked as speakers); while in the evenings they often felt like any other social gathering taking place around a bar. I attended four of these events and they were invaluable for understanding the workings of Aftermath, talking informally with a large number of members over a longer period of time. Members often spoke of the value of these occasions, as in this letter to the newsletter written by new members:

> The family members that courageously spoke were just amazing, to relive often painful memories; we could understand their pain, learn from their experiences, and gain hope for the future. . . . The most

> outstanding part of the weekend was meeting such lovely people, being able to talk honestly, and finding total understanding of our experiences and gaining hope that we can live through our forthcoming trial. Sadly, our time together was too short but the brave and strong family members we met have touched our lives forever. We both feel honoured to be part of our 'new family' and grateful to have made some wonderful new friends.
>
> (Excerpt from letter from parents, Aftermath newsletter June 2001)

Even over these long weekends the atmosphere remained calm and friendly. Although Aftermath as an organisation went through turmoil and changes of leadership over its aims and purpose, this conflict was restricted to committee meetings and private discussions and rarely played out in these more public arenas. The drive to preserve Aftermath meetings as safe places appeared to keep heated discussions suppressed, while anger was an emotion rarely expressed by members when talking about their circumstances. This contrasts with the 'righteous anger, vociferous campaigning and denunciation of outsiders that so beset the politics of other survivors' groups' (Howarth and Rock 2000: 73) or in more politically active or campaigning groups. Although Aftermath wanted their members' plight recognised, their efforts were much quieter, possibly a reflection of their struggle with feelings of stigma, shame and responsibility. There were discussions about appointing an Aftermath member as media spokesperson, for example, but this never materialised. On the few occasions that members did appear in documentaries or on chat shows they commonly expressed dissatisfaction and thought they had been unsympathetically portrayed.[1]

Gender and self-help

It was striking that almost all the active Aftermath members were women. Women made up all but one of the members who offered formal support to other members and around 90 per cent of those attending functions. They were often wives and mothers but also other female relatives such as grandmothers and sisters. Men attending would either be ex-offenders or would be 'accompanied' men, usually with their wives, but sometimes with other female family members. During more than three years of fieldwork I only met two male relatives of offenders who had come alone to Aftermath gatherings. On several occasions, men would be attending reluctantly or just to support their wives. At a weekend gathering, one man came with his wife but did not attend the formal sessions while she attended them all. At another meeting, a man waiting for his wife sat in his car, reading his paper throughout the session.

I asked a group of five Aftermath members at a lunch (one of whom was male) why they thought most members were women, eliciting some interesting reasons including the restricted, stereotypical image of men as 'tough' and reserved, qualities which they thought were transmitted through social conditioning, peer pressure and other sources such as the media; the 'different kind of bonding' that they thought women experienced; assumptions about women's verbal ability and greater capacity for sympathy; and the straightforward practical reason that in many families the offender is the male partner who might be in prison. They thought men would be less likely to approach an organisation like Aftermath for help and support as men are more likely to keep their feelings hidden and not want to admit help is needed, and less likely to choose to be in an environment focusing on emotional support. Harriet suggested the bond between mother and child might explain the greater number of mothers in Aftermath:

> Never for one minute did I think 'well, if he's done it, I don't want anything to do with him'. He came from my body; I couldn't turn on him whatever he'd done. And I think this is why, when you say 'why are there more women in Aftermath?', because they carried the child, they gave birth to the child, they knew the child from nine months before the father did, and I think many fathers . . . haven't bonded in the way that the mother has.
>
> (Harriet, son accused of sex offence)

It is helpful to seek more broadly-applicable explanations because such a gender imbalance is not unique to Aftermath. Studies have shown that members of self-help groups are characteristically drawn from similar populations: female, white, middle class and with a higher level of education (Gidron *et al.* 1990; Heller *et al.* 1997; Lieberman and Snowdon 1994; Norton *et al.* 1993; Videka-Sherman 1982). A similar gender imbalance has also been found in readers of self-help literature (Simonds 1992). Campbell found that the practical politics and community groups on the estates she researched were initiated and run by women. When men were asked why they did not take part they said it was 'women's work'. Campbell explains: 'Solidarity and self-help are sustained by networks that are . . . open, expansive, egalitarian and incipiently democratic. . . . Crime and coercion are sustained by men. Solidarity and self-help are sustained by women. It is as stark as that' (Campbell 1993: 319).

In trying to understand why the majority of Aftermath members were female, it is useful to think about what self-help could offer women who were the primary supporters of offenders. Aftermath members repeatedly emphasised the importance of meeting other relatives of serious offenders: to share stories and experiences, for mutual support and friendship, and to share practical information and ways of coping with their predicament. In Aftermath, they found others prepared to talk about their shared experiences – a community of story tellers describing their experiences in similar ways (Plummer 1995). They thought that other relatives of serious offenders understood how they felt and could empathise in a way that non-relatives could not:

> I went and attended the first lunch that I went to and I couldn't believe that, you know, that there was like all these different people that were in a similar role you know, situations to what we were. And then, and that they all met and you know, I felt brilliant. Well I felt a hundred per cent better when I came away from there than I did when I went. And it was sort of, the fact that knowing, you know, I mean there were other people that were suffering the same as we were but you don't know where they are, you don't know who they are, you know, it's not something that you can shout from the rooftops, that it's happening to you.
>
> (Angela, husband accused of sex offence)

Many members talked about the importance of knowing that they were not the only person in this situation, as Hilda, whose son was detained in a special hospital, described:

> It makes a difference to me to know someone else is going through what I'm going through. I'm not selfish or anything, but I do at times think what am I going through all this for? Why me? Then I think well why not? . . . Aftermath have given me more confidence because I know there are other people going through what I'm still going through and which I will do, surely, because things don't change. He's there, he's never going to come out, and you've still got to carry on. It hurts and it's hard.
>
> (Hilda, son convicted of homicide)

Relatives spoke about Aftermath as a non-judgemental and safe place, something which was an important contrast to their everyday lives:

> *R*: Does it help that [Aftermath members] have also got a serious offender in the family?
>
> *L*: Yes, it does, it does help. It does help because you know when you're talking to them, you're not an outcast, you know. It's like when I was on the [hospital-based] therapy group, I couldn't bring myself to tell people in that group why I was at the group. I told them I was at the group because my son was in prison, but I never

> told them what he was in prison for because they were local people from around where I live. Whereas Aftermath, you could tell them, you could talk to them, they didn't look down on you, they didn't think you were some monster. And they also didn't consider your son a monster which to me was such a great relief, you know, that you could talk to somebody about it.
>
> (Lillian, son convicted of sex offence)

> I found it a comfort to know that I wasn't alone, that there were places [within Aftermath] where I was safe to talk. You're not safe and you've got this terrible secret and you can't talk to anyone, but if you can't talk you just sort of think you're going to explode, but you daren't talk.
>
> (Harriet, son accused of sex offence)

Harriet had seen a counsellor through her GP's surgery who had told her that if she talked about her son's alleged sexual offences against his children, anything she said would have to be passed on to social services. She therefore did not feel safe to express her uncertainty about his guilt, but within Aftermath felt she was able to do so.

A place to talk in safety about their experiences was something relatives valued. Just as in South Africa when the slogan 'Revealing is Healing' was used by victims in the Truth and Reconciliation Commission (Slovo 2003), being able to talk in a safe place had important consequences for managing stigma and shame and moving forward from the low point of discovery:

> *R*: What's the most useful service that Aftermath provides?
>
> *G*: A haven, safe talking, you know. I did, I felt safe. There was so much, from walking down the street I felt people were looking at me and talking about me and I was even afraid, yeah, that a brick might come at me or something like that. I thought, you know, on the phone to Aftermath you felt you could say anything to them without them thinking 'oh you shouldn't be saying that, or shouldn't be thinking that way,' and the same when you went in to meet them, you just felt like a proper person again, not like somebody dirty, somebody that had gone into a life, you know, it's such a shock to go into that prison life, it's just so totally foreign.
>
> (Gill, husband convicted of sex offence)

Through self-help, members can gain knowledge and learn strategies to cope with their predicament. This might be the outcome of counselling processes, or conveyed between members who have, as they say, 'been there'. Aftermath also offered practical support and information about prison visiting or court hearings. Those relatives that had had no past experience of the criminal justice system had to go through a process of 'socialisation', of learning what to do and how to do it. The professional and 'experiential' knowledge (Borkman 1990) gleaned through Aftermath was invaluable in making this possible.

> Well the most important thing was to go on that seminar [weekend] and just to meet people, networking, ask them the specific questions: 'how do I get the parole looked at again?', 'how can I get him on the course [Sex Offenders Treatment Programme]?' and to find out about his legal rights.
>
> (Betty, brother convicted of sex offence)

> Yeah, the lunches. Being there, having somebody that actually, that understood. You know, they'd not actually gone through the same experience but knowing that they understood exactly what I was feeling, you know, like they didn't say to me 'I know how you feel' because that's really patronising, because nobody knows how we feel, nobody does because no two people feel the same anyway. But like they'd say you know, 'when this happened to us, this is how I handled it', or 'this is how I felt'. And knowing that you could relate to that person you know, the empathy that was there was really important.
>
> (Angela, husband accused of sex offence)

New members to Aftermath benefit not only from learning *how* other relatives got through the earlier traumatic stages, but also that they *did*. Aftermath could be classified as a long-term coping group (Borkman 1990), a primary function was to help members to cope with their predicament rather than transform their own behaviour and members often remained so for many years. Aftermath members could learn from other members at mutual gatherings such as lunches or annual seminar weekends where members at different stages came together, and through one-to-one supporting. A letter to the Aftermath newsletter showed this progression and the help offered to others by those in the later stages:

> It's [date] once more and the anniversary of my brother's offence. I am amazed to realise that it is now ten years since I first needed Aftermath. I was depressed, panic-stricken, ashamed and very lonely. How lucky I was to find such a wonderful group of people, all able to empathise with me in my plight and offer the support I so desperately needed at that time, and sometimes still do need. I would like to take this opportunity to thank all the Aftermath

> members, both past and present, who have 'been there' for me over the years. To our 'older' members I say 'Thank you for walking my road with me', and to our 'younger' members I say 'Take heart, you too will get through'. Thanks a million everyone.
>
> (Aftermath newsletter, 2002)

For some members, one-to-one support, usually given by telephone because members were so geographically dispersed, was a lifeline. It was described to me as such by several interviewees who said they did not know what they would have done without it. Some had even contemplated suicide and doubted they would have survived without Aftermath's support, all the more poignant now this support no longer exists.

Nine interviewees were also telephone counsellors or supporters and when they talked about their work they described how desperate the members they were supporting could sometimes be. Though anger was rarely expressed at Aftermath meetings, Angela described how one member was able to do so during one-to-one support:

> I've got one lady that rings at half past one in the morning screaming, just screaming, she just screams until the frustration's gone. She's got to scream at somebody, I'd rather she scream at me than slice her wrists or take a load of pills. But she's at the stage where she's angry and she's, you know, so then she cries and says she's 'sorry Angela, I don't mean to scream at you'. I say 'it's alright love', I just hold the phone away from me ear cause I know it's there and I know she's going to go off ballistic and swearing and going off. But it's her way of venting the anger and I'd rather she'd vent the anger on me than one of the kids and I know it's not personal. I know when she's screaming and ranting and raving, it's nothing to do with me as a person; I'm just a sounding board for her to sound off on. And then she'll calm down and then we talk and you know, you rationalise things and I sort of said to her, you know, 'let's think rational about this'. And then she'll say to me and I'll say 'but how do you feel about that?' And I turn everything back on her and she don't even realise you're doing it and you know, she'll say 'well yeah'. 'And how do you feel about that?' You know. 'What do you think you should have done?' And it's 'well I know I should do this', 'well there you have it then, there's your answer, what you talking about?' You know.
>
> (Angela, husband accused of sex offence)

Self-help groups such as Aftermath help members to manage stigma and repair damaged identities. It has been argued that the collective management of stigma is a key role shared by all such groups:

> . . . all self-help/mutual aid is formed in part in reaction against the stigma projected by others – friends, co-workers, strangers, professionals providing services, and so on – onto the shared problem that is the focus of the group.
>
> (Borkman 1999: 8)

It was important to relatives to know that they were not the only families in their situation and to find other people (and often other caring wives and mothers) who shared their circumstances:

> Looking back now [to when I first joined Aftermath], it was a sort of belonging I suppose, and when I went to the lunches it was the realisation that there are other normal families that it had happened to, you know.
>
> (Anne, son convicted of rape)

> I felt everybody could look at me and see we've got a prisoner in the family, and yeah you do, you just feel awful, you think nobody else has got one. It's only when I went, and that is the good thing about it, when I went to Aftermath and you find there are perfectly normal respectable people out there.
>
> (Mary, daughter convicted of violent offence)

As we will see, Aftermath provided a way of understanding their problem, constructing relatives of serious offenders as 'the other victims of crime', providing a collective narrative that minimised their own culpability. Members' sense of self and identity was further boosted through the confidence and sense of belonging engendered by membership:

> The initial shock, horror, I wanted to lock myself away, it would have been very nice to have had, to have known there was someone there that I could talk to without feeling tainted. See that's the thing that Aftermath does for me. It makes me feel like a person. I'm not something dirty that should be under a stone or crawled out from under a stone. That's how Aftermath made me, it gave me my self-confidence and I felt part of something, belonging. And that is very important because as the wife of a serious offender, you don't belong anywhere. You're vulnerable. Everyone can throw what they like at you and you're nothing, you know. They did that for me and they've been great because there's a lot of us here and we're all in this together and you're part of us. And that is something to cling to.
>
> (Eileen, husband convicted of sex offence)

One of the primary benefits from membership of Aftermath was that of friendship and a social network, and as we saw in Chapter 3, loss of friends was often one of the consequences of relatives' secondary stigma. Interviewees characterised Aftermath and the bonds between members as being 'like a family'; perhaps ironic given the difficulties many members had encountered within their own families, but important nonetheless as their interpretation of the support they found. This was also part of Aftermath's collective narrative and a common way in which members spoke about the organisation:

> How do I feel a part of it? Well, it's as if we're one, it's a family, I suppose, and I feel one of the family, and we all help each other and we're there to help others as well.
>
> (Frances, husband convicted of sex offence)

> *R*: Has Aftermath made a difference to your life?
>
> *S*: Yeah it has, yeah. If I'm down in the dumps I can always phone one of the volunteers, any of them really. It's like one big happy family really. They do give you a lot of support.
>
> (Stephanie, husband convicted of homicide)

Another study of women in self-help groups for prisoners' partners found that the members were able to maintain a positive identity through giving help to others (Codd 2002); this may be an important reason why women stay in these groups when the level of support they themselves need diminishes, but is less likely to be the explanation for why most women join.

The predominance of women in Aftermath might partially be explained by female relatives seeking support in managing some of the new responsibilities outlined in Chapter 2 and in managing a stigma which, as we saw in Chapter 3, is partly based on the gendered construction of kin relationships. If female family members, and particularly wives and mothers, take on the greater load of support both in emotional and practical terms, support might be sought from groups such as Aftermath to help in managing this load. If women's identities are more closely constructed through their kin relationships, they may be more subject to blame and shame for the deviation of a family member, and they may feel a greater need to seek help as a result when something goes wrong. It is likely that women feel more comfortable asking for emotional support and discussing sensitive familial issues, and there is a sense in which the family, kinship and related problems are seen as women's domain and women's responsibility, and a normative expectation that it is for women to sort them out. Men remained somewhat hidden in this process. One interviewee was a father who clearly cared deeply about his son and had given him considerable support, although his wife was the more active Aftermath member and had set up our interview. I had conversations with other men during fieldwork, but in most cases they were involved with their wife or other female relative. It is evident that some fathers, husbands, brothers and sons do support offenders and further research would be useful to understand more about their experiences.

A collective narrative

Self-help groups provide meaning and a way of understanding the particular problem that they have been organised to address. This collectively constructed meaning has variously been called 'community-level narrative' (Rappaport 1993), 'meaning perspective' (Borkman 1999), 'worldview transformation' (Kennedy and Humphreys 1994), 'narrative map' and 'template' (Pollner and Stein 1996), 'collective story' (Richardson 1990) and 'cognitive restructuring' (Katz 1993). Organisational settings such as self-help groups provide 'a distinctive conversational environment – a set of methods and constraints – that circumstantially shape storytelling and self constructions' (Holstein and Gubrium 2000: 154). Self-help groups are a site for the production and consumption of stories (Plummer 1995), and how members talk about their experiences both shapes and is shaped by a shared, collective narrative.

There was a discernible collective narrative through which Aftermath understood the experience of being a relative of a serious offender. Aftermath maintained that there were many victims of an offence, and that families of offenders were the unrecognised victims of crime. They claimed that the experience of discovering the offence was devastating for relatives and comparable to bereavement and that the events which followed could be very difficult to manage. Family members were often traumatised and might be blamed, unfairly, for the actions of the offender. Only others who had been through the experience of being related to a serious offender could really understand the impact it had. It was possible for relatives to support the offender without condoning the offence – they could 'hate the sin but love the sinner' – and this separation enabled Aftermath and its members to offer acceptance to offenders and their families. Aftermath aimed to provide a caring, compassionate and non-judgemental network to help relatives to cope with the traumatic impact and the difficulties they faced. Sharing the same problem – having a serious offender in their immediate circle – brought a close bond between members comparable in many ways to a family.

In 2000, Aftermath produced a six page 'Annual Review' which included the following statement about its beliefs:

> We define as 'serious' crimes that carry a substantial prison sentence. Many of the serious crimes carry a stigma, offences such as murder, rape and sexual abuse. Aftermath believes that the family of a serious offender can very often experience the backlash of their relative's wrong doing, and are very often treated with contempt. The mother and father who find their son has committed a serious sexual offence can immediately lose their own self worth. Learning to accept the gravity of a social wrong committed by a close relative is a process of extreme torment and Aftermath offers a safe, non-judgemental support system where families can begin to regain their self-esteem and dignity.
>
> (Aftermath 2000: 2)

Aftermath's collective narrative was conveyed through literature such as this and through newsletters, by supporters or counsellors, and at meetings and lunches by speakers and through informal conversations.

Although Aftermath had a definite way of understanding the experiences of families of serious offenders, the narrative was less immediately visible than in many other self-help organisations. Self-help organisations differ in the strength of interpretation that they offer. For some, a way of seeing a problem is their primary function, of which 'twelve-step' groups such as Alcoholics Anonymous might be the best example; for others, such as Aftermath, ways of seeing are more diffuse and less structured. Alcoholics Anonymous has a 'Big Book', which has sold over 25 million copies in English alone and outlines its beliefs, aims and work. AA meetings revolve around the personal stories of members (Cain 1991). Through these testimonies more experienced members offer 'narrative maps' which might shape the decisions, actions and discourse of new members (Pollner and Stein 1996). These narrative maps have particular characteristics and shape experience in specific ways, and coupled with the twelve-step programme provide a powerful guide for how newcomers should interpret their experience. Aftermath did not offer a framework of this strength or pervasiveness.

In part, this may be because Aftermath was a small organisation that only existed for 17 years, a relatively short time. Organisations such as AA are much older and more extensive and their 'narrative maps' have taken on an existence independent of individual members and can be found in any meeting, transcending place and time. Aftermath was not a transformative group (Borkman 1990) – it did not attempt to change its members' behaviour – and it did not have the same focus on the self as can be found in twelve-step groups. Relatives of alcoholics in AlAnon, for example, follow a twelve-step programme which focuses on changes in their attitude and behaviour and modifying their thinking to improve conditions in their lives (Ablon 1974) and are encouraged to practice 'detachment' and 'tough love' to allow the alcoholic to experience the consequences of alcoholism which it is thought will aid their recovery (Reddy and McElfresh 1978); a similar focus on changing beliefs about the self and behaviour exists in the organisation Adult Children of Alcoholics (Kennedy and Humphreys 1994). Aftermath did not define its members as acting inappropriately or seek to change their behaviour in this way and instead focused on helping them to cope with the difficulties they faced.

During the period of my research Aftermath did not attempt to provide answers about why the offences had happened (although in its early days under the leadership of its founder questions of aetiology had been part of its focus, see Howarth and Rock 2000 and May 2000). It did emphasise that families were not to be held to blame for the sins of their members, but alternative theories about why people offend were not propounded. Aftermath provided an environment where attempts to adjust the actor would be sympathetically received, where members could speak openly to each other about the offender and expect to have their claims honoured: claims to various mitigating factors (denial of full responsibility), claims to the offender being 'more than a sex offender' (resisting totalising identity) or claims about his or her good qualities (balance). Separating the act from the actor ('hate the sin but love the sinner') was a key part of Aftermath's collective narrative, and an actor adjustment that most Aftermath members would profess to honour, however heinous the crime.

No-one within Aftermath openly condoned the offence, although feelings about the offence and its gravity varied. A lunch participant told me 'If a parent turned up not bitterly ashamed but almost bragging about it, we would find that very difficult' and other members in the room agreed. With such serious offences we might expect claims for act adjustments to be less straightforwardly received. In line with Aftermath's claim to provide a supportive and non-judgemental environment I did not witness public challenging of members' interpretations, although the opportunity to do this would not arise often as offences and the reasons behind them were usually not discussed publicly at Aftermath meetings and tended to be restricted to private conversations and more formalised supporting or counselling, which in itself was non-directive and according to the accounts of my interviewees did not suggest or offer explanations as to why the offence had happened. The Aftermath environment might have kept these attempts to adjust the act suppressed with members not feeling comfortable expressing these views. Were public attempts made to adjust the act, the response from other members might have been restricted to private thoughts or private conversations. They might have made their own judgements, for example, about Frances's claim that her 15-year-old foster-daughter 'offered it' and her husband 'could not say no' or Ada relaying her GP's opinion that rape was 'part of growing up', but I did not witness gossiping about other members' interpretations of the crime. As we saw in Chapter 4, these attempts at adjusting such serious acts were unusual and actor adjustments were much more frequently heard.

Aftermath's narrative was constructed around resisting relatives' own feelings of shame and worthlessness and notions of contamination and culpability. Constructing relatives as the 'other victims' encompassed both blamelessness and suffering: they were not to blame for the circumstances in which they found themselves; the crime was not their fault; and they were not to be blamed if they chose to support the offender. Aftermath aimed to treat its members as people in their own right, uncontaminated by their kin relationship, and to help them to 'regain their self-esteem and dignity'.

What is the relationship between a collective narrative produced by a group such as Aftermath and the individual narratives of members? Does it offer a script which instructs members how to view their circumstances and the problems they face? And once confronted with this way of seeing, do members adopt it unquestioningly and uncritically and all perceive their problems in the same way? My interviews with relatives suggested that they did not, and that they received the different elements of the narrative in a much more questioning, active manner. The relationship between the collective narrative and individual narratives was more dynamic and interactive as they informed and were informed by each other. During the research I was sometimes asked whether it was valid to talk to members of a self-help group about the problems facing relatives of offenders when what I would in fact tap into would be the self-help group's narrative or perspective rather than what relatives of serious offenders *really* thought. But members of self-help organisations are not automatons who, once they have come into contact with the organisation's narrative, use it as a kind of script for living by and stop thinking for themselves about their circumstances. Social scientists are expected to be reflexive, but our research subjects are sometimes denied reflexive agency. Just as 'we' are allowed to have explanations for why we do things, while offenders have no excuse (Maruna and Copes 2005: 287) and offenders' excuses are constructed as pathology (Fox 1999), so 'we' are allowed to draw on many different sources to understand our lives and construct personal narratives, but self-help group members are perceived to have just the one.

People are not 'judgemental or cultural dopes' (Garfinkel 1967) but are active participants in the production of meaning and can think critically about messages they are confronted with, draw on different skills to make judgements and do not just believe everything they are told. Analyses of how we receive media messages have long recognised the existence of different sources of knowledge. In addition to the media, for example, people get information and knowledge of social reality from personal experience, significant others, social groups and institutions (Surette 1998) and actively construct their own interpretations and meanings. The narrative provided by a group like Aftermath is just one contributory source to relatives' own accounts and how they received the different elements of the collective narrative depended on how it spoke to them as, for example, mothers, wives, workers, counsellors, committee members, and so on – not just as relatives of serious offenders – and different components of their self-narratives would be in the foreground at different times. Aftermath's narrative was an important and influential source for members – it addressed the problems they faced in a unique and targeted way – but was not unquestioningly accepted as the only way of understanding their predicament.

Relatives could reject or accept different aspects of the collective narrative according to their own experiences and exercise 'interpretive discretion' (Holstein and Gubrium 2000) to use the narrative in contingent ways. The collective narrative offered by Aftermath was therefore better viewed as a *resource* rather than a template or rigid lens through which members understood their experience. Although members might initially have appeared to agree with key elements in similar ways, and there was a core of shared understanding about their predicament, when probed further different interpretations of what the elements actually meant were uncovered. The elements of the collective narrative were therefore *flexible categories* which members interpreted to suit. As Richardson says, 'people make sense of their lives through the stories that are available to them, and they attempt to fit their lives into the available stories' (Richardson 1990: 26); people also attempt to fit available stories into their lives. As Holstein and Gubrium have commented, different groups have different stories, however: 'none of their stories enters into everyday use as a narrative template. Rather, the stories are continuously shaped and reshaped as participants variously borrow from, keep separate, combine, individually formulate, or even suppress stories to construct difference and sameness' (Holstein and Gubrium 2000: 116). Holstein and Gubrium refer to this as 'narrative elasticity' and show how, even in organisations like AA which have stronger narrative control, different elements of the narrative are adapted and constructed by members in fluid ways (*ibid.*).

Some elements of Aftermath's collective narrative had more power than others and it was unlikely that relatives who wholeheartedly disagreed with the narrative would become or remain members.

However, this still left room for differences in interpretation. Not all members could separate the actor and the act ('hate the sin but love the sinner') and as we have seen some chose not to support because this adjustment did not work for them, although this on its own did not prevent their membership. All interviewees did describe the events surrounding discovery as very upsetting and traumatic, emphasising the need for recognition of what they had been through. However, we cannot be sure firstly whether the source was Aftermath's narrative about discovery (and non-members describing it in similar terms suggests it might not have been) or whether those feelings were what brought relatives to Aftermath in the first place. A manager of a visitors' centre at a high security prison described how families were devastated and how 'everything falls down broken' when the family discovers the offence, based on her experience of working with a large number of non-Aftermath relatives of serious offenders. The few non-Aftermath members interviewed for this study talked about discovery of the offence being traumatic and shocking, although they did not explicitly compare their experiences to bereavement. Finally, the meaning of the words 'traumatic' and 'shocking' might be quite different for different members and being traumatised or being shocked might be expressed in very different ways.

The way that different elements of a narrative are interpreted is well illustrated by looking at how relatives understood Aftermath's claim that relatives of offenders were the 'other victims' of crime. This was an important part of Aftermath's collective narrative. An Aftermath leaflet stated:

> THE FORGOTTEN VICTIMS
> Whilst we support the offender and his family, we never condone the offence. We do, however, sympathise with the unique and difficult circumstances in which these families find themselves. These are the *Forgotten Victims*. Our aim is to offer them support, love and understanding.
>
> (Aftermath leaflet, n.d.)

Depicting families of offenders as victims was not unique to Aftermath and has a long history in the broader prisoners' families literature. In 1978, for example, the families of prisoners were described as the 'hidden victims of crime' (Bakker *et al.* 1978) and in 1983 as the 'innocent victims of our penal system' (Matthews 1983). In 1993 Light stated that 'the victims of crime include not only those who have had offences committed against them, but also families and dependents of those convicted of offences, particularly if the offender is sentenced to a period in prison' (Light 1993: 324–5) and a Howard League report in 1994 described prison visitors as 'the innocent, and often "forgotten" victims within the criminal justice system' (Howard League 1994).

According to Holstein and Miller, we assign victim status to ourselves and others through 'interpretive and representational processes' (Holstein and Miller 1990: 105), processes which were apparent in interviewees' accounts. Interviewees had different interpretations of what this part of Aftermath's narrative actually meant and varied in the degree to which they incorporated it into their own personal narratives. Lisa, for example, did not see herself as a victim, having met her partner while he was in prison, but explained her belief that families of serious offenders were victims because of the nature of the offence and the difficulties imposed by the offender's imprisonment:

> It must be so difficult for ... a wife whose husband's gone inside and she has to explain to the children, she has to try and stop them being bullied and tormented in the school playground, she's confronted with media pressure, she's confronted with conversations in shops that suddenly stop as she goes in, I mean all those must be dreadful pressures and I think this is something that people don't understand, one conversation I had with a girl in the [prison] waiting room, was 'Well, it's alright for him, isn't it? He's not sitting waiting for the light to go out, he's not wondering where the gas is coming from to cook the children's tea, he's in the warm, he's in the dry, he's got no bills and he's got three fucking meals a day' and she was surrounded by three little ones, so I mean they're getting all sorts of pressures that most of us don't understand, and that most of society is unwilling to accept. We'll read *The Sun* and we'll take on board all these ridiculous stories about yes they're living on lobster and caviar and Whitemoor is a hotel, what they won't take on board is how a little girl goes back to wetting the bed and cries herself asleep at night because she's lost her daddy and she doesn't understand why, and because of what people are saying to her about it.
>
> (Lisa, partner convicted of homicide)

For Frances, families were victims because of the lack of provision targeted towards them and the lack of recognition of their needs. This is what attracted her to Aftermath in the first place:

> *R*: And why Aftermath? Why were you interested in them?
>
> *F*: Um, well it was you know, what it said, you know 'for the other victims', um, because there was no help for me, everybody else seemed to get help but me, you know I did take it quite badly.
>
> (Frances, husband convicted of sex offence)

George thought that families were victims because they were 'brought down' to the level of the prisoner. However, although he saw himself as a victim because of what he felt people were thinking, he did not think that his life was otherwise affected.

G: Yeah, I think they are [victims], I think that's true. I think that's what we are. You're brought down to a level, like we were talking before about visits, and you are, you might just as well be a prisoner. In fact you are a prisoner, for that time that [my son] was in [prison] anyway because you can't get out [of the situation].
R: Do you see yourself as a victim of what happened?
G: I do up to a point, but not, it doesn't, not to the point where it's affected my life. I'm only affected as I said before by that smear that comes along from time to time and 'well he's the father of somebody that's killed', or 'he's the father he must be to blame', or that kind of suggestion, from that point of view, yes, I feel a victim.
R: Where do those suggestions come from?
G: I don't know, I think they're probably in my thoughts just as much as from outside. I mean you tend to get these concepts of people thinking that you're one thing, but maybe it's not happening at all.
(George, son convicted of homicide)

George's comments might also reflect a gender difference. It is possible that male relatives are less willing to admit to feeling like victims (although with only one male interviewee this cannot be concluded with any certainty); may be less likely to organise their lives around caring for the offender (see Chapter 2); and are less likely to be financially dependent on the offender.

Harriet was an active Aftermath member when I met her, attending lunches and acting as a supporter. However, she did not agree with describing relatives as victims because she thought this could be perceived as a claim for suffering to the same degree as primary victims and their relatives:

H: I've always taken issue with Aftermath that we are victims. I think that must be dreadfully annoying to the people who have had someone murdered or raped. You know, how dare they say they are victims? You know. We've suffered greatly as a result, but I think the word victim is the wrong word. And I think it must lose us a lot of public sympathy. I can't think of another word other than victim, but it is the wrong word.
R: And you don't feel like a victim yourself?

> *H*: Possibly, but I think it's worse for the actual people whose brother has been murdered . . . we're a victim once removed, aren't we? There are many different types of victim – the immediate victim, the relatives of that victim, and then another tier on the other side, the relatives of those that have done it.
>
> (Harriet, son accused of sex offence)

Although Harriet thought she was possibly a victim of what had happened, she resisted the use of the term because it did not differentiate between different types of victims. 'Victim' was therefore a flexible category, and part of a narrative which was used contingently as a resource by relatives. Different aspects of victimisation were emphasised, and the degree to which relatives were prepared to incorporate this status into their own personal narratives varied and was dependent upon their circumstances and the other resources they used to understand those circumstances. There may be a further distinction between relatives' public and private accounts: some relatives might say that they define themselves as victims to reduce blame from others, but privately feel a greater degree of self-blame than they are willing to express.

Six interviewees were not Aftermath members, although one became an Aftermath member after our interview at the suggestion of another prisoners' families organisation. Responses from these participants were mixed. Sarah thought that families were victims because they had to deal with problems not of their own making. Like Lisa, she pointed to problems faced while the family member was imprisoned, however unlike Lisa she did see herself as a victim:

> *S*: Oh yes, yes because they're [families of serious offenders] unwittingly caught up in it all aren't they? They're having to face the music of that family member. If that family member is in prison, they're out the way but the rest of the family has to face the hostility that might come from neighbours towards the family you know, like your brother did so and so. 'He's a complete waste of time, your, the whole family's a waste of time', that sort of thing.
>
> *R*: And do you see yourself like that, as a victim of what your Mum did?
>
> *S*: Yeah. Yes. Yes I do.

Sarah's mother committed a violent attack against her father. Sarah identified herself as a victim because of her relationship to both her mother and her father:

> I've actually identified with both. Yes, I identified, saw myself very much as a victim because of I think, if I'm honest, what I was having

> to deal with and what was being put on my shoulders and the emotional trauma that I was having to deal with. So I did see myself as a victim. Victim Support verified that. You know, they said 'well you are, you are a victim' and initially yes, I did identify very strongly with what Dad was going through. Then it switched and I was identifying with Mum and what Mum was or wasn't doing to me. You know, the fact that she wasn't talking to me plus the fact I felt so incredibly guilty about her not staying here [while on bail], although I couldn't have done it, the guilt was unbearable.
>
> (Sarah, mother convicted of violent offence)

Christine was prepared to consider describing families as victims, but was not prepared to describe herself in this way:

> *R*: I've also heard the families of offenders described as 'the other victims of crime'. What do you think about that?
>
> *C*: [long pause] Um, well yeah, I suppose we are in a way, you know, because we're still living with it, living with her being in prison. She's our daughter and she's been took away from us, although be it her own fault, sort of thing. So we are living with that.
>
> *R*: So do you see yourself like that, as a victim of what's happened?
>
> *C*: I don't know if victim is the right word to use, because that's like I feel sorry for myself, and I don't feel sorry for myself. I feel sorry for her, that she got that low, no I don't, I don't feel like a victim. I feel we're suffering from the fact that we haven't got her here, that she's not with us.
>
> (Christine, daughter convicted of violent offence)

Why did Aftermath place such an emphasis on families as victims? The status of victim encompasses both recognition of suffering and blamelessness – that the individual is not to blame for their suffering which comes from sources beyond their control, although as Lamb has commented the status of 'victim' should not necessarily mean absolution from all responsibility (Lamb 1996: 21). The claim for victim status therefore powerfully countered the contamination and blame that relatives experienced in their everyday lives. Holstein and Miller summarise the meaning of the label 'victim' using the example of a caregiver at an Alzheimer's disease caregiver support group who describes the disease as having two victims: 'the label implicitly underscores the caregiver's injury, free from fault for her troubles, and renders her worthy of others' concern' (Holstein and Miller 1990: 106).

There is much to be gained from the status of victim: to be seen as deserving of help and support, sympathy and possible funding (important to self-help groups like Aftermath, lack of which was the source of their eventual demise), and importantly absolving or minimising an individual's personal responsibility. A claim for the status of victim often encompasses assigning victimiser status to another, although it is possible for victims to be 'depicted as objects of harm by *amorphous, impersonal* forces. The well known "victim of circumstances" is exemplary in this regard' (Holstein and Miller 1990: 107). It is not immediately clear who Aftermath members claimed to be victimised by. Although they spoke of crimes having many victims, they were not (in most cases) asking for more blame to be heaped upon the offender – in fact, often quite the contrary as we have seen with their attempts to adjust the actor and the act. Their claim was a broader one: they were victims of the stigma, shock and repercussions of serious offending and of events surrounding and following discovery. Sometimes blame was levelled at specific others, but this was more likely to be people within their local community from whom they received negative responses, or institutions or agencies they felt had treated them unfairly:

> You almost begin to feel a victim yourself in a funny sort of way. Again a victim of the media, you know, a victim of the state as far as social services and probation were concerned, I felt at that time very victimised.
>
> (Clare, husband convicted of sex offence)

Aftermath received a mixed response to their claim to victimhood, and it was a claim that was often not honoured:

> If 'victim' is regarded as a claim about the world, then belief in the factual status of the description depends on such things as credibility, influence, and warrant for honouring one set of claims over another.
>
> (Holstein and Miller 1990: 114)

During the 17 years of its existence Aftermath faced a constant struggle for this credibility and influence. The negative connotations of passivity and weakness associated with the status of victim have led some groups, such as those in the rape crisis movement, to shun the term, preferring to claim the status of 'survivor'. Progression to an alternative term might only be possible after recognition of suffering has been made and claims to victimhood honoured. Relatives of serious offenders struggled for recognition of their injury and were often not seen as free from fault for their troubles. The web of shame was so significant for the relatives that I met that countering it took precedence over such concerns.

Note

1 One exception to this was the BBC documentary specifically about Aftermath (BBC 2, *40 Minutes*, February 1994).

Conclusion

> I have visited families where the windows are nailed shut, letter boxes blocked up to avoid flaming rags or dog excrement being thrown in. Families have been spat at, publicly reviled. A mother will look at her newborn baby and dream that one day he/she will be a doctor, an Olympic athlete, a mechanic like his father; no mother cradles that tiny scrap of life and thinks one day he will be a murderer, a rapist or a paedophile. It is not only parents who feel this terrible pain, there are siblings, children, grandparents, aunts, uncles, cousins, all get drawn into the net of horror and loss. The ripple effect can be enormous and pass down the generations. All these persons may be viewed as the 'Scum of the Earth'. The only 'crime' that the families have committed is to be related to someone that the public has labelled 'a monster'. Love does not end when a person gets into trouble; this is the time when true, unconditional love shines through. This is NOT condoning the crime.
>
> (Action for Families Enduring Criminal Trauma (AFFECT) 2002)

This book has been an attempt to tell the story of a group of relatives of serious offenders as I found it, between 1997 and 2003. When I began writing about Aftermath, the work it did, and how it had been so essential to so many of the relatives that I met, I did not imagine I would finish by writing about its closure. The service it provided was the only one of its kind, and was open to any relative of a serious offender in the UK. Relatives often described Aftermath as a lifeline, there for them in the darkest of times, when some had even contemplated suicide. Now Aftermath is no more, and at the time of writing, its work has not been taken over by any other organisation. No statutory agency has responsibility for offenders' relatives; there is no other organisation able to take on Aftermath's caseload; and, I have been told by former members, there are no plans to revive Aftermath. Serious offenders' families can find help through other prisoners' families organisations, and the contact details for the prisoners' families helpline appear at the end of the book. There may be individuals within these organisations who can assist families to deal with the horror of the crime and its consequences, but no national organisation exists with this express purpose. Furthermore, these organisations are themselves few in number and tend to be under-resourced and rely heavily on volunteers (Gampell 2002).

At the time of writing (and this is a rapidly changing landscape) there is a small organisation located in Hampshire and West Sussex which was set up in 2001 by former Aftermath members who were prominent in the organisation during much of my fieldwork, but had left before it folded. AFFECT (Action For Families Enduring Criminal Trauma) has been established as a regional organisation to help 'families and friends facing possible "Life"/Long prison sentences', although it says it will take referrals from anywhere in the country. AFFECT offers support and counselling to members, has quite detailed advice about managing the criminal justice process on its website, and produces various information leaflets. However, it is currently run by only a handful of people, working from their own homes, and supports a much lower number of families than Aftermath. It may grow, but it too is experiencing severe difficulty in securing funds and risks closure if funds cannot be found. The excerpt above is taken from one of their publications and shows how AFFECT retains much of the spirit of Aftermath at the time of my research.

Returning to the findings of this study, the experiences of relatives appeared to be mediated by the kin relationship they shared with the offender, the offence type, and the gender of the offender. So, for example, mothers often talked about how they felt a strong bond to the offender, and would support him or her no matter what the offence, whereas only wives and partners (in five cases) felt able to cease supporting the offender. Relatives of sex offenders believed they were subject to stronger stigma and shame. In the case of sex offences, it seemed as if 'hating the sin but loving the sinner' was a separation that was difficult for outsiders to accept; the status of sex offender was a master status that defined an offender's very being. Moral panics about child sexual abuse have been flourishing since the 1980s (Cohen 2003: Introduction), with public opinion vehemently against offenders and their associates. This was vividly shown when the *News of the World* ran a campaign naming and shaming paedophiles, following the abduction and murder of Sarah Payne in 2000, which led to vigilante attacks. Relatives of sex offenders were often genuinely fearful that they might encounter similar public fury if their circumstances were known.

The gender of the offender was found to be significant in several ways. Relatives of female offenders tended to contextualise the offences using actor adjustments constructed around denials of full responsibility.

Christine's daughter, for example, was addicted to heroin and according to Christine she was made to commit armed robberies by an abusive boyfriend who controlled her supply; Louise's daughter's violent offence followed a traumatic bereavement which devastated her and which she sought to avenge in her bereaved state; and Monica's daughter suffered psychiatric problems, mental instability and then post-natal depression which culminated in an attack on her baby. The victims of three of the female offenders had been within the immediate family and closely related to the participating relative: Monica and Jane's daughters committed violent offences against their babies and Sarah's mother against her father. These relatives had to struggle with conflicting feelings as close relatives of both the offender and the victim. (This was also the case for some of the relatives of male offenders, though only in those in the child sex offence group where the victims had been nieces, a foster-daughter, step-children and grandchildren of the participating relative and one homicide case where the victim had been the interviewee's grandmother-in-law).

Two points were commonly expressed by relatives of female offenders: first, the unexpected nature of the offence, and second, specific concerns about the offender in prison. Several expressed their surprise that their female relative became a serious offender. Christine, for example, said that as she brought her daughter up it was never one of her concerns that she would see her convicted of a serious offence like armed robbery. Three relatives were worried that their daughters might attempt suicide in prison, and one that her daughter would be given adequate help in withdrawing from drugs. Monica was concerned that her daughter did not receive psychiatric care, and was not provided with appropriate physical care when she was denied a breast pump when she first arrived in prison after sudden separation from the child she was feeding. Both Monica and Jane were concerned for their daughters' safety should their offences against their children become known. (Relatives of male offenders did express concerns about the health and well-being of the offender, and some expressed concerns about his safety in prison, but again this was mostly relatives of sex offenders.)

The concerns of the relatives of female offenders fit with what we know about the female prison population, two-thirds of whom have been found to show symptoms of at least one neurotic disorder and more than half to suffer from a personality disorder; 40 per cent have attempted suicide at some time in their lives, and 54 per cent of remand prisoners and 41 per cent of sentenced prisoners have reported some degree of drug dependency in the year before prison (Prison Reform Trust 2003). However, whether or not relatives of female offenders experienced greater stigma and shame could not be concluded with any certainty because of the difference between the male and female offenders in offence type: only one female offender was convicted of a homicide offence, and none was convicted of a sex offence. Although the relatives of female offenders did not express feelings of greater stigma and shame, the explanation might be found in the greater stigma of relatives of male sex offenders. Further research would be necessary to investigate a possible gender difference more thoroughly, matching the relatives of male and female offenders by offence type.

This has been a sociological study of relatives of serious offenders and has not sought to directly address questions of policy. However, these findings do raise particular policy implications and leave open a number of questions. First, the research indicates that early intervention and referrals by criminal justice agencies might be important for relatives of serious offenders. Participants in this study often discovered the offence at the point when the offender was arrested, and in some cases had their houses searched. There is no provision for helping offenders' relatives at this stage, and unless they are lucky enough to find a prisoners' families organisation they are very much on their own. As often the first agency to encounter the offenders' family, the police might have a role to play in referring relatives to appropriate agencies for help. Clearly the first priority of the police is the crime investigation, and some family members might even be suspects, but this would not preclude guidelines for dealing with offenders' families. According to participants in this study, the treatment they received from the police was somewhat haphazard and depended very much on the inclinations of individual officers. Further research would be useful to understand more about how the role of the police in dealing with offenders' relatives is defined.

Participants in this study spoke of their time in court as particularly traumatic, and a time when they were often lacking in support. In some cases relatives were in fear of, or subject to, attacks from the victim's associates, and some relatives described collapsing in the court at hearing the verdict or sentence given. Participants who had been supporters of other relatives in court spoke of the importance of recognising their needs: the need for information about the court process, being able to sit away from the victim's friends and family, being given protection should it be needed and being shielded from the press to whatever extent is practical. How could this be achieved? Victim Support's Witness Service only supports a defendant's family or friends if they are witnesses for the defence. However, in reality they support very few defence witnesses (only 2 per cent of the 350,000 witnesses supported by the Witness Service last year were defence witnesses) and it would therefore be very unusual for them to be involved with defendant's families. Victim Support has said it would be unlikely to expand its role to include supporting defendant's families because this would go beyond its charitable objectives, would inevitably lead to supporting defendants with a consequent conflict of interest and the risk that the Service would lack credibility with victims and prosecution witnesses, and because the Witness Service is already overworked and under-resourced (Victim Support 2006). Who else might provide support to defendant's families in court?

Serious offenders' families often become prison visitors for many years. Recognition of the needs of prisoners' families has developed considerably in recent times. A Prison Reform Trust report found 80 visitors' centres at prisons across the UK (Loucks 2002). These centres help to maintain family ties, help families to make sense of the difficult visiting process, and aid interaction between the prison and the family on issues such as the welfare of the prisoner. The report found a low priority accorded to these centres and to visits generally in some prisons, and stressed the importance of good funding, often not forthcoming. It recommended the development of fully-staffed centres across the prison estate (*ibid.*). These issues are even more important to relatives of serious offenders who may be trying to maintain family ties across longer periods of separation, might have concerns about the prisoner linked to sentence length or possible repercussions from the type of offence and as we have seen, for participants in this study, might lack basic information and need to learn how to become competent prison visitors. The dynamics in the visits room are also important, and if vulnerable prisoners are segregated, their visitors will be identified.

During the period of my research, the prison population soared. In May 1997, when a Labour Government came to power, the prison population was 60,131; in July 2006 it was 78,443, with reported plans by the Home Office to build an extra 8000 places. In the ten years between 1995 and 2005 it rose by 25,000, having previously taken four decades (1958–1995) to rise by the same amount (Prison Reform Trust 2006). At the same time, contact between prisoners and their families has actually decreased (Loucks 2002). From 1993–2003 there was a tightening of security across the prison estate following high profile escapes which had a number of implications for the management of family contact, including increased searching of visitors (Brooks-Gordon and Bainham 2004). My research has therefore taken place at a time of increased emphasis on law and order with increasing punitiveness having consequences for families of offenders. Furthermore, in an age of being 'tough on crime' groups such as Aftermath might have been perceived as soft, 'woolly liberal' causes. In light of the increasing panics about sexual and violent crime, those in public life might be reluctant to align with groups for perpetrators' relatives. The wider political context might therefore have contributed to Aftermath's difficulty in gaining legitimacy and funds, and to its eventual demise. It is perhaps no coincidence that in Aftermath's early years, one of its patrons was the late Lord Longford who was known for his willingness to support unpopular causes (including campaigning to release Myra Hindley, and attending the wedding of the notorious prisoner Charles Bronson) and not afraid to court controversy and criticism for doing so.

Though they did not use the term, most of the relatives that I met were in the business of reintegration. Within their own families and within their own lives they were trying to support the offender without condoning his or her actions and trying to help the offender make good. If we have expectations of relatives to extend this role into more formal criminal justice procedures, and to be involved in the reintegration of offenders through processes such as restorative justice, we need to recognise that that they might themselves be subject to stigma and shame and their involvement in shaming processes, even when 'reintegrative', will not be neutral. If it is also the case that these processes are gendered, with women in the family shouldering much of the burden of shaming and of re-negotiated responsibilities, then this too will have implications which further research should explore.

It is important to make family blaming by experts and others with the power to define explicit, examining how it informs social work or probation practice, for example. New research might investigate how social workers construct sex offenders and their families; the criteria used in the definition of a parent as 'non-protecting' or colluding; and the theories about families of offenders that inform social work practice.

In Chapter 2 we saw how life changed after discovery, and how family responsibilities were re-negotiated, leading to the emergence of new roles devolved largely on female relatives and revolving around the offender and his or her needs. The Government has identified family ties as one of nine key factors in reducing offending (Social Exclusion Unit 2002) and the prisoners' families literature consistently points to a strong association between the two (See Ditchfield 1994 and Mills 2004 for a review of this literature). Offenders who have relatives willing to take on these responsibilities are therefore thought to have a better chance of rehabilitation. In most cases, participants in this study wanted to support the offender, and further wanted to encourage the offender to address his or her offending behaviour. Indeed, their act and actor adjustment techniques allowed for this, as in most cases these adjustments did not attempt to fully absolve the offender of blame.

However, as we have seen, responsibilities may fall disproportionately on women along with other caring responsibilities within the family which raises the question of how much we can reasonably expect relatives of offenders to do. For example, is it reasonable to expect a mother on income support to send her son money and buy items to send to him, forgoing some of her own needs, or should prison wages be increased to a point where prisoners can afford to buy these items themselves? Relatives who support might help to reduce recidivism, but this can sometimes lead to them being given a policing function within the family. Clare, for example, said she felt she was expected to police her family when her husband was released from a prison sentence for child sex offences. She did not believe that her son had been abused, nor that he was at risk, but felt she was being expected to monitor her husband at home and constantly watch his relationship with his son, something she was not prepared to do, and one of the reasons, she said, that she decided to end the marriage on his release. Furthermore, if relatives do take on these responsibilities and reduce recidivism as the literature suggests, it is important that they are supported in doing so. As we have seen, no statutory agencies support relatives of serious offenders; Aftermath has closed; and many other organisations for offenders' families struggle to secure funding. There is an inherent contradiction between targeting 'problem families' who do not fulfil their responsibilities, and failing to support relatives who are endeavouring to do so (see Girshick 1996 for a similar point).

Is it right or reasonable to expect an individual to take responsibility for another's actions? The co-dependency movement, which Lamb describes as 'the quintessential example of women's assuming responsibility for male behavior' (Lamb 1996: 34) began as a movement to help alcoholics take responsibility for their own actions, but has grown in popularity as a movement focusing on wives (and other relatives) as enablers, needing to change their own behaviour and sharing some responsibility for their husband's actions. The portrayal of women as 'enablers' has been subject to criticism from feminist authors for contributing to the oppression of women and encouraging 'overresponsibility' (Kresten and Bepko 1992). If family members are encouraged to take responsibility for each other, we must be cautious if to do so would include sharing responsibility for deviant actions; if primarily it is women who take responsibility for aberrant men; if it lessens the responsibility offenders take for their own actions; or if relatives take on responsibilities that should be fulfilled by others. As we saw in Chapter 3, the ways in which kin might be deemed responsible depend largely on kin relationship, and discourses of parental responsibility are particularly strong. Having responsibility for another's actions presupposes a degree of influence or control over their behaviour, however, which can be a problematic assumption in any relationship.

So what can be made of the stories told by relatives in this book? It has not been the purpose of this book to judge the accuracy of those stories or to try to ascertain whether relatives were telling the 'truth' about their family lives, the offender, and the reasons for his or her crime. My interest has been in how relatives constructed their lives, how they made sense of what had happened, and how they incorporated events into their own self-narratives. Although factual information about court dates or prison sentences can be checked and cross-referenced, this becomes almost impossible with the stories people tell about their own lives. Different family members might tell quite different stories about the same events; those stories may be very real for the teller and are of interest in their own right as part of the processes through which we make sense of our lives. As the film producer Robert Evans has said: 'There are three sides to every story: my side, your side, and the truth. And no one is lying. Memories shared serve each one differently.' My concern in this book has been with *how* they serve, how they are relayed through culturally-shared vocabularies, how we organise our memories to make sense of our lives and to construct a coherent 'story' of the self, and the work we do to mend breaches that threaten this coherence.

The difficulty of judging and interpreting stories is tellingly illustrated by the responses of readers reviewing Lionel Shriver's *We Need to Talk about Kevin*. On her website, Shriver has a letter addressed to her readers in which she writes about the reviews written by 'ordinary' readers on booksellers' websites. These reviews divide

> almost straight down the middle into what seem to be reviews of two completely different books. . . . One camp assesses a story about a well-intentioned mother who, whatever her perfectly human deficits in this role, is saddled with a 'bad seed', a thoroughly evil child from birth whose ultimate criminality only she seems to perceive but is helpless to prevent. . . . The second camp of readers appears to have read another novel entirely: about a mother whose coldness is itself criminal, and who bears full responsibility for her son's tragic rampage as a teenager. Having allowed an ambivalence about the whole parental enterprise to poison her relationship with the boy even as an innocent baby, this mother is an object lesson. Parents get the children they deserve.

But Shriver is not worried about this disparity and says if the book leant itself to only one interpretation she would have been keenly disappointed. There is no real 'answer', she says, because 'in real life, you don't get one' (Shriver 2006). Pathways to crime are complex and real life is full of grey areas, which contrast with the black and white simplistic answers so favoured by commentators on crime and the family. The responses of readers to the relatives' stories in my book might similarly be divided between the sceptical and the sympathetic. However, my purpose has not been to investigate why the offences happened, or to apportion blame, but to understand how the relatives narrated their lives and how they understood and worked through very difficult experiences.

The accounts in this book have been necessarily partial and one-sided, restricted to the families' stories of crime and its consequences. As a result, many of the other parties affected by crime remain hidden, and in particular the primary victims who can be so devastated by the impact wrought by serious (and particularly sexual and violent) crime. A different book might have taken a smaller number of stories and looked at each one in much more detail, showing the complexities of each case and its wider ramifications. One book from the US about families of those on death row, for example, does this effectively by taking nine cases and devoting a whole chapter to each (King 2005). However, although I do not tell the stories of the victims, most of the relatives I met were preoccupied with the horror of the offence and the harm it had caused. They were not a normatively separate group; discovery was traumatic and they felt shame and needed to account for what had happened precisely because they too held values which had been breached by the actions of the offender. Had they been, for example, relatives engaged in organised crime through their familial networks, or relatives of political criminals who supported the offender's actions, they would not have been *Families Shamed* and their experiences would have been quite different.

I do not claim, therefore, that the stories of the relatives in this book reflect the experiences of all families of serious offenders. As we saw in the introduction, the sample of interviewees had particular characteristics which should make us cautious about generalising to the very broad population of serious offenders' families. Conversely, I would be surprised if all of the experiences relayed by the relatives I met were particular only to them. Similar experiences were recounted by the managers of prison visitors' centres and others who work with serious offenders' families, and other studies have found relatives of serious offenders to be managing similar problems: the relatives of murderers interviewed by May who were managing problems of stigmatisation and using techniques to account for the offence (May 1999, 2000); 13 'women who love men who kill' who relay very similar stories in a true crime book (MccGwire 1994); and the relatives of those on death row, who though obviously primarily preoccupied with the offender's fate, are still devastated by the seriousness of the offence, trying to understand why it happened, and suffering their situation without sympathy or comfort (King 2005), frequently reacting to the initial news with shock and disbelief, experiencing an extended grieving process, putting their lives on hold to focus on the family member in prison, and reporting negative reactions from others, ostracism and shame (Sharp 2005).

A glance through any newspaper will find stories about murderers, rapists or child sex offenders. Sometimes the offender's relatives are mentioned, and in the most high-profile cases might themselves be subject to tough media scrutiny. My aim in this book has been to show how the actions of each one of these offenders affects many more people than a surface reading would uncover. Taking one very high-profile example, Primrose Shipman, the wife of the serial killer Harold Shipman, has been vilified in the media (her case provoked intense debate when it was decided that she should be allowed to receive some of her husband's pension) and stigmatised and shamed as his wife. One analysis of the media reporting of the Shipman case tells how she has variously been described as obese, fat fingered, keeping a dirty and neglected house, having given up cooking and cleaning, and not bothering to keep her weight in check: 'Primrose is judged to be everything that a woman shouldn't be. She is represented as the binary opposite of the good wife' (Smith 2000).

The final question that this book raises is a normative one and takes us back to the title of the book: should families of serious offenders be shamed? This might initially seem an odd question to ask at the end of a book that has detailed the difficulties that shame and stigma have brought to these families, but it is worth pausing to imagine the opposite: a society where each person lived in their own moral bubble, where kin ties were not strong enough to transmit shame, and where relatives did not have any responsibility for each other and were never ashamed of each others actions. Would this be desirable? Or is there (at least in the case of serious offences that cause such harm) a just measure of shame for relatives? As we have seen, Braithwaite (1989) argues that thinking about how ashamed our relatives would be might stop us from committing crime and his reintegrative shame depends upon families imposing shame on the offender. He argues that serious offenders should feel some shame about the kind of person they are as well as guilt for the offence (Braithwaite and Braithwaite 2001) – do we also want their relatives to feel some shame?

Braithwaite uses Japanese society as an example of a culture with strong reintegrative shame, and quotes from one study that tells us that in Japan 'parents occasionally commit suicide when their children are arrested for heinous crimes' (Bayley 1983: 156). Is there a mid-point between these two positions of no familial shame and familial shame so strong it leads parents to commit suicide? Are they opposite ends of a continuum, and if so might there be a middle point that is 'just'? Or is shame a primarily negative emotion that focuses on personal failure and is therefore the wrong path to tread, doing more harm than good? And crucially, if we do have expectations about familial shame, how might we protect relatives who are so devastated and who, in the words of Eileen, feel like 'pariahs', 'outcasts' and 'the lowest of the low'? My aim in this book has been to show the need to look beneath assumptions about familial shame, to make explicit our expectations, and to think carefully about what their consequences might be.

During the fieldwork and interviews for this study I encountered a great deal of upset and hurt, and was often asked by different participants how I could stand to be around so much sadness and listen to unhappy stories and why I would choose to do so. However, I would not want this book to only reflect these aspects. The relatives in my study did not passively accept the personal and structural constraints imposed by their circumstances, but rather actively tried to shape their lives and find creative solutions to the difficulties they encountered. I heard stories of resilience, of women forging relationships with other women, and finding friendship and strength through mutual support in some of the most difficult circumstances. Their stories often reflected progress and a sense of moving forward from an initial point of devastation, with much of that progress driven by the relatives themselves, many of whom took pride in the strength of family bonds and their determination to support despite censure. I was encouraged by the progress I saw and by relatives managing to cope with experiences which had turned their worlds upside down. As Celia said: 'Aftermath allowed me to realise that people can come through terrible situations, and that had a big impact upon me.' What I encountered was also a positive story of moving forward, of salvaging dignity, humour, friendship and strength from difficult times and of relatives (primarily women) coming together to create new networks and re-build their lives and pass these coping skills onto others. In addition to contributing to theoretical and policy debates, I hope this book reflects this positive side to the stories told by the relatives who gave their time to participate.

Appendix I

Notes on methodology

The fieldwork for this study took place in short bursts over a relatively long period of time and in a number of different locations spread across England. The research was not tightly bound, temporally or geographically, but can still be broadly defined as an ethnographic study. The ethnographic methods employed were treated flexibly and adapted to fit the research problem and the environment. Though Aftermath members often lived far apart, they shared a 'culture': some of their ways of understanding and defining their circumstances were shared; they shared a way of supporting each other; and a network of relationships with other relatives of serious offenders to which they 'belonged'. While some elements of this culture were fixed, others were continually negotiated and changed over time. My aim has been to understand this 'culture' and to understand how relatives made sense of their lives, collectively and individually, and over several years I observed the times that they came together at meetings and talked with them in detail about their networks of support. This prolonged though intermittent immersion in the field was necessary to understand the ways in which relatives collectively understood and articulated their experiences and to also understand the 'cultural silences' (Maher 1997) of their social world.

As I repeatedly returned to the field I built up relationships with members and became a familiar face. I felt very comfortable at these meetings, and would be included in conversations, jokes, and rounds of cups of tea – but I was always aware (as I am sure the Aftermath members were aware) that I was not a relative of a serious offender, and hence attending as a guest. My role could be described as one of 'peripheral membership' (Adler and Adler 1998: 85), close enough to establish an insider's identity, particularly as the fieldwork progressed, but without full belonging – I was not involved in core activities such as supporting other members, for example. However, as Souhami (2007: 199) argues, the dual roles of researcher and member are complex. There is constant tension between the two roles and 'inherent ambiguity' in the researcher's position; the limitations of membership are not always clear and are subject to the different perceptions and expectations of those in the field. The roles are continually negotiated rather than being fixed and unproblematic. So it was with Aftermath, which itself was a changing, flowing organisation, and had members with different perceptions and expectations of research. So, for example, although many members were welcoming, open and eager to talk, some members did not want to talk about their experiences and declined to be interviewed. One group of women sitting together at a seminar weekend declined my request immediately saying they did not think it was possible to understand what it was like to have a serious offender in the family unless you had experienced this yourself, and there was therefore no point in trying. My role, and the degree to which I was seen as a member or as a researcher, was therefore fluid and changed across different contexts and across time.

What I looked for in my observations changed over the course of the study as I learnt more and progressively re-focused and narrowed down my aims. Adler and Adler (1998), following Spradley (1980) and Jorgenson (1989) describe these stages of observation – from initial observations, which are mostly descriptive and general, to more focused observations, which generate clearer research questions and typologies, which then require selected observations where the characteristics of previously selected elements and the relations between them are further defined. These stages form a 'funnel' as the researcher's attention becomes deeper and more focused. The interview process was also part of this funnel as my early observations shaped the development of the interview guide and the kinds of questions I asked. When I began the research, almost nothing had been written on families of serious offenders, and I had to spend time in the field to work out what the important issues were, although I began the research with the 'foreshadowed problem in mind' (Wilcox 1982: 459) of understanding the impact of having a serious offender in the family and how relatives coped with that impact in their everyday lives.

A false dichotomy can be set up between what people 'do', accessible through observation, and what people 'say they do', accessible through interviews. As Atkinson, Coffey and Delamont explain, this distinction can be overdrawn; forms of talk are themselves examples of social action. A purpose of this book has been to understand how people 'use biographical accounts to perform social actions. Through them they construct their own lives and those of others; they justify and legitimate past, current and future actions; they formulate explanations; they locate their own actions within socially shared frames of reference' (Atkinson, Coffey and Delamont 2003: 117). The accounts in this book are more than personal stories about private problems, and my focus in analysing the accounts I collected through interviews and fieldwork has been on 'the cultural resources people use to construct them, the kinds of interpersonal or organizational functions they fulfil, and the socially distributed forms that they take' (*ibid.*: 117).

Ethnography is produced through a dialogue of which the researcher is part and fieldwork depends upon this personal dimension. My authorship has been visible throughout the book as the ethnographer, sole interviewer, and interpreter of what I found. In the interest of visible authorship, I will reflect briefly on my part of the dialogue. During the period of fieldwork, I was in my late twenties and early thirties, white, British, and living in London. I didn't start my undergraduate degree until the age of 24, finding my way to university through an access course. During the period of fieldwork, I married, and I was pregnant with my first child in the final stages of interviewing. My second child was born two weeks after I submitted the PhD thesis on which this book is based (see Condry 2003). My status as a relatively young, female, student researcher undoubtedly conferred some advantages in researching subjects who were primarily women, most of whom did not have a university education, were brought together by the difficulties they shared as mothers or wives, and expressed interest in developments in my own family life. Of course, the authority that comes with greater seniority can confer its own advantages in research, but in this context my student status was possibly less daunting. Being a female researcher might not offer an immediate identification with female research subjects, but at the very least I suspect talking about intimate details of family life – including sexual abuse, domestic violence, feelings of grief and loss – was easier than it might have been had the researcher been male.

Fieldwork with a self-help organisation was not dirty, dangerous or risky, but did draw on (and develop) particular personal resources and skills: talking and listening, particularly with people who could be quite upset, but also with groups of people who I had sometimes only just met and who were not always immediately receptive; absorbing and remembering (I would usually write field notes that evening) could be exhausting, especially during more intense periods such as three-day residential weekends; and trying to strike a balance between being an active part of a group, sharing conversation, jokes and drinks, but still treading with care and tact and keeping in mind the purposes of the research. I was sometimes affected by what I heard – some stories could be very sad – and memories of particular comments or stories often stayed vivid long after the fieldwork had finished. When I had my first child, a son, I would on occasion recall the numerous photographs that I had been shown of bouncing babies and smiling blonde toddlers who grew up to be rapists and murderers, and probably worried more frequently than other new parents about what it is that shapes who we become.

Research in people's own homes had the potential to be risky, but in reality I was usually visiting women I had met before, and the offender was rarely present. If the offender or other male relatives were there, their contact with me was mediated by the interviewee. There was one potentially difficult situation when a husband recently released from a prison sentence for child sex offences came into the living room to find me talking with his wife and reacted angrily to my presence. However, it transpired that he thought I was from social services and when he established my identity as 'the lady from the university', he could not have been more apologetic and offered endless cups of tea throughout the interview, much to his wife's impatience. In the prison visitors' centre I witnessed visitors getting quite heated on several occasions which was perhaps not surprising given the stress of prison visiting and was considered a normal part of the job. Travelling alone around the country to conduct interviews presented its own problems. I sometimes had to travel long distances, which I nearly always did by car, and as a woman travelling alone had to plan ahead with an eye to personal safety. On one occasion I had booked ahead into what appeared to be a very nice guesthouse in a large industrial town, only to find I was the only woman staying there with 30 transient shipbuilders, but most of the travelling and the bits in between fieldwork were much more mundane.

I chose to prioritise quotations from relatives in this book rather than those who work with offenders' families. However, I do not claim that this book gives a 'voice' to relatives of serious offenders. In a book such as this, the control of the text is in the hands of the author and it is the ethnographic 'I' rather than 'they' or 'us' who interprets, codes and (re)frames participants' narratives (Maher 1997: 229). Even with a significant number of direct quotations 'the informant's voices cannot penetrate the discursive speech of the ethnographer' (Hastrup 1992: 121, quoted in Maher 1997: 226). We do not simply mirror what our research subjects tell us but analyse, interpret and construct our own story about what we found. There are many levels of interpretation, and while some sections of chapters leave the views expressed relatively undisturbed (such as the problems they face supporting an offender through the criminal justice system in Chapter 2) others are part of a sociological analysis that those relatives might not recognise (we do not go about our lives with a conscious awareness of the shared vocabularies we use to account for untoward events, for example). I hope I have retained a respect for the relatives' accounts, while trying to unpack and theorise some of the processes which underlie them.

Similarly, although I would describe the research as grounded in a feminist perspective, this would not be because it 'empowered' the women participants. However one might try to be fair and respectful, in any research the power imbalance remains. As the researcher I was the main beneficiary of the research process, and responsible for its outcome and products. However, the interview process can have some advantages for interviewees and they often spoke of the positive benefits of being able to talk at length to someone neutral who was interested in their story. The research could be defined as feminist in perspective, not because it employs methods that can be claimed to be uniquely feminist, but because it focused primarily on women and women's lives and asked questions about how their lives were structured by gender and how the women themselves managed those constraints. There is of course no single feminist perspective, but as a study of a group of women whose experiences usually remain hidden, it has brought to the fore a number of ways in which the broader impact of serious crime and responses to it are gendered (see Condry 2006 for further discussion).

Research such as this clearly depends on building personal relationships, and some of the relatives I met became friends with whom I remained in contact. I was concerned that all of those who participated did not feel exploited and I endeavoured to be open and honest about the purposes of the research and to preserve the anonymity of participants. Several participants had particular concerns about being identified, one of whom had received threats against her life and was understandably anxious that her participation did not jeopardise her local anonymity, or raise her profile in any way. I have been careful with all interview and observational data to change names, dates, and places and to leave out identifying details where necessary, without damaging the integrity of the data.

Through the research I accumulated a collection of field notes, transcripts of long interviews with the relatives and with others working in the field, numerous Aftermath documents, newsletters, letters written to me by some of the relatives, and newspaper cuttings about their cases. The process of data analysis – identifying and linking conceptual categories, including processes of describing, classifying and connecting (Dey 1993) – had begun much earlier during the research as initial research questions and conceptual categories emerged during fieldwork. Interpretation and sense-making is also part of the process of writing field notes; noting what is significant and what is not is an active process, and not a matter of passively copying down 'facts' (Emerson, Fretz and Shaw 1995). However, once the collection process was complete, there was a stage of more focused analysis which broadly followed several stages (similar to those in Hammersley and Atkinson 1995). I began by reading through data many times to get a 'feel' for important issues. The interview transcripts were analysed using the computer programme Atlas/ti as a basic tool to code and retrieve relevant sections of text. At first, this produced a very long list of codes which was gradually refined to a list of 50. Codes came from two sources: pre-designated categories which by this stage I knew to be important to the analysis (for example 'reasons' was used to code anything said about the reasons for the offence) and those which emerged from the transcripts (for example 'hierarchical comparisons' was a code that emerged from the comparisons interviewees made between themselves and others; this later developed into the technique of comparative adjustment described in Chapter 4). The coding categories were therefore both 'observer-identified' and 'member-identified' (Lofland 1976).

Each file of quotations was retrieved and transferred into a Word file. Within each Word file further categories and sub-categories were developed, and the importance of variables such as kin relationship, offence type, and gender of the offender was checked. Field notes were coded manually, looking for anything that related to my coding scheme and anything else that emerged as important. Some bits of documentary data that related to particular topics were coded. Finally, as the ideas were developed and during the writing stage, points were checked and re-checked against the data. I would not want to present this process as a neat and tidy categorisation of all the data; it was a messy and time-consuming process, messier than many descriptions of methodology reveal, and involved going back and forth between data, ideas, and writing until eventually clearer, coherent and consistent ideas and theoretical frameworks evolved. What has emerged, I hope, is an analysis of relatives' situated meanings and a document of their social world and the ways in which they managed the consequences of serious crime.

Appendix 2

Interviewee characteristics

	Kin relationship to offender	Offence category	How reached?	Age	Ethnicity	Offender's ethnicity	Interview location
Relatives of male offenders:							
Lisa	Partner	Homicide	Aftermath lunch	50s	White UK	White UK	Home
Frances	Wife	Sex offence	Aftermath lunch	40s	White UK	White UK	Friend's home
Angela	Wife	Sex offence	Aftermath lunch	40s	White UK	White UK	Home
Beryl	Mother	Homicide	Introduction from Aftermath member	70s	White UK	White UK	Home
George	Father	Homicide	Introduction from Aftermath member	60s	White UK	White UK	Ex-wife's home
Beatrice	Mother	Homicide	Aftermath lunch	60s	White UK	White UK	Home
Pauline	Mother	Homicide	Introduction from Aftermath member	40s	White UK	White UK	Home
Ada	Mother	Rape	Introduction from Aftermath member	60s	White UK	White UK	Home
Nancy	Wife	Sex offence	Aftermath lunch	50s	White UK	White UK	Home
Alice	Mother	Homicide	Seminar weekend	60s	White UK	White UK	Home
Penny	Mother	Rape	Introduction from Aftermath member	60s	White UK	Mixed race*	Home

	Kin relationship to offender	Offence category	How reached?	Age	Ethnicity	Offender's ethnicity	Interview location
Relatives of male offenders:							
Anne	Mother	Rape	Aftermath lunch	40s	White UK	White UK	Home
Beverly	Grandmother	Violent offence	Letter via Aftermath office	50s	White UK	Mixed race	Home
Stephanie	Wife	Homicide	Introduction from Aftermath member	40s	White UK	White UK	Voluntary organisation
Lillian	Mother	Sex offence	Letter via Aftermath office	70s	White UK	White UK	University
Hilda	Mother	Homicide	Letter via Aftermath office	70s	White UK	White UK	Home
Harriet	Mother	Sex offence	Aftermath lunch	60s	White UK	White UK	Home
Gill	Wife	Sex offence	Aftermath lunch	40s	White UK	White UK	Sister's home
Debbie	Wife	Homicide	Letter via Aftermath office	30s	Black UK	Mixed race	Home
Nicola	Partner	Sex offence	Aftermath lunch	30s	White UK	White UK	Home
Clare	Wife	Sex offence	Seminar weekend	40s	White UK	White UK	Home
Betty	Sister	Sex offence	Seminar weekend	60s	Black UK	Black UK	Home
Eileen	Wife	Sex offence	Introduction from Aftermath member	60s	White UK	White UK	Home
Celia	Aunt	Homicide	Aftermath lunch	40s	White UK	White UK	Home

	Kin relationship to offender	Offence category	How reached?	Age	Ethnicity	Offender's ethnicity	Interview location
Relatives of female offenders:							
Mary	Mother	Violent offence	Aftermath lunch	70s	White UK	White UK	Home
Dorothy	Mother	Homicide	Prison visitors' centre	60s	White UK	White UK	Visitors' centre
Christine	Mother	Violent offence	Prison visitors' centre	40s	White UK	White UK	Home
Monica	Mother	Violent offence	Introduction from Aftermath member	50s	White UK	White UK	Home
Louise	Mother	Violent offence	Prison visitors' centre	60s	White UK	White UK	Home
Lorraine	Mother	Drug offence	Prison visitors' centre	40s	White UK	Mixed race	Home
Sarah	Daughter	Violent offence	Prison visitors' centre	30s	White UK	White UK	Home
Jane	Mother	Violent offence	Prisoners' families organisation	40s	White UK	White UK	Prisoners' families organisation

In each case where the offender is described as mixed race, their father was described by the interviewee as 'black' and their mother as 'white'.

Bibliography

Abbott, P. and Wallace, C. 1992. *The Family and the New Right*. London: Pluto Press.

Ablon, J. 1974. 'Al-Anon Family Groups: Impetus for Learning and Change through the Presentation of Alternatives'. *American Journal of Psychotherapy*, 28: 30–45.

Action for Families Enduring Criminal Trauma (AFFECT). 2002. *Family Stories*. Bognor Regis: AFFECT.

Action for Prisoners' Families. 2003. *Keeping in Touch: A Guide for the Partners and Families of Prisoners*. London: Action for Prisoners' Families.

Action for Prisoners' Families. 2006. *Action for Prisoners' Families News*, Winter/Spring 2006. London: Action for Prisoners' Families.

Adler, P.A. and Adler, P. 1998. 'Observational Techniques' in Denzin, N.K. and Lincoln, Y.S. (eds) *Collecting and Interpreting Qualitative Materials*. CA, USA: Sage.

Aftermath. 2000. *Aftermath Annual Review*. Sheffield: Aftermath.

Alcoholics Anonymous. 2006. '25 Millionth Alcoholics Anonymous "Big Book"' at http://www.alcoholics-anonymous.org/en_press.cfm?PressID=1 (Retrieved 30 July 2006).

Arber, S. and Gilbert, N. 1989. 'Transitions in Caring: Gender, Life Course and Care of the Elderly' in Bytheway, B., Keil, T., Allatt, P. and Bryman, A. (eds) *Becoming and Being Old: Sociological Approaches to Later Life*. London: Sage.

Arthur, R. 2005. 'Punishing Parents for the Crimes of their Children'. *Howard Journal of Criminal Justice*, 44, 3: 233–53.

Ashworth, A. 2005. *Sentencing and Criminal Justice*, 4th edn. Cambridge: Cambridge University Press.

Atkinson, P. 1992. *Understanding Ethnographic Texts*. CA, USA: Sage.

Atkinson, P., Coffey, A., and Delamont, S. 2003. *Key Themes in Qualitative Research: Continuities and Changes*. CA, USA: AltaMira Press.

Averill, J.R. 1968. 'Grief: Its Nature and Significance'. *Psychological Bulletin*, 70: 721–48.

Bakker, L.J., Morris, B.A. and Janus, L.M. 1978. 'Hidden Victims of Crime'. *Social Work*, 23: 143–8.

Bar-On, D. 1989. *Legacy of Silence: Encounters with Children of the Third Reich*. Cambridge, MA: Harvard University Press.

Bar-On, D. 1990. 'Children of Perpetrators of the Holocaust: Working through One's Own Moral Self'. *Psychiatry*, 53: 229–45.

Bayley, D.H. 1983. 'Accountability and Control of the Police: Some Lessons for Britain' in T. Bennet (ed.) *The Future of Policing*. Cambridge: Institute of Criminology.

BBC. 2005. 'UK Suicide Bomber Family Cleared' at http://news.bbc.co.uk/1/hi/uk/3835601.stm, 28 November 2005 (Retrieved 30 July 2006).

Beck, U. and Beck-Gernsheim, E. 1995. *The Normal Chaos of Love*. Cambridge: Polity.

Bell, A. and Weinberg, M.S. 1978. *Homosexualities: A Study of Diversity Among Men and Women*. New York: Simon and Schuster.

Bennett, W.L. 1997. 'Storytelling in Criminal Trials: A Model of Social Judgement' in Hinchman, L.P. and Hinchman, S.K. (eds) *Memory, Identity, Community: The Idea of Narrative in the Human Sciences*. Albany, USA: State of New York University Press.

Bettelheim, B. 1970. *The Informed Heart*. London: Palladin.

Borkman, T.J. 1990. 'Experiential, Professional and Lay Frames of Reference' in Powell, T.J. (ed.) *Working with Self-Help*. Silver Spring, MD: National Association of Social Workers.

Borkman, T.J. 1999. *Understanding Self-Help/Mutual Aid: Experiential Learning in the Commons*. New Brunswick, NJ: Rutgers University Press.

Boswell, G. and Wedge, P. 2001. *Imprisoned Fathers and their Children*. London: Jessica Kingsley Publishers.

Bowlby, J. 1981. *Attachment and Loss*, vol. III. *Loss: Sadness and Depression*. Harmondsworth: Penguin Books.

Bowling, B. and Phillips, C. 2002. *Racism, Crime and Justice*. Harlow: Longman.

Braithwaite, J. 1989. *Crime, Shame and Reintegration*. Cambridge: Cambridge University Press.

Braithwaite, J. 1999. 'Restorative Justice: Assessing Optimistic and Pessimistic Accounts' in Tonry, M. (ed.) *Crime and Justice: A Review of the Research*, vol. 25. Chicago: University of Chicago Press.

Braithwaite, J. and Braithwaite, V. 2001. 'Shame, Shame Management and Regulation', Part I of Braithwaite, J., Braithwaite, V., Harris, N. and Ahmed, E. *Shame Management Through Reintegration*. Cambridge: Cambridge University Press.

Braithwaite, J., Braithwaite, V., Harris, N. and Ahmed, E. 2001. *Shame Management Through Reintegration*. Cambridge: Cambridge University Press.

Branscombe, N.R. and Doosje, B. (eds) 2004. *Collective Guilt: International Perspectives*. Cambridge: Cambridge University Press.

Brody, E.M. 2004. *Women in the Middle: Their Parent Care Years*, 2nd edn. New York: Springer Publishing Company.

Brooks-Gordon, B.M. and Bainham, A. 2004. 'Prisoners' Families and the Regulation of Contact'. *Journal of Social Welfare and Family Law*, 26, 3: 263–80.

Burris, C.T. and Jackson, L.M. 1999. 'Hate the Sin/Love the Sinner, or Love the Hater? Intrinsic Religion and Responses to Partner Abuse'. *Journal for the Scientific Study of Religion*, 38: 160–74.

Caddle, D. and Crisp, D. 1996. 'Imprisoned Women and Mothers'. London: Home Office Research Study 162.

Cain, C. 1991. 'Personal Stories: Identity Acquisition and Self-Understanding in Alcoholics Anonymous'. *Ethos*, 19: 210–53.

Campbell, B. 1993. *Goliath: Britain's Dangerous Places*. London: Methuen.

Caplan, P.J. and Caplan, J.B. 1994. *Thinking Critically About Research on Sex and Gender*. New York: HarperCollins College Publishers.

Caplan, P. and Hall-McCorquodale, I. 1985. 'Mother Blaming in Major Clinical Journals'. *American Journal of Orthopsychiatry*, 55: 345–53.

Carlen, P. 1983. *Women's Imprisonment: A Study in Social Control*. London: Routledge, Keegan and Paul.

Carveth, D. 2001. 'The Unconscious Need for Punishment: Expression or Evasion of the Sense of Guilt?' *Psychoanalytic Studies*, 3, 1: 9–21.

Casale, S. 1989. *Women Inside: The Experience of Women Remand Prisoners in Holloway*. London: Civil Liberties Press.

Chambers, D. 2001. *Representing the Family*. London: Sage.

Cheale, D. 1999. 'The One and the Many: Modernity and Postmodernity' in Allan, G. (ed.) *The Sociology of the Family: A Reader*. Oxford: Basil Blackwell.

Clear, T.R., Rose, D.R. and Ryder, J.A. 2001. 'Incarceration and the Community: The Problem of Removing and Returning Offenders'. *Crime and Delinquency*, 47, 3: 335–51.

Codd, H. 1998. 'Prisoners' Families: The "Forgotten Victims"'. *Probation Journal*, 45, 3: 148–54.

Codd, H. 2002. '"The Ties that Bind": Feminist Perspectives on Self-Help Groups for Prisoners' Partners'. *The Howard Journal*, 41: 334–47.

Cohen, S. 2001. *States of Denial: Knowing About Atrocities and Suffering*. Cambridge: Polity Press.

Cohen, S. 2003. *Folk Devils and Moral Panics*, 3rd edn. London and New York: Routledge.

Cohler, B.J., Pickett, S.A. and Cook, J.A. 1991. 'The Psychiatric Patient Grows Older: Issues in Family Care' in Light, E. and Lebowitz, B. (eds) *The Elderly with Chronic Mental Illness*. New York: Springer.

Comfort, M. 2002. '"Papa's house": The Prison as Domestic and Social Satellite'. *Ethnography*, 3, 4: 467–99.

Comfort, M. 2003. 'In the Tube at San Quentin: The "Secondary Prisonization" of Women Visiting Inmates'. *Journal of Contemporary Ethnography* 32: 77–107.

Comfort, M. 2007. *Doing Time Together: Forging Love and Family in the Shadow of the Prison*. Chicago: University of Chicago Press.

Condry, R. 2003. *After the Offence: The Construction of Crime and its Consequences by Families of Serious Offenders*. PhD thesis, University of London.

Condry, R. 2006. 'Stigmatised Women: Relatives of Serious Offenders and the Broader Impact of Crime' in Heidensohn, F. (ed.) *Gender and Justice: New Concepts and Approaches*. Cullompton, Devon: Willan Publishing.

Cook, J.A. 1988. 'Who "Mothers" the Chronically Mentally Ill?' *Family Relations*, 37: 42–9.

Cook, J.A., Pickett, S.A. and Cohler, B.J. 1997. 'Families of Adults with Severe Mental Illness – The Next Generation of Research'. *American Journal of Orthopsychiatry* 67: 172–6.

Corr, C.A., Nabe, C.M. and Corr, D. 1997. *Death and Dying, Life and Living*. 2nd edn. Pacific Grove, CA: Brooks Cole.

Cressey, D.R. 1962. 'Role Theory, Differential Association, and Compulsive Crimes' in Rose, A.M. (ed.) *Human Behavior and Social Processes: An Interactionist Approach*. London: Routledge and Keegan Paul.

Crocker, J., Major, P. and Steele, C. 1998. 'Social Stigma' in Gilbert, D.T., Fiske, S.T. and Lindzey, G. (eds) *Handbook of Social Psychology*. New York: McGraw-Hill.

Davies, L. and Krane, J. 1996 'Shaking the Legacy of Mother Blaming: No Easy Task for Child Welfare'. *Journal of Progressive Human Services*, 7, 2: 3–22.

Denzin, N. 1989. *Interpretive Biography*. Newbury Park, CA: Sage.

Dey, I. 1993. *Qualitative Data Analysis: A User Friendly Guide*. London: Routledge.

DeYoung, M. 1988. 'The Indignant Page: Techniques of Neutralization in the Publications of Pedophile Organizations'. *Child Abuse and Neglect*, 12: 583–91.

Ditchfield, J. 1994. 'Family Ties and Recidivism: Main Findings from the Literature'. London: Home Office Research Bulletin, 36.

Ditton, J. 1977. *Part-time Crime: An Ethnography of Fiddling and Pilferage*. London: Macmillan.

Dobash, R.E., Dobash, R.D., Cavanagh, K. and Lewis, R. 2001. *Homicide in Britain*. Manchester: University of Manchester.

Emerson, R.M., Fretz, R.I., Shaw, L.L. 1995. *Writing Ethnographic Fieldnotes*. Chicago: University of Chicago Press.

Epstein, S. 1998. 'Mothering to Death' in Ladd-Taylor, M. and Umansky, L. (eds) *"Bad Mothers": The Politics of Blame in Twentieth Century America*. New York and London: New York University Press.

Ezzy, D. 1998. 'Theorizing Narrative Identity: Symbolic Interactionism and Hermeneutics'. *Sociological Quarterly*. 39: 239–52.

Farrington, D.P. 2002. 'Developmental Criminology and Risk-Focused Prevention' in Maguire, M., Morgan, R. and Reiner, R. (eds) *The Oxford Handbook of Criminology*. Oxford: Oxford University Press.

Fattah, E.A. 1991. *Understanding Criminal Victimization: An Introduction to Theoretical Victimology*. Scarborough, Ontario: Prentice-Hall Canada Inc.

Festinger, L. 1954. 'A Theory of Social Comparison Processes'. *Human Relations*, 40: 427–48.

Finch, J. 1989. *Family Obligations and Social Change*. Cambridge: Polity Press.

Finch, J. and Mason, J. 1993. *Negotiating Family Responsibilities*. London: Tavistock/Routledge.

Finkelhor, D., Araji, S., Baron, L., Doyle Peters, S. and Wyatt, G.E. 1986. *A Sourcebook on Child Sexual Abuse*. CA, USA: Sage.

Fishman, L.T. 1990. *Women at the Wall: A Study of Prisoners' Wives Doing Time on the Outside*. Albany: State University of New York Press.

Foucault, M. 1967. *Madness and Civilization*. London: Tavistock Publications.

Fox, K. 1999. 'Reproducing Criminal Types: Cognitive Treatment for Violent Offenders in Prison'. *Sociological Quarterly*. 40: 435–53.

Francis, B., Soothill, K. and Dittrich, R. 2001. 'A New Approach for Ranking "Serious" Offences: The Use of Paired-Comparisons Methodology'. *British Journal of Criminology* 41: 726–37.

Gampell, L. 2002. 'Who's Guilty?' *Criminal Justice Matters*, 50 (Winter 2002/3): 22–3.

Garfinkel, H. 1967. *Studies in Ethnomethodology.* Englewood Cliffs, NJ: Prentice-Hall.

Gebhard, P., Gagnon, J., Pomeroy, W. and Christenson, C. 1965. *Sex Offenders: An Analysis of Types.* New York: Harper & Row.

Gibbs, C. 1971. 'The Effect of Imprisonment of Women Upon Their Children'. *British Journal of Criminology,* 11: 113–30.

Giddens, A. 1991. *Modernity and Self-Identity.* Cambridge: Polity Press.

Giddens, A. 1992. *The Transformation of Intimacy: Sexuality, Love and Eroticism in Modern Societies.* Cambridge: Polity Press.

Gidron, B., Guterman, N.B. and Hartman, H. 1990. 'Stress and Coping Patterns of Participants and Non-Participants in Self-Help Groups for Parents of the Mentally Ill'. *Community Mental Health Journal,* 26: 483–96.

Gillies, V. 2005. 'Meeting Parents' Needs? Discourses of "Support" and "Inclusion" in Family Policy'. *Critical Social Policy,* 25, 1: 70–90.

Girshick, L.B. 1996. *Soledad Women: Wives of Prisoners Speak Out.* Westport, Conneticut: Praeger Publishers.

Glaser, B. and Strauss, A. 1964. 'Awareness Contexts and Social Interaction'. *American Sociological Review*: 669–79.

Goffman, E. 1956. 'Embarrassment and Social Organization'. *American Journal of Sociology,* 62, 3: 264–71.

Goffman, E. 1961. *Asylums: Essays on the Social Situation of Mental Patients and Other Inmates.* Harmondsworth: Penguin.

Goffman, E. 1963. *Stigma: Notes on the Management of a Spoiled Identity.* Harmondsworth: Penguin.

Goleman, D. 1985. *Vital Lies, Simple Truths: The Psychology of Self-Deception.* New York: Simon and Schuster.

Hagan, J. and Dinovitzer, R. 1999. 'Collateral Consequences of Imprisonment for Children, Communities, and Prisoners' in Tonry, M. and Petersilia, J. (eds) *Prisons.* Chicago: University of Chicago Press.

Hagedorn, J. 1990. 'Back in the Field Again: Gang Research in the Nineties' in Huff, R. (ed.) *Gangs in America,* 2nd edn. Newbury Park, CA: Sage, 240–59.

Hairston, C.F. 1991. 'Family Ties During Imprisonment: Important to Whom and For What?' *Journal of Sociology and Social Welfare,* 18: 87–104.

Hambrecht, M., Hafner, H. and Loffler, W. 1994. 'Beginning Schizophrenia Observed by Significant Others'. *Social Psychiatry,* 29: 53–60.

Hamlin, J.E. 1988. 'The Misplaced Role of Rational Choice in Neutralization Theory'. *Criminology,* 26: 425–38.

Hammersley, M. and Atkinson, P. 1995. *Ethnography: Principles in Practice.* London and New York: Routledge.

Hanson, R.C. and Slater, S. 1993. 'Reactions to Motivational Accounts of Child Molesters'. *Journal of Child Sexual Abuse,* 2: 43–59.

Harris, N. 2001 'Shaming and Shame: Regulating Drink Driving', Part II of Braithwaite, J., Braithwaite, V., Harris, N. and Ahmed, E. *Shame Management Through Reintegration.* Cambridge: Cambridge University Press.

Harvey, J.H., Weber, A.L. and Orbuch, T. 1990. *Interpersonal Accounts: A Social Psychological Perspective.* Cambridge: Blackwell.

Harvey, J.H., Orbuch, T.L., Chwalisz, K.D. and Garwood, G. 1991. 'Coping with Sexual Assualt: The Roles of Account-Making and Confiding'. *Journal of Traumatic Stress*, 4: 515–31.

Hastrup, K. 1992. 'Writing Ethnography: State of the Art' in Okely, J. and Callaway, H. (eds) *Anthropology and Autobiography*. New York: Routledge.

Heatherton, T.F., Kleck, R.E., Hebl, M.R. and Hull, J.G. 2000. *The Social Psychology of Stigma*. New York: The Guildford Press.

Heller, T., Roccoforte, J., Hsieh, M.A., Cook, J.A. and Picket, S.A. 1997. 'Benefits of Support Groups for Families of Adults with Severe Mental Illness'. *American Journal of Orthopsychiatry*, 67, 2: 187–98.

Herman, N.J. 1994. 'Former Crazies in the Community' in Dietz, M.L., Prus, R.C. and Shaffir, W. (eds) *Doing Everyday Life: Ethnography as Lived Human Experience*. Ontario, Canada: Copp Clark Longman.

Hil, R. and McMahon, A. 2001. *Families, Crime and Juvenile Justice*, New York: Peter Lang Publishing.

Hobbs, D. 2002. 'Organized Crime Families'. *Criminal Justice Matters*, 50 (Winter 2002/3): 26–7.

Holstein, J.A. and Gubrium, J.F. 2000. *The Self We Live By: Narrative Identity in a Postmodern World*. New York and Oxford: Oxford University Press.

Holstein, J.A. and Miller, G. 1990. 'Rethinking Victimization: An Interactional Approach to Victimology'. *Symbolic Interaction*, 13: 103–22.

Horowitz, A. 1985. 'Family Caregiving to the Frail Elderly' in Eisdorfer, C., Lawton, M.P. and Maddox, G.L. (eds) *Annual Review of Gerontology and Geriatrics*, 5. New York: Springer Publishing Company.

Howard League. 1994. *Families Matter*. London: Howard League for Penal Reform.

Howard League. 2006. Prison Information Bulletin, January 2006 at http://www.howardleague.org/fileadmin/howard_league/user/pdf/Prison_information_bulletin1_01.pdf (Retrieved 21 June 2006).

Howarth, G. and Rock, P. 2000. 'Aftermath and the Construction of Victimisation: "The Other Victims of Crime"'. *The Howard Journal*, 39: 58–78.

Howitt, D. 1995. *Paedophiles and Sexual Offences Against Children*. Chichester: John Wiley & Sons.

Humphreys, C. 1994. 'Counteracting Mother-Blaming Among Child Sexual Abuse Service Providers: An Experiential Workshop'. *Journal of Feminist Family Therapy*, 6, 1: 49–65.

Janoff-Bulman, R. 1992. *Shattered Assumptions: Towards a New Psychology of Trauma*. New York: The Free Press.

Johnson, E.D. 2000. 'Differences Among Families Coping with Serious Mental Illness: A Qualitative Analysis'. *American Journal of Orthopsychiatry*, 70: 126–34.

Jones, E.E., Farina, A., Hastorf, A.H., Markus, H., Miller, D.T. and Scott, R.A. 1984. *Social Stigma: The Psychology of Marked Relationships*. New York: W.H. Freeman and Company.

Jones, M.B. and Jones, D.R. 2000. 'The Contagious Nature of Antisocial Behavior'. *Criminology*, 38, 1: 25–46.

Jorgenson, D.L. 1989. *Participant Observation*. CA, USA: Sage.

Katz, A.H. 1993. *Self-Help in America: A Social Movement Perspective*. New York: Twayne Publishers.

Kelley, S.J. 1990. 'Responsibility and Management Strategies in Child Sexual Abuse: A Comparison of Child Protective Workers, Nurses, and Police Officers'. *Child Welfare*, 69, 1: 43–51.

Kennedy, M. and Humphreys, K. 1994. 'Understanding Worldview Transformation in Members of Mutual Help Groups'. *Prevention in Human Services*, 11: 181–98.

King, R. 2005. *Capital Consequences: Families of the Condemned Tell their Stories.* New Brunswick, NJ and London: Rutgers University Press.

Klockars, C.B. 1974. *The Professional Fence*. London: Tavistock.

Kresten, J. and Bepko, C. 1992. 'Codependency: The Social Reconstruction of Female Experience' in Bepko, C. (ed.) *Feminism and Addiction*. New York: The Hayworth Press, 48–66.

Kubler-Ross, E. 1969. *On Death and Dying*. New York: Macmillan.

Kurtz, L.F. 1994. 'Self-help Groups for Families with Mental Illness or Alcoholism' in Powell, T.J. (ed.) *Understanding the Self-Help Organization: Frameworks and Findings*. Thousand Oaks, CA: Sage.

Lacey, N. 1993. 'A Clear Concept of Intention: Ellusive or Illusory?' *Modern Law Review*, 56, 5: 621–42.

Ladd-Taylor, M. and Umansky, L. 1998. *Bad Mothers: The Politics of Blame in Twentieth-Century America*. New York: New York University Press.

Lamb, S. 1996. *The Trouble with Blame: Victims, Perpetrators and Responsibility*. Cambridge, MA and London: Harvard University Press.

Laub, J.H. and Sampson, R.J. 2003. *Shared Beginnings, Divergent Lives: Delinquent Boys to Age 70*. Cambridge, MA and London: Harvard University Press.

Lefley, H.P. 1987. 'Family Burden and Family Stigma in Major Mental Illness'. *American Psychologist*, 44: 556–60.

Lerner, M.J. 1980. *The Belief in a Just World*. New York: Plenum.

Levi, M. and Maguire, M. 2002. 'Violent Crime' in Maguire, M., Morgan, R. and Reiner, R. (eds) *The Oxford Handbook of Criminology*. Oxford: Oxford University Press.

Lewis, H.B. 1971. *Shame and Guilt in Neurosis*. New York: International University Press.

Lewis, M. 1992. *Shame: The Exposed Self*. New York: Free Press.

Lickel, B., Schmader, T. and Hamilton, D.L. 2003. 'A Case of Collective Responsibility: Who Else Was to Blame for the Columbine High School Shootings?' *Personality and Social Psychology Bulletin*, 29: 2 (February): 194–204.

Lickel, B., Schmader, R., Curtis, M., Scarnier, M. and Ames, D.R. 2005. 'Vicarious Shame and Guilt'. *Group Processes and Intergroup Relations*, 8, 2: 145–57.

Lieberman, M.A. and Snowdon, L.R. 1994. 'Problems in Assessing Prevalence and Membership Characteristics of Self-Help Group Participants' in Powell, T.J. (ed.) *Understanding the Self-Help Organization: Frameworks and Findings*. Thousand Oaks, CA: Sage Publications.

Light, R. 1993. 'Why Support Prisoners' Family-Tie Groups?' *The Howard Journal*, 32, 4: 322–9.

Lincoln, C.V. and McGorry, P. 1995. 'Pathways to Psychiatric Care for Young People Experiencing a First Episode of Psychosis'. *Psychiatric Services*, 46: 1166–71.

Lindemann Nelson, H. 2001. *Damaged Identities, Narrative Repair.* Ithaca, New York: Cornell University Press.

Lindisfarne, N. 1999. 'Gender, Shame, and Culture: An Anthropological Perspective' in Gilbert, P. and Andrews, B. (eds) *Shame: Interpersonal Behavior, Psychopathology, and Culture.* Oxford: Oxford University Press.

Lloyd, A. 1995. *Doubly Deviant, Doubly Damned: Society's Treatment of Violent Women.* London: Penguin.

Lofland, J. 1976. *Doing Social Life: The Qualitative Study of Human Interaction in Natural Settings.* New York: Wiley.

Loucks, N. 2002. 'Just Visiting? A Review of the Role of Prison Visitors' Centres'. London: Prision Reform Trust and Federation of Prisoners' Families Support Groups.

MacLeod, R.J. 1982. 'A Child is Charged With Homicide: His Family Responds'. *British Journal of Psychiatry*, 141: 199–201.

Maher, L. 1997. *Sexed Work: Gender, Race and Resistance in a Brooklyn Drug Market.* Oxford: Oxford University Press.

Malle, B.F. and Nelson, S.E. 2003. 'Judging *Mens Rea*: The Tension Between Folk Concepts and Legal Concepts of Intentionality'. 21, 5: 563–80.

Marks, J. 2006. *Mr Nice and Mrs Marks.* London: Ebury Press.

Maruna, S. 2001. *Making Good: How Ex-Convicts Reform and Rebuild their Lives.* Washington, DC: American Psychological Association.

Maruna, S. and Copes, H. 2005. 'What Have We Learned from Five Decades of Neutralization Research?' in Tonry, M. (ed.) *Crime and Justice: A Review of the Research*, vol. 32. Chicago: University of Chicago Press.

Matthews, J. 1983. 'Forgotten Victims: How Prison Affects the Family'. London: NACRO.

Matza, D. 1969. *Becoming Deviant.* Englewood Cliffs, NJ: Prentice-Hall.

Mauer, M. and Chesney-Lind, M. (eds). 2002. Invisible Punishment: The Collateral Consequences of Mass Imprisonment. New York: The New Press.

May, H. 1999. 'Who Killed Whom? Victimisation and Culpability in the Social Construction of Murder'. *British Journal of Sociology*, 50: 489–506.

May, H. 2000. '"Murderers' Relatives" Managing Stigma, Negotiating Identity', *Journal of Contemporary Ethnography*, 29: 198–221.

McCaghy, C.H. 1968. 'Drinking and Deviance Disavowal: The Case of Child Molesters'. *Social Problems*, 16: 43–9.

MccGwire, S. 1994. *Women Who Love Men Who Kill.* London: True Crime.

McDermott, K. and King, R. 1992. 'Prison Rule 102: "Stand By Your Man": The Impact of Penal Policy on the Families of Prisoners' in Shaw, R (ed.) *Prisoners' Children: What Are the Issues?* London: Routledge, 50–73.

McLaughlin, M.L., Cody, M.J. and Read, S.J. 1992. *Explaining One's Self to Others: Reason-Giving in a Social Context.* Hillsdale, NJ: Lawrence Erlbaum Associates.

Miall, C.E. 1986. 'The Stigma of Involuntary Childlessness'. *Social Problems*, 33, 4: 268–82.

Mills, A. 2004. '"Great Expectations?": A Review of the Role of Prisoners' Families in England and Wales', vol. 7, Selected Papers from the 2004 British Society of Criminology Conference, Portsmouth July 2004 at http://www.britsoccrim.org/v7.htm (Retrieved 21 March 2006).

Mills, C.W. 1940. 'Situated Actions and Vocabularies of Motive'. *American Sociological Review*, 6: 904–13.

Mitchell, J. and Dodder, R. 1980. 'An Examination of Types of Delinquency through Path Analysis', *Journal of Youth and Adolescence*, 12: 307–18.

Morris, P. 1965. *Prisoners and their Families*. London: George Allen and Unwin Ltd.

Murray, J. 2003a. *Visits and Family Ties Amongst Men at HMP Camphill*. London: Action for Prisoners' Families.

Murray, J. 2003b. *Visits and Family Ties Amongst Women at HMP Cookham Wood*. London: Action for Prisoners' Families.

NACRO. 1994. *Opening the Doors: Prisoners' Families*. London: National Association for the Care and Resettlement of Offenders.

Nathanson, D.L. 1992. *Shame and Pride: Affect, Sex and the Birth of the Self*. New York: W.W. Norton.

National Statistics. 2004a. 'Working Lives: Men Managers Twice as Likely as Women' at http://www.statistics.gov.uk/cci/nugget.asp?id=435 (Retrieved September 2006).

National Statistics. 2004b. 'Work and Family: 1 in 2 Mums of under 5s are in Labour Force' at http://www.statistics.gov.uk/CCI/nugget.asp?ID=436 (Retrieved September 2006).

National Statistics. 2004c. 'Lifestyles: Women Do More Chores than Men' at http://www.statistics.gov.uk/cci/nugget.asp?id=440 (Retrieved September 2006).

Norton, S., Wandersman, A. and Goldman, C.R. 1993. 'Perceived Costs and Benefits of Membership in a Self-Help Group: Comparisons of Members and Nonmembers of the Alliance for the Mentally Ill'. *Community Mental Health Journal*, 29: 143–60.

Nussbaum, M. 2004. *Hiding from Humanity: Disgust, Shame and the Law*. Princeton and Oxford: Princeton University Press.

Oakley, A. 1981. 'Interviewing Women: A Contradiction in Terms' in Roberts, H. (ed.) *Doing Feminist Research*. London: Routledge and Keegan Paul.

Office of Juvenile Justice and Delinquency Prevention. 2006. 'Juvenile Justice Reform Initiatives in the United States 1994–1996' at http://ojjdp.ncjrs.org/pubs/reform/contents.html (Retrieved 24 July 2006).

Ontario Statutes. 2004. 'The Parental Responsibility Act 2000' at http://www.e-laws.gov.on.ca/DBLaws/Statutes/English/00p04_e.htm (Retrieved 29 July 2006).

Orbuch, T.L. 1997. 'People's Accounts Count: The Sociology of Accounts'. *Annual Review of Sociology*, 23: 455–78.

Orbuch, T.L., Harvey, J., Russell, S.M. and Sorenson, K. 1992. 'Account Making Through Accounts: Three Studies'. *Journal of Social Behavior and Personality*, 7: 79–94.

Paitich, D. and Langevin, R. 1976. 'The Clarke Parent–Child Relations Questionnaire: A Clinically Useful Test for Adults'. *Journal of Consulting and Clinical Psychology*, 44: 428–36.

Parkes, C.M. 1971. 'Psycho-Social Transitions: A Field of Study'. *Social Science and Medicine*, 5, 2: 101–15.

Parkes, C.M. 1972. *Bereavement: Studies of Grief in Adult Life*. London: Tavistock.

Parkes, C.M. 1975. 'What Becomes of Redundant World Models? A Contribution to the Study of Adaptation to Change'. *British Journal of Medical Psychology*, 48: 131–7.

Paylor, I. and Smith, D. 1994. 'Who are Prisoners' Families?' *Journal of Social Welfare and Family Law*, 2: 131–44.

Perring, C., Twigg, J. and Atkin, K. 1990. *Families Caring for People Diagnosed as Mentally Ill: The Literature Re-Examined*. London: HMSO/SPRU.

Phoenix, A., Woollett, A. and Lloyd, E. 1991. *Motherhood: Meanings, Practices and Ideologies*. London: Sage.

Player, E. 1994. 'Women's Prisons After Woolf' in Player, E. and Jenkins, M. (eds) *Prisons After Woolf: Reform Through Riot*. London: Routledge.

Plummer, K. 1995. *Telling Sexual Stories: Power, Change and Social Worlds*. London and New York: Routledge.

Pollner, M. and McDonald-Wikler, L. 1985. 'The Social Construction of Unreality: A Case Study of a Family's Attribution of Competence to a Severely Retarded Child'. *Family Process*, 24: 241–54.

Pollner, M. and Stein, J. 1996. 'Narrative Mapping of Social Worlds: The voice of experience in Alcoholics Anonymous'. *Symbolic Interaction*, 19: 203–23.

Pollock, N.L. and Hashmall, J. 1991. 'The Excuses of Child Molesters'. *Behavioral Sciences and the Law*, 9: 53–9.

Polsky, N. 1998. *Hustlers, Beats and Others* (expanded edition). New York: Lyons Press.

Prison Reform Trust. 2000. 'Justice for Women: The Need for Reform'. London: Prison Reform Trust.

Prison Reform Trust. 2003. 'Troubled Inside: Responding to the Mental Health Needs of Women in Prison'. London: Prison Reform Trust.

Prison Reform Trust. 2006. 'Bromley Briefings Prison Factfile April 2006'. London: Prison Reform Trust. http://www.prisonreformtrust.org.uk (Retrieved July 2006).

Prus, R. 1994. 'Generic Social Processes: Intersubjectivity and Transcontextuality in the Social Sciences' in Dietz, M.L., Prus, R.C. and Shaffir, W. (eds) *Doing Everyday Life: Ethnography as Lived Human Experience*. Ontario, Canada: Copp Clark Longman.

Qureshi, H. and Walker, A. 1989. *The Caring Relationship*. London: Macmillan.

Randall, W.L. 1995. *The Stories We Are: An Essay on Self-Creation*. Toronto: University of Toronto Press.

Rappaport, J. 1993. 'Narrative Studies, Personal Stories, and Identity Transformation in the Mutual Help Context'. *Journal of Applied Behavioral Science*, 29: 239–56.

Ray, M.C. and Simmons, R.L. 1987. 'Convicted Murderers' Accounts of their Crimes: A Study of Homicide in Small Communities'. *Symbolic Interaction*, 10: 57–70.

Reddy, B. and McElfresh, O. 1978. 'Detachment and Recovery from Alcoholism'. *Alcohol Health and Research World*, 2: 28–33.

Richards, M., McWilliams, B., Allcock, L., Enterkin, P., Owens, P. and Woodrow, J. 1994. 'The Family Ties of English Prisoners: The Results of the Cambridge

Project on Imprisonment and Family Ties, Occasional Paper No. 2'. Cambridge: Centre for Family Research.

Richardson, L. 1990. *Writing Strategies: Reaching Diverse Audiences*. London: Sage.

Rock, P. 1998a. *After Homicide: Practical and Political Responses to Bereavement*. Oxford: Clarendon Press.

Rock, P. 1998b. 'Murderers, Victims and "Survivors": The Social Construction of Deviance'. *British Journal of Criminology*, 38: 185–200.

Rogler, L.H. and Hollingshead, A.B. 1965. *Trapped: Families and Schizophrenia*. New York: John Wiley.

Rose, D.R. and Clear, T.R. 1998. 'Incarceration, Social Capital and Crime: Implications for Social Disorganization Theory'. *Criminology*, 36: 441–79.

Rose, N. 2000. 'The Biology of Culpability: Pathological Identity and Crime Control in a Biological Culture'. *Theoretical Criminology*, 4: 5–34.

Russell, D.E.H. 1986. *The Secret Trauma: Incest in the Lives of Girls and Women*. New York: Basic Books.

Samarel, N. 1995. 'The Dying Process' in Wass, H. and Neimeyer, R.A. (eds) *Dying: Facing the Facts*. 3rd edn. Washington, DC: Taylor & Francis.

Sampson, H., Messinger, S.L. and Towne, R.D. 1962. 'Family Processes and Becoming a Mental Patient'. *American Journal of Sociology*, 68: 88–96.

Schafer, N.E. 1994. 'Exploring the Link Between Visits and Parole Success: A Survey of Prison Visitors'. *International Journal of Offender Therapy and Comparative Criminology*, 38, 1: 17–32.

Schneider, J.W. and Conrad, P. 1980 'In the Closet with Illness: Epilepsy, Stigma Potential and Information Control'. *Social Problems*, 28, 1: 32–44.

Scott, M.B. and Lyman, S.M. 1968. 'Accounts'. *American Sociological Review*, 33: 46–62.

Scully, D. and Marolla, J. 1984. 'Convicted Rapists' Vocabulary of Motive: Excuses and Justifications'. *Social Problems*, 31: 530–44.

Semin, G.R. and Manstead, A.S.R. 1983. *The Accountability of Conduct: A Social Psychological Analysis*. London: Academic Press Inc.

Sharp, S.F. 2005. *Hidden Victims: The Effects of the Death Penalty on Families of the Accused*. New Jersey: Rutgers University Press.

Shaw, R. (ed.) 1992. *Prisoners' Children: What are the Issues?* London: Routledge.

Shriver, L. 2003. *We Need to Talk About Kevin*. London: Serpent's Tail.

Shriver, L. 2006. 'Dear Readers' at http://www.harpercollins.com/authorintro/index.asp?authorid=27687 (Retrieved 21 June 2006).

Simonds, W. 1992. *Women and Self-Help Culture: Reading Between the Lines*. New Brunswick, NJ: Rutgers University Press.

Slovo, G. 2003. 'Revealing is Healing'. *New Humanist*, 118: 18–21.

Small, N. 2001. 'Theories of Grief: A Critical Review' in Hockey, J., Katz, J. and Small, N. *Grief, Mourning and Death Ritual*. Buckingham: Open University Press.

Smart, L. and Wegner, D.M. 2000. 'The Hidden Costs of Hidden Stigma' in Heatherton, T.F., Kleck, R.E., Hebl, M.R. and Hull, J.G. (eds) *The Social Psychology of Stigma*. New York: The Guildford Press.

Smith, B.J. and Trepper, T.S. 1992. 'Parents' Experience When their Sons Sexually Offend: A Qualitative Analysis'. *Journal of Sex Education and Therapy*, 18: 93–103.

Smith, G. 2000 'Reporting Shipman', *Hoolet: The Magazine of RCGP (Scotland)*, Winter 2000, http://www.hoolet.org.uk/28hoolet/shipman.htm (Retrieved 20 July 2006).

Social Exclusion Unit. 2002. *Reducing Re-Offending by Ex-Prisoners*. London: Office of the Deputy Prime Minister.

Social Exclusion Unit. 2004. *Tackling Social Exclusion: Taking Stock and Looking to the Future – Emerging Findings*. London: Office of the Deputy Prime Minister.

Sokoloff, N.J . 2003. 'The Impact of the Prison Industrial Complex on African American Women'. *SOULS: A Critical Journal of Black Politics, Culture, and Society*, 5, 4: 31–46.

Soothill, K. and Walby, S. 1991. *Sex Crime in the News*. London and New York: Routledge.

Soothill, K., Francis, B., Ackerley, E. and Fligelstone, R. 2002. *Murder and Serious Sexual Assault: What Criminal Histories Can Reveal About Future Serious Offending*. Police Research Series Paper 144. London: Home Office.

Souhami, A. 2007. *Transforming Youth Justice: Occupational Identity and Cultural Change*. Cullompton, Devon: Willan Publishing.

Spradley, J.P. 1980. *Participant Observation*. New York: Holt, Rinehart & Winston.

Stangor, C. and Crandall, C.S. 2000. 'Threat and Social Construction of Stigma' in Heatherton, T.F., Kleck, R.E., Hebl, M.R. and Hull, J.G. (eds) *The Social Psychology of Stigma*. New York: The Guilford Press.

Stokes, R. and Hewitt, J.P. 1976. 'Aligning Actions'. *American Sociological Review*, 41: 838–49.

Surette, R. 1998. *Media, Crime, and Criminal Justice: Images and Realities*, 2nd edn. New York: Wadsworth Publishing.

Sykes, G.M. and Matza, D. 1957. 'Techniques of Neutralization: A Theory of Delinquency'. *American Sociological Review*, 22: 664–70.

Tangney, J.P. 1991. 'Moral Affect: The Good, the Bad and the Ugly'. *Journal of Personality and Social Psychology*, 61, 4: 598–607.

Taylor, L. 1972. 'The Significance and Interpretation of Replies to Motivational Questions: The Case of Sex Offenders'. *Sociology*, 6: 23–39.

Tchaikovsky, C. 1994. 'No Room of One's Own'. *Criminal Justice*, 12, 2: 5–6.

Thomson, J.G., Marolla, J.A. and Bromley, D.G. 1998. 'Disclaimers and Accounts in Cases of Catholic Priests Accused of Pedophilia' in Shupe, A. (ed.) *Wolves Within the Fold: Religious Leadership and Abuses of Power*. New Brunswick: Rutgers University Press.

Toch, H. 1993. 'Good Violence and Bad Violence: Self-Presentations of Aggressors through Accounts and War Stories' in Felson, R.B. and Tedeschi, J.T. (eds) *Aggression and Violence: Social Interactionist Perspectives*. Washington, DC: American Psychological Association.

Topalli, V., Wright, R. and Fornango, R. 2002. 'Drug Dealers, Robbery and Retaliation. Vulnerability, Deterrence and the Contagion of Violence'. *The British Journal of Criminology*, 42: 337–51.

Veevers, J. 1980. *Childless by Choice*. Toronto: Butterworths.

Victim Support. 2006. Personal communication from Peter Dunn, Head of Research and Development, Victim Support.

Videka-Sherman, L. 1982. 'Effects of Participation in a Self-help Group for Bereaved Parents: Compassionate Friends'. *Prevention in Human Services*, 1: 69–77.

Von Hirsch, A. and Jareborg, N. 1991. 'Gauging Criminal Harm: A Living-Standard Analysis'. *Oxford Journal of Legal Studies* 11: 1–38.

Walklate, S. 1989. *Victimology: The Victim and the Criminal Justice System*. London: Unwin Hyman.

Walter, T. 1999. *On Bereavement*. Buckingham: Open University Press.

Weir, G. 2002. 'The Economically Inactive Who Look After the Family or Home' National Statistics feature. London: Office for National Statistics at http://www.statistics.gov.uk/articles/labour_market_trends/Economically_inactive_nov2002.pdf (Retrieved September 2006).

Wilcox, K. 1982. 'Ethnography as a Methodology and its Application to the Study of Schooling: A Review' in Spindler, G. (ed.) *Doing the Ethnography of Schooling*, New York: CBS Publishing, 456–88.

Wilkinson, C. 1988. 'The Post Release Experience of Women Prisoners' in Morris, A. and Wilkinson, C. (eds) *Women and the Penal System*. Cambridge: Cambridge University Cropwood Series No.19.

Williams, G. 1984. 'The Genesis of Chronic Illness: Narrative Reconstruction'. *Sociology of Health and Illness*, 6: 175–200.

Wills, T.A. 1981. 'Downward Comparison Principles in Social Psychology'. *Psychological Bulletin*, 90: 245–71.

Wiseman, J.P. 1991. *The Other Half: Wives of Alcoholics and their Social-Psychological Situation*. New York: Aldine De Gruyter.

Wuthnow, R. 1994. *Sharing the Journey: Support Groups and America's New Quest for Community*. New York: Free Press.

Yarrow, M.R., Clausen, J.A. and Robbins, P.R. 1955a. 'The Social Meaning of Mental Illness'. *The Journal of Social Issues*, XI: 33–48.

Yarrow, M.R., Schwartz, C.G., Murphy, H.S. and Deasy, L.C. 1955b. 'The Psychological Meaning of Mental Illness in the Family'. *The Journal of Social Issues*, XI: 12–24.

Zalba, S.R. 1964. *Women Prisoners and their Families*. Los Angeles: Delmar Publishing Co. Inc.

Index